Instant Pot Mini Cookbook for Beginners

600 Healthy and Delicious Perfectly Portioned Recipes Your 3-Quart Models

Dorothy Stella

Table of Content

Chapter 4 Vegetable 26

Chapter 5 Poultry Recipes 45

Chapter 6 Beef Recipes 66

Chapter 7 Pork Recipes 77

Chapter 8 Fish and Seafood 89

Chapter 9 Snacks and Appetizers 110

Chapter 10 Desserts 120

Appendix 1 Measurement Conversion Chart 131

Appendix 2 Instant Pot Cooking Timetable 132

Appendix 3 Recipe Index 134

Introduction

I am a thirty year old with three kids, and I am EXCEPTIONALLY busy and up until one year ago, I simply didn't have the time to cook. As a result, I have spent several years eating microwave meals and processed foods. The consequences of my bad diet have been severe. I was diagnosed with several health conditions including irritable bowel syndrome, psoriasis, and anxiety, my skin and hair suffered, and I was always tired. I drank up to six cups of coffee a day to give me enough energy to do menial tasks, and two of my sons were diagnosed with ADHD. Due to the stress of being sick and having sick children, I got depressed and would consume even more junk food to make me feel better.

Combined with a bad diet, the doctors were pumping me full of medication that had terrible side effects. After having a meltdown and hitting rock bottom, I made the decision to take control of my life, I started reading about me and my children's conditions and found out that the majority of what we were going through was diet related. I emptied my cupboards and replaced everything with healthy foods, but I still had one problem – time! I was spending more than two hours per day preparing meals, and it was getting very difficult for me. I had to find a solution – and the answer to all my problems came through the instant pot!

Fast forward one year later, mine and my children's health have significantly improved, I've got so much energy that I have completely cut coffee out of my diet, and I've got more time to spend with my kids, family members and loved ones. So now my goal is to tell as many people as I can about the benefits of the instant pot.

Chapter 1 The Basics of Instant Pot

An instant pot is a multi-purpose pressure cooker which works as a slow cooker, yogurt maker, steamer, warmer, rice cooker and electric pressure cooker. **The instant pot has several benefits including the following:**

» Enhances food flavor

» Saves energy

» Saves space in the kitchen

» It can store leftovers

» Kills micro-organisms in food

» Multi functionalities

» Vegetables retain nutrients and minerals

» Less cooking odor

» Save time cooking

You don't need to have the cooking skills of Jamie Oliver to enjoy the benefits of an instant cooker. **Different foods may require that you tweak the process, but in general, the procedure is as follows:**

- Prepare your ingredients and add them to the pot
- Put the lid on the pot
- Seal the valve
- Press the necessary buttons for the desired settings
- Once the pot builds enough pressure, release it
- Once the food is cooked, serve and enjoy

The instant pot has several modes, but it's main use is as an electric pressure cooker, but it is a lot more advanced than the traditional pressure cooker. As an electric pressure cooker, pressure is built up inside the airtight chamber. When the pressure rises, hot steam quickly cooks the food. The instant pot has three main components, the lid, the inner pot and the outer pot.

The History of the Instant Pot

Pressure cooking has been around for centuries, it involves cooking food in a sealed vessel without allowing the release of steam below a preset temperature. As the pressure increases, the boiling point of water increases and the pressure that builds up inside the cooker allows for a significant increase in temperature before the liquid begins to boil.

French physicist Denis Papin invented the pressure cooker in 1679; however, it didn't become a household cooking appliance until World War II when people began to realize how much fuel they could save because of the shorter cooking time. They were also encouraged by how well it cooked cheaper cuts of meat.

Pressure cookers were originally made for use on a stove top, prevention from explosion and protection against overheating were achieved with a pressure activated interlock mechanism and a safety valve. When the required pressure is reached in the cooker, the internal pressure is pushed up by the steam regulator which allows the steam to escape. This is why the conventional oven top pressure cookers make a loud hissing sound when the pressure is on.

In 2008, Robert Wang and a friend started designing the instant pot, they spend 18 months developing it. Today the instant pot is one of the bestselling products on Amazon with millions of fervent foodies purchasing an instant pot since it released.

Instant Pot Cooking Hacks

As mentioned, the instant pot is simple and easy to use; but you can make the cooking process even easier by following these simple hacks:

- Use the sauté mode to brown meat and enhance the flavor

- You can thicken liquid by using the sauté mode without having to transfer the ingredients into another pot

- Having enough liquid in the pot will make the cooking process easier

- You can use your instant pot to reheat food by using the keep warm button setting

- When cooking frozen vegetables and meat, double the cooking time

What Are People Saying About the Instant Pot

The instant pot cookbook has taken the world by storm and people have taken to Amazon and social media platforms such as Instagram and Pinterest to sing its praises, here are some of the reviews:

"This device has transformed the way I cook! I absolutely love it."

"The instant pot has added a whole new dimension to meal prepping in our house."

"I used to hate cooking, but now I love it because the instant pot has made the process so simple, this is amazing!"

"I've got five kids and I used to spend hours standing over a stove cooking for them, Thanks to the instant pot, those days are finally over!"

How to Deep Clean Your Instant Pot

Instant pots are not cheap, and you don't want to ruin it by failing to clean it properly, that is a quick way to shorten its life span. Here are some cleaning tips that will preserve your instant pot for the long haul.

Cleaning After Each Use

- **Wash the Inner Pot:** The instant pot is dishwasher friendly, so you can put it in with the rest of your dishes after a meal.

- **Clean the Sealing Ring:** You will find a silicone ring on the inside of the lid, most of them are removable. Remove and wash it to prevent the absorption of colors and odors. Give the sealing ring a good wash by putting it on the top rack of the dishwasher.

- **Wipe it Down:** Wipe the inside and the outside of the pot down with a wet dishcloth.

- **Wipe the Inside of the Lid:** The inside of the lid is the surface that gets the dirtiest, but it's also a part of the pot that easiest to forget when it comes to cleaning.

Deep cleaning will ensure that your instant pot remains in pristine condition, follow these steps at least once a month to prevent stubborn food residues, clogging and bad smells from forming:

- Unplug the instant pot and use a dishcloth to wipe down the inside and the outside of the pot.

- Remove any dried food from the bottom of the unit using a small brush. There are a lot of crevices in the instant pot, so make sure you get in all the corners.

- Use warm soapy water to handwash the lid of the instant pot.

- There are several smaller parts around the steam valve that get clogged up with food residue. Clean these areas by removing the quick release handle, and then wash the areas with warm soapy water.

- Take off the shield covering the steam valve on the inside of the lid. Depending on the model, it will either pop off, or screw off.

- Remove the condensation collection cup, wash it and then replace it.

What Kind of Readers is This Book For?

I think everyone needs an instant pot because it has so many benefits; however, it will make life a lot easier for certain people:

- **Busy Mothers:** Kids, work and social obligations; some mothers simply don't have the time to spend hours preparing meals for their children. Taking care of infants essentially means less time to take care of yourself. However, the instant pot helps you carve out additional time so that you are not forced to rely on unhealthy fast food to feed your children.

- **Students:** Students are renowned for their unhealthy eating habits, if they are not eating take away, they have stocked up on Ramen noodles! Students often live in cramped dorms with a limited amount of space for kitchen utensils. Although students are known for their party lifestyles, they also spend a lot of time studying which means they don't have much time to cook. The instant pot eliminates this problem.

- **People With Limited Kitchen Space:** Some people were not blessed with a large kitchen and so they have very little space to store utensils. The good news is that not only is the instant pot multifunctional, it is also small in stature which means it can slot in somewhere nicely without being too conspicuous.

- **People Without a Stove:** There are several reasons why people don't have a stove in the home, it might have broken down or the kitchen is too small for one. The instant pot will solve all of your cooking needs.

- **People on a Budget:** When we are trying to save money, it's easy to stick with take away or cheap unhealthy packaged food. You won't have this problem with an instant pot cooker because you can buy cheap, healthy ingredients that you can prepare quickly and easily.

- **Bone Broth Fans:** Bone broth is a healthy soup with many nutritious benefits. However, it can take a while to prepare. The instant pot takes a few hours in comparison to the traditional method of preparing it. The instant cooker also preserves the flavor better.

- **People With Dietary Restrictions:** While dietary restrictions such as low FODMAP, gluten-free, AIP, paleo, vegetarian and vegan have grown in popularity over recent years, they can be difficult meals to prepare. The instant pot simplifies the process, not only does the instant pot cook food faster, it also enables you to make food in batches, so you don't need to spend so much time cooking.

- **People Who Don't Have the Time to Cook:** Cooking decent meals takes time, and whether you are a CEO of a large company, self-employed, or you have an active social life, there are some people who just don't have the time to cook. The instant pot speeds up the cooking process, so you've got more time to spend on the things that are most important to you.

- **People Who Live in Cold Climates:** Cold weather makes us crave comfort foods, the instant pot is the perfect utensil to make comfort foods such as porridge, bean dishes, rice, hearty stews and curries. Also, the keep warm setting will keep your meal warm until you are ready to eat it.

What Can Users Expect to Get From This Book

With this cookbook, you will never run out of meals to prepare; with over 600 recipes available, you will be spoilt for choice! Expect a wide range of simple recipes to make for breakfast, lunch and dinner including fish, vegan, vegetarian, lamb, pork, desserts and much more.

I have personally made each and every one of these recipes, and I can say with confidence that they are all delicious or I wouldn't have included them in the book. Although all the meals are delicious, there are some that you will prefer more than others, but I would advise you to experiment with all recipes to give you a better idea of what you will like.

You can also add or take away some of the ingredients to suit your needs, whether its adding more herbs, salt or sugar.

This is the beginning of an exciting new cooking journey, and I wish you all the best! Bon Appetite!

Chapter 2 Breakfast Recipes

Creamy Oats with Peach

Prep + cook time: 15 minutes; Serves: 2

Ingredients:

- 2 medium-sized peaches; diced
- 1 cup of coconut milk
- 2 cups of water
- 1 cup oats

Instructions:

1. Open the pot and mix in the peaches, milk, water, and oats then seal the lid and the valve.
2. Set to manual to cook for 10 minutes.
3. Cancel the pot and natural- release the pressure for 8 to 10 minutes.
4. Open the lid and add sugar or sweetener as desired.

Nutrition Facts per Serving:

Calories 189; Fat: 6.5g; Carbs: 32g; Protein 15g; Fiber 9.5g

Creamy Quinoa with Maple Syrup and Vanilla

Prep + cook time: 20 minutes; Serves: 3

Ingredients:

- 1 tbsp. coconut oil
- 1 cup of coconut milk
- 3 tbsp. maple syrup
- 1 cup rinsed quinoa
- 1 tsp. vanilla extract
- 1 cup of water

Instructions:

1. Mix all the ingredients in the Instant Pot.
2. Seal the lid and set to cook for 2 minutes at high pressure.
3. Natural- release the pressure and then quick-release the rest of the steam. Stir and serve with your desired topping.

Nutrition Facts per Serving:

Calories: 488, Fat: 27.1g, Carbs: 54.4g, Protein: 9.8g

Cinnamon Millet Dish

Prep + cook time: 15 minutes; Serves: 2

Ingredients:

- 1 tbsp. oil
- 1 stick cinnamon
- 2 pods cardamom
- 1 bay leaf
- 1 large onion; sliced
- 1 cup decorticated millet
- 1 ½ cups of water
- Salt

Instructions:

1. Press sauté on the Instant Pot and add the oil, cinnamon, cardamom, and bay leaf to cook until the cumin crackles.
2. Add the onions to cook for 2 to 3 minutes then switch off the pot and add the millet. Let it cook for some minutes until the millet has been coated with the spices.
3. Pour in the water and add the salt then seal the lid and the valve.
4. Set to manual to cook for 1 minute.
5. Cancel the pot when the timer stops and natural- release the pressure for 8 to 10 minutes.
6. Open the lid and loosen the millet dish with a fork. Serve warm.

Nutrition Facts per Serving:

Calories 150; Fat: 7g; Carbs: 18.5g; Protein 3g

Sweet and Creamy Mango Rice with Sesame Seeds

Prep + cook time: 15 minutes; Serves: 3

Ingredients:

- 1 cup uncooked white jasmine rice
- 1 cup mango chunks
- 1 ¼ cup lightly sweetened coconut milk
- 1/3 cup lightly sweetened coconut milk
- 2 tbsp. brown sugar
- Black sesame seeds

Instructions:

1. Open the pot and add the rice, mango chunks, and 1 ¼ cup of coconut milk. Seal the lid and the valve.
2. Set to manual to cook for 4 minutes until it stops.
3. Press the cancel button and natural- release the pressure for 8 to 10 minutes.
4. Open the lid and serve the rice into containers.
5. Mix in the coconut milk and top with brown sugar and sesame seeds and serve.

Nutrition Facts per Serving::
Calories: 230; Fat: 6g; Carbs: 38.4g; Protein 4g; Fiber 3.2g

Quinoa Jumble with Avocado and Tomatoes

Prep + cook time: 12 minutes; Serves: 2

Ingredients:

- 1 cup quinoa
- 1 cup of water
- 2 tbsp olive oil
- 2 tbsp. apple cider vinegar
- ½ tsp. salt
- ½ tsp. black pepper
- ½ diced avocado
- 1 fresh tomato; diced
- ¼ cup fresh cilantro; chopped

Instructions:

1. Mix the quinoa and water in the Instant Pot and seal the lid. Set to cook for 1 minute at high pressure.
2. Whisk the oil, vinegar, salt, and pepper in a bowl and set aside.
3. When the timer has stopped, mix the quinoa with the dressing, avocado, tomato, and cilantro.
4. Serve warm or chill.

Nutrition Facts per Serving::
Calories: 529; Fat: 26.18 g; Carbs: 61.91 g; Protein: 13.67 g; Fiber 10.3g

Creamy Mashed Potatoes with Parsley

Prep + cook time: 15 minutes; Serves: 4

Ingredients:

- 3 cubed potatoes
- 1 tsp. salt
- 1 cup water
- 3 tbsp. butter
- ½ cup of milk
- 1/8 tsp. black pepper
- ¼ cup grated parmesan cheese
- 2 tbsp. chopped parsley

Instructions:

1. Open the Instant Pot and add the potatoes, salt, and water. Seal the lid and set to cook at high pressure for 3 minutes.
2. Quick-release the pressure and remove the potatoes. Put it in a large bowl.
3. Add the butter to the potatoes and mash the potatoes with the butter with a masher until it is smooth.
4. Pour in the milk and add the pepper then mix well. Sprinkle with parmesan cheese and parsley.

Nutrition Facts per Serving:
Calories: 340, Fat: 18.4g, Carbs: 26.7g, Protein: 15.8g

Creamy Green Beans with Mushrooms

Prep + cook time: 25 minutes; Serves: 3

Ingredients:
- 2 tbsp. butter
- 12 oz. sliced mushrooms
- 1 small chopped onion
- 1 cup chicken broth
- 16 oz. green beans
- 1 cup heavy cream
- 1-2 tbsp. cornstarch
- ½ cup chopped green onions

Instructions:
1. Press sauté on the Instant Pot and add the butter, mushrooms, and onions to cook for 2 to 3 minutes.
2. Pour in the broth, green beans, and heavy cream and seal the lid and the valve.
3. Set to manual to cook for 15 minutes.
4. Press the cancel button and natural- release the pressure for 8 to 10 minutes.
5. Open the lid and mix in the cornstarch to make the liquid thicker. Serve topped with green onions.

Nutrition Facts per Serving:
Calories: 411; Fat: 34g; Carbs: 17g; Protein 9.4g; Fiber 3g

Cinnamon Oats with Carrots and Raisins

Prep + cook time: 20 minutes; Serves: 2

Ingredients:
- 1 tbsp. butter
- 1 cup steel-cut oats
- 2 cups milk; plus more for serving
- 2 cups of water
- 2 carrots; grated
- ½ tsp. nutmeg
- ½ cup raisins
- ¼ cup brown sugar
- 1 tsp. ground cinnamon

Instructions:
1. Press sauté on the Instant Pot and add the butter to melt. Mix in the oats to toast until lightly brown and smells nutty.
2. Pour in the milk, water, carrots, nutmeg, raisins, brown sugar, and cinnamon.
3. Seal the lid and set to cook for 10 minutes at high pressure. Serve with some milk.

Nutrition Facts per Serving::
Calories: 461; Fat: 17.4 g; Carbs: 77.05 g; Protein: 16.57 g; Fiber 9.8g

Spicy Rice with Potatoes, Lentils, and Peas

Prep + cook time: 20 minutes; Serves: 2

Ingredients:
- 1 tbsp. olive oil
- ½ tsp. cumin seeds
- ½ small onion; chopped
- ½ tbsp. ginger paste
- ½ cup split green lentils
- ½ cup carrots; peeled and diced
- 1 tomato; finely chopped
- ½ cup fresh green peas; shelled
- ¼ tsp. red chili powder
- ¼ tsp. ground turmeric
- 1 tbsp. fresh chopped cilantro
- Salt
- ½ cup rinsed white rice
- 3 cups of water

Instructions:
1. Press sauté on the pot and add the oil and cumin seeds to cook for 30 seconds.
2. Mix in the onions and ginger to cook for 2 minutes then add the vegetables and spices to cook for 2 minutes.
3. Mix in the rest of the ingredients without adding the cilantro. Seal the lid and the valve.
4. Set to manual to cook for 5 minutes until it stops.
5. Press the cancel button and natural- release the pressure for 8 to 10 minutes. Open the pot and serve rice dish topped with cilantro.

Nutrition Facts per Serving:
Calories 450; Fat: 16g; Carbs: 55.5g; Protein 20g; Fiber 11g

Cheesy Rice and Asparagus Dish

Prep + cook time: 20 minutes; Serves: 2

Ingredients:
- 1 tbsp. olive oil
- 1 small chopped onion
- ½ cup risotto rice
- 2 chopped garlic cloves
- 1 1/3 cup vegetable stock
- 2 tbsp. orange juice
- 1 tbsp. thyme
- ½ lb. asparagus; diced
- ¼ cup parmesan; grated

Instructions:
1. Press sauté o the Instant Pot and add the oil and onions to cook for 2 minutes.
2. Add the rice and garlic to cook until the garlic becomes fragrant then pour in the stock and the orange juice. Seal the lid and the valve.
3. Set to manual to cook for 7 minutes.
4. Press the cancel button and quick release the pressure.
5. Open the pot and add the thyme and asparagus. Mix and let it sit for 5 to 8 minutes.
6. Serve in a bowl topped with cheese.

Nutrition Facts per Serving:
Calories: 407; Fat: 15g; Carbs: 44.5g; Protein 24g; Fiber 4g

Spicy Potatoes with Bell Peppers

Prep + cook time: 20 minutes; Serves: 2

Ingredients:
- 1 cup bell pepper; chopped
- ½ tsp. pepper
- 1 medium potato; diced
- 1 tsp. cumin
- 1 clove minced garlic
- 1 tsp. paprika
- 1 tbsp. oil
- 1 medium sweet potato; diced
- ¼ cup water
- Pinch of cayenne
- ½ tsp. salt

Instructions:
1. Mix all the ingredients in a bowl until the potatoes are well coated in oil and spices.
2. Put the potatoes and bell pepper mixture into the Instant Pot and add a half cup of water. Seal the lid and the valve.
3. Set to manual to cook for 10 minutes until the timer stops.
4. Press the cancel button and quick release the pressure. Open the lid and press the sauté button to brown the potatoes some more.
5. Serve warm.

Nutrition Facts per Serving:
Calories: 100; Fat: –12g; Carbs: 21.5g; Protein 4g; Fiber 7g

Creamy Cinnamon Quinoa with Peaches

Prep + cook time: 15 minutes; Serves: 3

Ingredients:
- 1 tbsp. butter
- 1 cup quinoa
- 1 cup milk
- ½ cup of water
- ½ tsp. vanilla extract
- 1 tbsp. cinnamon
- ¾ cup half and half
- 1 cup peaches

Instructions:
1. Press sauté on the pot and add the butter to melt.
2. Mix in the quinoa and cook for 2 minutes while stirring.
3. Pour in the milk and water and add the vanilla and cinnamon. Seal the lid and set to cook at high pressure for 4 minutes.
4. Quick-release the pressure and open the lid. Mix in the half and half and peaches and serve.

Nutrition Facts per Serving:
Calories: 389, Fat: 16.1g, Carbs: 49.6g, Protein: 13.1g

Creamy Instant Pot Polenta

Prep + cook time: 13 minutes; Serves: 2

Ingredients:
- 2 cups of milk
- ½ cup polenta
- ½ tsp. salt
- 3 tbsp. milk
- 3 tbsp. butter

Instructions:
1. Press sauté on the pot and add the 2 cups of milk to boil. Mix in the polenta and the salt and seal the lid and the valve.
2. Set to manual to cook for 8 minutes until the timer stops.
3. Cancel the pot and quick release the pressure then open and mix in the 3 tablespoons of milk and butter.
4. Serve warm.

Nutrition Facts per Serving:
Calories 60; Fat: 1.6g; Carbs: 6.3; Protein 5g; Fiber 3.3g

Creamy Cinnamon Oats with Pumpkin

Prep + cook time: 20 minutes; Serves: 4

Ingredients:
- 1 cup steel-cut oats
- 1 tsp. vanilla
- 1 ¼ cup of water
- 14 oz. can coconut milk
- ½ tsp. salt
- ¼ tsp. cinnamon
- 1 tbsp. brown sugar
- 2 tbsp. maple syrup
- ¼ cup pumpkin

Instructions:
1. Mix the oats, vanilla, water, milk, and salt in the Instant Pot and seal the lid.
2. Set to cook for 10 minutes at high pressure. Quick-release the pressure when the timer stops and open the lid.
3. Mix in the rest of the ingredients and serve.

Nutrition Facts per Serving:
Calories: 316, Fat: 22.6g, Carbs: 27g, Protein: 4.9g

Fruity Quinoa with Pistachios

Prep + Cook time: 11 minutes; Serves: 2

Ingredients:
- ¾ cup white quinoa
- ¾ cup of water
- 1 small cinnamon stick
- ½ cup grated apples
- ½ cup apple juice
- 1/8 cup raisins
- ½ tbsp. honey
- ½ cup plain yogurt
- 3 tbsp. blueberries

Instructions:
1. Pour the quinoa into a bowl and add some water to rinse it. Strain it with a strainer and set aside.
2. Pour the ¾ cup of water inside the Instant Pot and add the quinoa and the cinnamon stick.
3. Seal the lid and the venting valve.
4. Set to cook at "Manual" for 1 minute.
5. "Cancel" the preset function and natural-release the pot pressure for 8 to 10 minutes.
6. Scoop the quinoa into a bowl and remove the cinnamon stick.
7. Mix the quinoa with the apples, juice, raisins, and the honey and keep in the fridge overnight or at least an hour.
8. Mix in the yogurt. Serve topped with blueberries.

Nutrition Facts per Serving
Calories 418, Fat 6.5g, Carbs 44.5g, Protein 14g, Fiber 7g

Buttery Rice Dish with Apples and Cherries

Prep + cook time: 23 minutes; Serves: 2

Ingredients:
- 1 tbsp. butter
- ¾ cup risotto rice
- 1 large apple; peeled, cored, and diced
- ¾ tsp. cinnamon
- ¼ cup brown sugar
- 1 ½ cup milk
- ½ cup apple juice
- ¼ cup dried cherries

Instructions:
1. Press sauté on the Instant Pot and add the butter and the rice to cook until the rice is opaque for 4 minutes.
2. Mix in the apple, cinnamon, sugar, milk, and apple juice and seal the lid and the valve.
3. Set to manual to cook for 6 minutes until the timer stops.
4. Press the cancel button and quick release the pressure. Mix in the cherries and serve in bowls with a splash of milk and sprinkle of brown sugar.

Nutrition Facts per Serving:

Calories: 180; Fat: 7g; Carbs: 18.5g; Protein 10g; Fiber 8g

Creamy Vanilla Oats with Potatoes and Raisins

Prep + cook time: 25 minutes; Serves: 2

Ingredients:
- ½ cup steel cut oats
- ½ tsp. cinnamon
- ¼ tsp. cardamom
- ½ tsp. vanilla extract
- 1/8 tsp. ginger
- 2 tbsp. raisins
- 1 1/3 cup water
- 1 cup chopped sweet potato
- ¼ cup almond milk
- Salt to taste

Instructions:
1. Mix the oats, raisins, water, cardamom, cinnamon, ginger and sweet potatoes in the Instant Pot.
2. Seal the lid and set to cook at low pressure for 15 minutes.
3. Quick-release the pressure and open the lid.
4. Mix in the chopped sweet potatoes and vanilla, pour in the almond milk, and season with a pinch of salt and mix well to combine.

Nutrition Facts per Serving

Calories 270, Fat 8.7g, Carbs 44.2g, Protein 5.7g

Cinnamon Banana Pottage

Prep + Cook time: 8 minutes; Serves: 2

Ingredients:
- 1 cup buckwheat groats; rinsed
- 2 tbsp. brown sugar; plus some more serving
- 2 cups milk; plus some more for serving
- 1 tsp. ground cinnamon
- 1 ripe banana; sliced

Instructions:
1. Mix the buckwheat groats, brown sugar, milk, ground cinnamon, and ripe bananas in the Instant Pot.
2. Seal the lid and set to cook for 6 minutes at high pressure. Serve the pottage with some brown sugar and some milk.

Nutrition Facts per Serving

Calories 409, Fat 12.7g, Carbs 62.26g, Protein 15.08g, Fiber 4.5g

Creamy Blueberries Pottage

Prep + Cook time: 25 minutes; Serves: 3

Ingredients:

- 2 tsp. butter
- 1 cup of water
- 1 tbsp. flax meal
- ½ cup almond flour
- 1 tbsp. sugar
- 1 tbsp. heavy cream
- 1 egg
- 1 ½ tbsp. blueberries

Instructions:

1. Press "Sauté" on the Instant Pot and add the butter to melt.
2. Pour in the water and add the flax meal, almond flour, sugar, and heavy cream and mix well. Leave to cook for 2 to 3 minutes.
3. Beat the egg in a small bowl and add it to the pot while mixing continuously. Seal the lid and set to cook for 10 minutes at high pressure.
4. Quick-release the pressure and mix the blueberries with the pottage and serve.

Nutrition Facts per Serving

Calories 195, Fat 16g, Carbs 9.6g, Protein 6.5g

Cinnamon Carrot Oatmeal with Raisins

Prep + cook time: 20 minutes; Serves: 2

Ingredients:

- 1 tbsp. butter
- 1 cup steel-cut oats
- 2 grated carrots
- 1 tsp. ground cinnamon
- ¼ cup brown sugar
- ½ tsp. nutmeg
- ½ cup raisins
- 2 cup milk
- 2 cup of water

Instructions:

1. Press "Sauté" on the Instant Pot and add the butter to melt then mix in the oats. Let the oats toast till lightly browned and smells nutty.
2. Add the rest of the ingredients to the Instant Pot and seal the lid to cook at high pressure for 10 minutes. Serve with some milk.

Nutrition Facts per Serving

Calories 451, Fat 17.4g, Carbs 77.05g, Protein 16.5g

Chili Garlic Polenta

Prep + Cook time: 15 minutes; Serves: 2

Ingredients:

- Cooking oil
- 1 tsp. minced garlic
- 1 bunch green onions
- 1 cup broth
- 2 tbsp. cilantro
- ½ cup cornmeal
- ½ tsp. cumin
- A pinch of cayenne
- ½ tsp. oregano
- 1 ½ tsp. chili powder
- ¼ tsp. paprika
- 1 cup boiling water

Instructions:

1. Press "Sauté" on the Instant Pot and pour in some cooking oil and add the garlic and onions to cook for 2 to 3 minutes until soft.
2. Pour in the broth and add the cilantro, cornmeal, cumin, cayenne, oregano, chili powder, paprika, and the boiling water and stir. Seal the lid and the venting valve.
3. Set to "Manual" to cook for 5 minutes until the timer has stopped.
4. Select "Cancel" to stop the preset function.
5. Natural-release the pressure for 8 to 10 minutes. Open and serve.

Nutrition Facts per Serving

Calories 98, Fat 1.5g, Carbs 6g, Protein 4g, Fiber 3g

Spicy Potatoes with Bell Peppers

Prep + Cook time: 20 minutes; Serves: 2

Ingredients:
- 1 medium potato; chopped
- 1 medium sweet potato; diced
- 1 cup bell pepper; chopped
- ½ tsp. pepper
- 1 tbsp. oil
- ¼ cup water
- 1 tsp. cumin
- 1 minced garlic clove
- 1 tsp. paprika
- ½ tsp. salt

Instructions:

1. Mix all the potatoes and the bell peppers with the oil and spices in a bowl.
2. Put the spice-coated potatoes and bell peppers in the Instant Pot and add the water. Seal the lid and the venting valve.
3. Set to "Manual" to cook for 10 minutes until the timer has stopped.
4. Select "Cancel" to stop the preset function. Quick-release the pressure, open the pot and select "Sauté" to brown the potatoes. Serve.

Nutrition Facts per Serving

Calories 256, Fat -12g, Carbs 21.5g, Protein 4g, Fiber 7g

Vanilla and Cinnamon Quinoa with Peaches

Prep + Cook time: 15 minutes; Serves: 3

Ingredients:
- 1 tbsp. butter
- 1 cup quinoa
- 1 cup milk
- ½ cup of water
- ½ tsp. vanilla extract
- 1 tbsp. cinnamon
- ¾ cup half and half
- 1 cup peaches

Instructions:
1. Press "Sauté" on the Instant Pot and add the butter.

2. Mix in the quinoa and continue stirring for 2 minutes.
3. Pour in the milk and water and mix then add the vanilla and cinnamon and mix again. Seal the lid to cook for 4 minutes at high pressure.
4. Quick-release the pressure and open the lid then add the half and half and peaches.

Nutrition Facts per Serving

Calories 389, Fat 16.1g, Carbs 49.6g, Protein 13.1g

Apple and Squash Meal

Prep + Cook time: 28 minutes; Serves: 2

Ingredients:
- 1 (1 ¼ lb) whole squash
- 2 medium apples; cored and roughly chopped
- ½ cup chicken broth
- ½ tsp. ground cinnamon
- 1/8 tsp. ground ginger
- 1/8 tsp. ground cloves
- 2 tbsp. maple syrup
- 2 tbsp. gelatin
- A pinch of salt

Instructions:
1. Place the Instant Pot on a clean and dry surface and put it on.

2. Mix in the squash, apples, chicken broth, cinnamon, ginger, and cloves then seal the lid and the venting valve.
3. Set to "Manual" to cook for 8 minutes until the timer has stopped.
4. Select "Cancel" to stop the preset function then natural-release the pressure for 8 to 10 minutes.
5. Open the pot and let it cool for some minutes. Remove the squash and put it on a chopping board to cut half lengthwise then throw the seeds away.

6. Put the squash and the apple mix from the pot, maple syrup, gelatin, and salt in a blender and pulse until it is smooth and serve.

Nutrition Facts per Serving
Calories 312, Fat 0.8g, Carbs 44g, Protein 13.5g, Fiber 9g

Carrot Oatmeal with Raisins

Prep + Cook time: 20 minutes; Serves: 2

Ingredients:
- 1 tbsp. butter
- 1 cup steel-cut oats
- 2 cups milk; plus more to serve
- 2 carrots; grated
- ¼ cup brown sugar
- 1 tsp. ground cinnamon
- ½ tsp. nutmeg
- ½ cup raisins

Instructions:

1. Press "Sauté" on the Instant Pot and add the butter to melt then add the oats. Let the oats toast till it is slightly brown and smells nutty.
2. Add the milk, carrots, brown sugar, cinnamon, nutmeg, and raisins.
3. Seal the lid to cook at high pressure for 10 minutes. Serve with some milk.

Nutrition Facts per Serving
Calories 451, Fat 17.4g, Carbs 77.05g, Protein 16.57g, Fiber 9.8g

Cheesy Bacon Omelet

Prep + Cook time: 15 minutes; Serves: 3

Ingredients:
- 3 eggs
- 1 chopped scallion
- 4 tbsp. shredded cheddar cheese
- 1 chopped zucchini
- 2 cooked bacon slices
- ¼ tsp. lemon-pepper seasoning
- ¼ cup almond milk
- Pepper and salt
- 1 cup of water

Instructions:
1. Pour a cup of water into the Instant Pot and put a steaming rack above the water.

2. Whisk the eggs, scallion, cheese, zucchini, bacon, lemon pepper, milk, pepper, and salt together in a bowl.
3. Pour the egg mix into a silicone mold and put the filled mold on the steaming rack. Seal the lid and set to cook for 5 minutes at high pressure.
4. Quick-release the pressure and open the lid. Serve.

Nutrition Facts per Serving
Calories 228, Fat 17.7g, Carbs 4.5g, Protein 13.9g

Indian Pilaf

Prep + Cook time: 15 minutes; Serves: 2

Ingredients:
- 1 tbsp. oil
- 1 stick cinnamon
- 2 tsp. whole cumin
- 2 pods cardamom
- 1 bay leaf
- 1 large onion; sliced
- 1 cup millet; decorated
- 1 ½ cup water
- Salt

Instructions:

1. Put the Instant Pot on a clean surface and switch it on.
2. Press "Sauté" on the pot and add the oil, cinnamon, cumin, cardamom, and bay leaf to cook until the cumin crackles.
3. Add the onions to cook for 2 to 3 minutes then put the pot off and add the millet to cook for some more minutes until it is coated with the spices.
4. Add the water and salt and seal the lid.
5. Set to "Manual" to cook for 1 minute.

6. When the timer stops, press "Cancel" to stop the preset function and natural-release the pressure for 8 to 10 minutes.

7. Open the pot and toss the millet with a fork and serve.

Nutrition Facts per Serving
Calories 315, Fat 7g, Carbs 18.5g, Protein 3g

Rice with Potatoes and Sausages

Prep + Cook time: 18 minutes; Serves: 3

Ingredients:
- 1 ½ tbsp. olive oil
- 1 tbsp. green onions; finely chopped
- 1 ½ tbsp. green onion; finely chopped
- 4 slices ginger
- 2 lean sausages; thinly sliced
- 5 small yellow potatoes; peeled
- 1/6 tsp. ground black pepper
- 2 cups long-grain rice
- ¼ tsp. chicken broth
- 3 cups of water
- 1 tsp. salt

Instructions:
1. Select "Sauté" on the Instant Pot then add the olive oil, onions, and ginger to cook for 2 minutes.

2. Mix in the sausages to cook for 2 to 3 minutes then add the potatoes to cook for 2 more minutes. Stir in the rice.

3. Mix in the black pepper, chicken broth, water, and salt and seal the lid.

4. Press the "Rice" button to cook for 4 minutes.

5. When the timer has stopped, "Cancel" the preset function and natural-release the pressure for 8 to 10 minutes.

6. Open the lid and serve into containers or dishes and garnish with green onions.

Nutrition Facts per Serving
Calories 377, Fat 12g, Carbs 55.6g, Fiber 4g, Protein 13.7g

Fruity Rice Dish

Prep + Cook time: 23 minutes; Serves: 2

Ingredients:
- 1 tbsp. butter
- ¾ cup risotto rice
- 1 large apple; peeled, cored and diced
- ¾ tsp. cinnamon
- ¼ cup brown sugar
- 1 ½ cups milk
- ½ cup apple juice
- ¼ cup dried cherries

Instructions:
1. Press "Sauté" on the Instant Pot and add the butter and the rice to cook for 4 minutes until opaque.

2. Stir in the apple, cinnamon, and brown sugar then add the milk and apple juice.

3. Seal the lid and set to "Manual" to cook for 6 minutes.

4. "Cancel" the preset function when the timer stops and quick-release the pressure.

5. Mix in the dried cherries and serve into bowls with some milk, almonds and sprinkled with brown sugar.

Nutrition Facts per Serving
Calories 556, Fat 7g, Carbs 18.5g, Protein 10g, Fiber 8g

Vanilla Oats with Pumpkin

Prep + Cook time: 20 minutes; Serves: 4

Ingredients:

- 1 cup steel-cut oats
- 1 tsp. vanilla
- 14 oz. can coconut milk
- ½ tsp. salt
- ¼ tsp. cinnamon
- 1 tbsp. brown sugar
- 2 tbsp. maple syrup
- ¼ cup pumpkin

Instructions:

1. Mix the oats, vanilla, coconut milk, and salt in the Instant Pot.
2. Seal the lid and set to cook for 10 minutes at high pressure. Quick-release the pressure and open the lid.
3. Mix in the cinnamon, brown sugar, maple syrup, and pumpkin.

Nutrition Facts per Serving

Calories 316, Fat 22.6g, Carbs 27g, Protein 4.9g

Cheesy Mashed Potatoes with Parsley

Prep + cook time: 15 minutes; Serves: 4

Ingredients:

- 3 cubed potatoes
- 1 tsp. salt
- 1 cup of water
- 3 tbsp. butter
- ½ cup milk
- 1/8 tsp. pepper
- ¼ cup parmesan cheese
- 2 tbsp. chopped parsley

Instructions:

1. Put the potatoes, salt, and the water in the Instant Pot and seal the lid.
2. Set to cook for 3 minutes at high pressure. When the timer stops, quick-release the pressure and open the lid.
3. Remove the potatoes from the water and put it in a large bowl.
4. Add the butter to the potatoes and mash the potatoes until smooth.
5. Mix in the milk and pepper. Serve garnished with cheese and parsley.

Nutrition Facts per Serving

Calories 352, Fat 18.4g, Carbs 26.7g, Protein 15.8g

Apricot Oats

Prep + cook time: 5 minutes; Serves: 2

Ingredients:

- 1 tbsp. butter
- 1 cup steel-cut oats
- 1 ½ cup milk
- 1 ½ cup water
- 1 cup dried apricots

Instructions:

1. Set the Instant Pot to "Sauté" and add the butter to melt.
2. Add the oats to toast until brown and nutty.
3. Add the milk, water, and dried apricots and stir. Seal the lid and set to cook at high pressure for 3 minutes.
4. Serve into bowls with milk.

Nutrition Facts per Serving

Calories 435, Fat 15.38g, Carbs 80.5g, Protein 16.16g

Spicy Rice with Potatoes and Lentils

Prep + cook time: 20 minutes; Serves: 2

Ingredients:

- 1 tbsp. olive oil
- ½ tsp. cumin seeds
- ½ small onion; chopped
- ½ tbsp. ginger paste
- ½ cup split green lentils; rinsed
- ½ cup carrots; peeled and diced
- ½ cup fresh green peas; shelled
- 1 small potato; cut into small pieces
- ¼ tsp. red chili pepper
- ¼ tsp. ground turmeric
- ½ cup white rice; rinsed
- 1 tomato; finely chopped
- 3 cups of water
- Salt to taste
- 1 tbsp. chopped fresh cilantro

Instructions:

1. Press "Sauté" on the Instant Pot and add the olive oil and cumin seeds to cook for 30 seconds.
2. Mix in the onions and ginger paste to cook for 2 minutes then add the vegetables, potatoes, chili pepper, and turmeric to cook for 2 minutes.
3. Mix in the rice, water, and season with some salt then seal the lid.
4. Press "Manual" to cook for 5 minutes.
5. "Cancel" the preset function and natural-release the pot pressure for 8 to 10 minutes. Serve topped with cilantro.

Nutrition Facts per Serving

Calories 358, Fat 16g, Carbs 55.5g, Protein 20g, Fiber 11g

Buttery Sprouts with Pomegranate

Prep + Cook time: 15 minutes; Serves: 3

Ingredients:

- 1 cup of water
- 1 lb. Brussels sprouts
- 2 tbsp. melted butter
- 2 tbsp. pomegranate seeds
- 1 cup crumbled feta cheese
- ¼ cup chopped cashew nuts

Instructions:

1. Pour the water into the Instant Pot and place a steaming rack above it.
2. Put the Brussels sprouts on the steaming rack and seal the pot to cook at high pressure for 3 minutes.
3. Quick-release the pressure and open the lid.
4. Remove the Brussels sprouts to a bowl and drizzle with the melted butter. Mix in the seeds, feta cheese, and cashew nuts.

Nutrition Facts per Serving

Calories 379, Fat 24.8g, Carbs 20.2g, Protein 14.8g

Butter Oatmeal with Apricots

Prep + Cook time: 5 minutes; Serves: 2

Ingredients:

- 1 tbsp. butter
- 1 cup steel-cut oats
- 1 ½ cup milk; plus more for serving
- 1 ½ cup water
- 1 cup dried apricots

Instructions:

1. Press "Sauté" on the Instant Pot and add the butter to melt. Mix in the oats to toast until it is lightly brown and smells nutty.
2. Mix in the milk, water, and dried apricots.
3. Seal the lid and set to cook at high pressure for 3 minutes. Serve into bowls with milk.

Nutrition Facts per Serving

Calories 435, Fat 15.38g, Carbs 80.59g, Protein 16.6g, Fiber 12g

Chapter 3 Soup and Stews

Garlic Chicken Soup with Radish and Carrots

Prep+ cook time: 26 minutes; serves: 2

Ingredients:

- 1 medium carrot
- ¼ lb. radish
- ¼ lb. boneless chicken breast
- ¼ tsp. oregano
- ¼ tsp. chopped' parsley
- ¼ tsp. dried thyme
- ¼ tsp. dried rosemary
- 2 tbsp. chopped celery stalk
- 2 tsp. minced garlic
- 2 tbsp. chopped onion
- 1 ½ cups of water

Instructions:

1. Cut the carrot and radish into thick slices and put it in the Instant Pot then cut the chicken into small chunks and put it on the carrots and radishes.
2. Add the oregano, parsley, thyme, rosemary, garlic, and onion then pour water and seal the lid and the valve.
3. Set to soup to cook for 22 minutes.
4. Quick-release the pressure and open the pot. Mix in the celery until it is wilted then serve in bowls.

Nutrition Facts per Serving

Calories: 142; Net Carbs: 5.3g; Fat: 4.4g; Protein: 17.5g; Carbs: 7.7g

Creamy Celery Soup

Prep + cook time: 6 minutes; serves: 4

Ingredients:

- 1½ tbsp. butter
- 1 tsp. minced' garlic
- ¼ cup chopped' onion
- 1½ cups diced' celeries
- 1 ½ cup vegetable broth
- 1 bay leaf
- ¼ tsp. salt
- ¼ tsp. pepper
- 2 tbsp. fresh milk
- 1 tbsp. chopped parsley

Instructions:

1. Press sauté on the pot and add the butter to melt then add the garlic, onion, and celery to cook until soft.
2. Press cancel then pour the broth and add the bay leaf, milk, salt, and pepper. Stir then seal the lid and the valve.
3. Set to manual to cook for 4 minutes. Natural-release the pressure and open the pot.
4. Blend with a dipping blender until smooth then serve topped with parsley.

Nutrition Facts per Serving

Calories: 110; Net Carbs: 4.2g; Fat: 7.3g; Protein: 5.1g; Carbs: 6g

Creamy Squash Curry

Prep + cook time: 40 minutes; serves: 2

Ingredients:

- 1 tsp. olive oil
- ½ minced onion
- ½ tbsp. curry powder
- 1 minced garlic clove
- 1 ½ lb. cubed butternut squash
- 1 ½ cup of water
- Salt to taste
- ¼ cup of coconut milk

Instructions:

1. Press sauté on the pot and add the oil and onions to cook until soft then add the curry and garlic to cook for 1minute.

2. Mix in the squash, water, and salt then seal the lid and the valve to cook at soup for 25 minutes.
3. Quick-release the pressure and puree with a dipping blender. Mix with the coconut milk and serve.

Nutrition Facts per Serving
Calories: 260, Fat: 10.1g, Carbs: 45.4g, Protein: 4.7g

Chicken Zoodles with Carrots and Celery

Prep + cook time: 15 minutes; serves: 2
Ingredients:
- ½ lb. bone-in chicken breast
- ¼ cup chopped' carrots
- 2 tbsp. diced' celeries
- 2 tbsp. chopped' onion
- ¼ tsp. salt
- 1 cup of water
- ¼ tsp. garlic powder
- 1 tsp. soy sauce
- ¼ tsp. oregano
- 1 tbsp. butter
- 2 medium zucchinis; julienned

Instructions:
1. Cut the chicken into medium-sized chunks and set aside. Press sauté on the pot and add the butter.
2. Mix in the carrots, celery, and onion to cook till fragrant then press the cancel button.
3. Mix in the chicken then pour the water over it. Add the salt, garlic powder, soy sauce, and oregano. Stir well then seal the lid and the valve.
4. Set to soup to cook for 8 minutes at high pressure. Quick-release the pressure and mix in the zucchini noodles until wilted. Serve warm.

Nutrition Facts per Serving
Calories: 226; Net Carbs: 6.6g; Fat: 7.7g; Protein: 30g; Carbs: 9.6g

Spicy Bean Soup

Prep + cook time: 47 minutes; serves: 2
Ingredients:
- 1 tbsp. olive oil
- 1 tsp. cumin seeds
- 1 medium onion; chopped
- 1 tbsp. garlic paste
- 1 tbsp. ginger paste
- 1 tsp. red chili powder
- ½ tsp. ground turmeric
- ½ tsp. garam masala
- 2 tsp. ground coriander
- Salt
- 1 cup black beans; soaked overnight and drained
- 2 cups of water
- 1 tsp. lemon juice

Instructions:
1. Press sauté on the pot and add the oil and the cumin seeds to cook for 30 seconds. Mix in the onion, garlic, ginger, spices, and salt to cook for 3 to 4 minutes.
2. Mix in the beans and water then seal the lid and the valve.
3. Set to beans/chili to cook for 30 minutes. Press the cancel button and natural-release the pressure for 8 to 10 minutes. Open the lid and mix in the lemon juice. Serve warm.

Nutrition Facts per Serving
Calories: 437; Fat: 9g; Carbs: 68.5g; Fiber: 16.5g; Protein 22g

Spicy Chicken with Zucchini Noodles Soup

Prep + cook time: 15 minutes; serves: 4

Ingredients:
- 1 onion; chopped
- 1 tbsp. oil
- 1 jalapeno; chopped
- 1 cup chicken breast 1-inch slices
- 1 tbsp. curry paste
- 1 can full-fat coconut milk
- 1 zucchini; spiralized
- 1 tbsp. fish sauce
- ½ lime; juiced
- 4 cups chicken broth
- salt

Instructions:
1. Press sauté on the pot and add the oil and onions to cook for 2 to 3 minutes.

2. Mix in the jalapeno to cook for 1 to 2 minutes then add the chicken, curry, and milk to cook for 2 to 3 minutes.
3. Press the cancel button them add the rest of the ingredients except the zucchini. Seal the lid and set to manual to cook for 5 minutes at high pressure.
4. Press the cancel button and quick release the pressure. Open the lid and mix it in the zoodles. Serve.

Nutrition Facts per Serving

Calories: 319 g; Fat: 22.8 g; Carbs: 10.8 g; Protein: 19.5

Creamy Lentils Soup

Prep + cook time: 12 minutes; serves: 2

Ingredients:
- ¼ lb. boneless chicken breast; cubed
- 2 tbsp. uncooked lentils
- 2 tbsp. diced' onions
- 1½ cups chicken broth
- ¼ tsp. salt
- ¼ tsp. pepper
- ¼ cup half and half

Instructions:
1. Put the cubed chicken in the pot and add the lentils, onions, salt, and pepper. Pour in the broth and stir then seal the lid and the valve.

2. Set to manual to cook for 10 minutes at high pressure.
3. Natural-release the pressure and open the lid.mix in the half and half then press the sauté button and cook for 2 minutes.
4. Serve into bowls.

Nutrition Facts per Serving

Calories: 151; Net Carbs: 6.1g; Fat: 3.4g; Protein: 19.9g; Carbs: 10g

Buttery Salmon Stew

Prep + cook time: 15 minutes; serves: 3

Ingredients:
- 1 lb. cubed salmon fillet
- 1 chopped onion
- 1 cup fish broth
- 1 tbsp. butter
- Salt and Pepper

Instructions:

1. Mix all the ingredients in the pot and seal the lid and the valve.
2. Set to cook for 6 minutes at high pressure then natural-release the pressure, open the lid, stir, and serve.

Nutrition Facts per Serving

Calories: 261, Fat: 13.7g, Carbs: 3.7g, Protein: 31.4g

Creamy Tarragon and Carrot Soup

Prep + cook time: 16 minutes; serves: 4

Ingredients:

- 2 tbsp. butter
- 1 onion; chopped
- 2 ½ cups raw carrots; chopped
- 2 sprigs fresh tarragon
- 5 oz. Greek yogurt
- 4 cups vegetable stock or water
- Salt and pepper

Instructions:

1. Press sauté on the pot and add the butter and onions to cook for 2 to 3 minutes.
2. Mix in the rest of the ingredients then seal the lid and the valve.
3. Set to manual to cook for 3 minutes at high pressure.
4. Press the cancel button and quick release the steam. Open the lid and remove some of the liquid to create the required thickness.
5. Puree with a dipping blender and serve topped with yogurt.

Nutrition Facts per Serving

Calories: 129 g; Fat: 8.4 g; Carbs: 11.2 g; Protein: 3.1

Ginger Ribs with Collard

Prep + cook time: 26 minutes; serves: 2

Ingredients:

- 3/4 lb. pork ribs
- 1 tsp. sliced shallots
- ½ tsp. ginger
- ¼ tsp. nutmeg
- 1 cup water
- ¼ tsp. salt
- ¼ tsp. pepper
- ¼ cup chopped' collard

Instructions:

1. Put the pork in the pot and add the rest of the ingredients except the collard.
2. Seal the lid and set to manual to cook at high pressure for 20 minutes.
3. Quick-release the pressure and open the lid.
4. Mix in the collard and press sauté on the pot to cook for 1 minute or until collard is wilted.
5. Serve.

Nutrition Facts per Serving

Calories: 471; Net Carbs: 0.8g; Fat: 30.3g; Carbs: 1.2g; Protein: 45.3g.

Spicy Onion Soup

Prep + cook time: 10 minutes; serves: 4

Ingredients:

- 2 tbsp. butter
- 1 cup sliced onions
- ½ tbsp. thyme
- ¼ tsp. pepper
- 1½ cups vegetable broth
- ¼ cup white wine
- ½ tbsp. Worcestershire sauce
- 1 bay leaf
- ½ tsp. salt

Instructions:

1. Press sauté on the pot and add the butter and the onions to cook until fragrant. Press the cancel button and add the rest of the ingredients.
2. Seal the lid and set it to manual to cook for 6 minutes.
3. Quick-release the pressure and open the pot then puree with a dipping blender.

Nutrition Facts per Serving

Calories: 160; Net Carbs: 6.8g; Fat: 11.7g; Carbs: 8.4g; Protein: 0.9g

Chicken Noodles Soup with Carrots and Celery

Prep + cook time: 18 minutes; serves: 3

Ingredients:

- 2 boneless chicken thighs; cubed
- 2 cups uncooked egg noodles
- 1 celery stalk; sliced
- 3 cups chicken stock
- 1 onion; diced
- 2 carrots; sliced
- 1 bay leaf
- ½ tsp. salt
- ½ tsp. black pepper

Instructions:

1. Mix all the ingredients in the pot then seal the lid and set to cook for 8 minutes.
2. Remove the bay leaf and serve.

Nutrition Facts per Serving

Calories: 311; Fat: 17.31 g; Carbs: 17.68 g; Fiber: 1.3 g; Protein: 20.21 g

Creamy Potato Curry with Zucchini and Tomatoes

Prep + cook time: 20 minutes; serves: 3

Ingredients:

- 1 tbsp. olive oil
- ½ tbsp. minced ginger
- 1 diced onion
- 1 minced garlic clove
- 7oz.coconut milk
- 7oz.diced tomatoes
- ½ diced bell pepper
- ½ diced zucchini
- 1 diced sweet potato
- 1 lime juice
- 1 tbsp. red curry paste
- ½ tsp. turmeric
- 1 tsp. curry powder
- ½ tsp. sea salt

Instructions:

1. Press sauté on the pot and add the oil and onions to cook for 1 minute.
2. Mix in the garlic and ginger to cook for another minute then mix in the rest of the ingredients.
3. Seal the lid and set to cook for 5 minutes at high pressure.
4. Quick-release the pressure and open the lid. Serve.

Nutrition Facts per Serving

Calories: 251, Fat: 20.6g, Carbs: 16.7g, Protein: 3.5g

Spicy Chicken Soup with Mushrooms and Carrots

Prep + cook time: 35 minutes; serves: 4

Ingredients:

- ½ lb. chicken meat; cooked, shredded
- 1 onion; chopped
- 1 carrot; diced
- ½ celery; diced
- 2 garlic cloves; chopped
- 7 oz. mushrooms; sliced
- 5 cups chicken stock
- 1 tsp. thyme
- 1 tsp. rosemary
- 2 bay leaves
- 2 tbsp. olive oil
- Salt and pepper

Instructions:

1. Press sauté on the pot and add the oil.
2. Mix in the onion and carrots to cook for 2 to 3 minutes then add the celery, garlic, and mushrooms to cook for 3 minutes.
3. Press the cancel button and add the rest of the ingredients.
4. Seal the lid and the valve and set to soup to cook at low pressure.
5. Press cancel and quick release the pressure. Open the lid and serve.

Nutrition Facts per Serving

Calories: 216 g; Fat: 11 g; Carbs: 5.4 g; Protein: 24

Nutty Beef Soup

Prep + cook time: 25 minutes; serves: 2

Ingredients:

- ½ lb. beef sirloin
- 2 kluwak nuts
- ¼ tsp. ginger
- ½ tsp. coriander
- ¼ tsp. cumin
- 2 shallots
- ½ cup water
- ¼ tsp. turmeric
- ½-inch galangal
- 1 lemongrass
- 3 kaffir lime leaves
- 2 cloves garlic
- ½ tsp. salt

Instructions:

1. Soak the kluwak nuts in water until the water turns black.
2. Put the ginger, coriander, cumin, shallots, and turmeric in a processor and blend till smooth.
3. Cut the beef into slices and put it in the Instant Pot then pour the spice mixture over it. Add the rest of the ingredients then mix well.
4. Seal the lid and the valve then set to manual to cook for 20 minutes at high pressure.
5. Natural-release the pressure and open the lid.
6. Serve.

Nutrition Facts per Serving

Calories: 154; Net Carbs: 6.4g; Fat: 4.2g Protein: 23.6g; Carbs: 6.6g

Oxtail with Veggies Soup

Prep + cook time: 28 minutes; serves: 2

Ingredients:

- 3/4 lb. oxtails
- 1 clove
- 1 cup water
- ¼ tsp. nutmeg
- ¼ tsp. salt
- ¼ tsp. pepper
- 2 tbsp. chopped' carrots
- 1 tbsp. chopped' celeries

Instructions:

1. Put the oxtails in the pot and add the clove, water, nutmeg, and salt. Mix well then seal the lid and the valve.
2. Set to manual to cook for 20 minutes at high pressure.
3. Quick-release the pressure and open the lid.
4. Mix in the carrot and celery the press the sauté button to cook for 3 minutes or until the carrot is soft. Serve into bowls.

Nutrition Facts per Serving

Calories: 426; Net Carbs: 0.8g; Fat: 22.7g; Carbs: 1.2g; Protein: 52.7g.

Creamy Chicken Soup with Carrots

Prep + cook time: 18 minutes; serves: 2

Ingredients:

- ½ lb. boneless chicken breast; diced
- ½ cup water
- 1 tsp. minced' garlic
- ¼ tsp. salt
- ¼ tsp. black pepper
- ¼ cup heavy cream
- ¼ cup diced' mushrooms
- 2 tbsp. diced' carrots

Instructions:

1. Put the chicken cubed in the pot and add the water, garlic, salt, and pepper.
2. Seal the lid and valve and set it to manual to cook for 10 minutes.
3. Quick-release the pressure and open the pot then add the cream, mushrooms, and carrots.
4. Seal the lid and cook on high for 3 minutes.
5. Quick-release the pressure and open the lid. Serve into a bowl.

Nutrition Facts per Serving

Calories: 217; Net Carbs: 1.2g; Fat: 11.6g; Carbs: 1.6; Protein: 25.5g.

Creamy Spiced Mushrooms Soup

Prep + cook time: 15 minutes; serves: 3

Ingredients:

- 4 cup sliced mushrooms
- 1 tbsp. minced garlic
- 1 cup chicken broth
- 1 chopped jalapeno pepper
- 2 sliced onions
- 1/2 cup heavy whipping cream
- 1 tsp. dried thyme
- 1 tsp. pepper
- 1 tsp. salt

Instructions:

1. Mix all the ingredients minus the whipping cream in the Instant Pot and seal the lid.
2. Set to cook at high pressure for 10 minutes.
3. Natural release the pressure and open the lid.
4. Use a dipping blender to puree the soup while leaving some mushroom pieces whole.
5. Mix in the whipping cream.

Nutrition Facts per Serving

Calories: 139, Fat: 8.3g, Carbs: 12.7g, Protein: 6.1g

Cheesy Cauliflower Soup

Prep + cook time: 10 minutes; serves: 4

Ingredients:

- 1 ½ cups cauliflower florets
- 2 tsp. minced garlic
- ¼ cup chopped onions
- ¼ tsp. salt
- ½ tsp. pepper
- 1 cup vegetable broth
- ¼ cup cream cheese

Instructions:

1. Put the florets in the pot and add the garlic, onions, and salt and pepper.
2. Pour the broth in the pot and seal the lid and valve.
3. Set to manual to cook at high for 6 minutes.
4. Quick-release the pressure and mix in the cream cheese.
5. Blend with a dipping blender until smooth and serve into bowls.

Nutrition Facts per Serving:

Calories: 150; Net Carbs: 5.4g; Fat: 10.9g; Carbs: 7.8g; Protein: 6.5g.

Creamy Cheesy Beef Soup

Prep + cook time: 20 minutes; serves: 4

Ingredients:

- 1 tsp. olive oil
- 7 oz. ground beef
- 4 cups beef broth
- 3 ounces cream cheese
- 2 garlic cloves; minced
- 1 tsp. chili powder
- 1 tsp. ground cumin
- ½ cup heavy cream
- Salt and Pepper

Instructions:

1. Put the oil in the pot and add the beef to cook for 5 to 7 minutes.
2. Press the cancel button and drain the grease from the pot. Mix in the rest of the ingredients and seal the lid.
3. Set to manual to cook for 5 minutes at high pressure.
4. Press the cancel button and natural release the pressure. Open the pot and serve.

Nutrition Facts per Serving:

Calories: 606 g; Fat: 45.8 g; Carbs: 19.4 g; Protein: 32.9

Chapter 4 Vegetable

Creamy Tomato Soup with Celery

Prep + cook time: 20 minutes; serves: 4

Ingredients:
- 3/4 cup roasted cherry tomatoes
- 1 tbsp. tomato paste
- ¼ tsp. cayenne pepper
- 1½ tsp. olive oil
- 2 tbsp. diced' onions
- ½ cup heavy cream
- 1 tbsp. chopped' celeries
- ¼ tsp. salt
- 1 cup of water
- 1 tsp. red chili flakes
- ¼ tsp. pepper

Instructions:

1. Press sauté on the pot and add the oil and onions to cook until it is fragrant then press the cancel button.
2. Mix in the rest of the ingredients except the and seal the lid and the valve.
3. Set to soup to cook for 10 minutes then quick release the steam and open the lid.
4. Mix in the cream and press the sauté button to cook for 2 minutes. Puree with a dipping blender and serve.

Nutrition Facts per Serving

Calories: 156; Net Carbs: 6.7g; Fat: 13.5g; Protein: 2.1g; Carbs: 8.4g

Cheese Pasta with Zucchini

Prep + cook time: 14 minutes; serves: 3

Ingredients:
- 1 lb. penne pasta
- 4 cups of water
- 2 zucchinis; julienned
- 1 large tomato; diced
- 1 red bell pepper; julienned
- 1 onion; sliced thin
- 2 cloves garlic; minced
- ½ cup grated Parmesan
- ½ tsp. black pepper
- ¼ cup fresh basil; chopped
- 2 tbsp. olive oil
- ½ tsp. salt

Instructions:

1. Mix the pasta with the water in the pot and put a rack over the pasta.
2. Put the zucchini, garlic, tomato, pepper, and onion on the rack then seal the lid and the valve. Set to cook for 4 minutes at high pressure.
3. Quick-release the pressure and drain the pasta. Mix the rack contents with oil, basil, and parmesan. Serve seasoned with salt and black pepper.

Nutrition Facts per Serving

Calories: 283; Fat: 12.44 g; Carbs: 33.15 g; Protein: 10.59 g; Fiber: 3.9 g.

Creamy Ginger Mushroom Balls

Prep + cook time: 20 minutes; serves: 4

Ingredients:
- 2 cups chopped mushrooms
- ½ tsp. ginger
- 1 tsp. minced' garlic
- ½ tsp. rice wine
- ¼ tsp. sugar
- ½ cup of water
- 1 tsp. olive oil
- ½ tbsp. chopped onion
- 2 tbsp. coconut milk
- 2 tbsp. soy sauce

Instructions:

1. Put 1 cup of the mushrooms in a food processor then add the ginger, garlic, rice wine, and sugar to blend till smooth.

2. Mold into balls and set aside.
3. Pour water into the pot and place the rack over it. Put the mushroom balls on the rack and seal the lid and the valve. Set to steam to cook for 10 minutes.
4. Remove the balls and set aside when you quick release the steam.

5. Wipe the pot then add the oil and onions to cook till fragrant on sauté function. Press cancel then add the mushroom balls, milk, and soy sauce and cook for 3 minutes.
6. Serve the mushroom balls with the sauce.

Nutrition Facts per Serving
Calories: 88; Net Carbs: 4g; Fat: 6.2g; Carbs: 5.2g; Protein: 2.7g

Garlic Eggplant with Olives

Prep + cook time: 30 minutes; serves: 2

Ingredients:
- 2 tbsp. olive oil
- 2 eggplants; peeled on one side and chopped
- 2 garlic cloves
- 1 cup of water
- 1 tsp. salt
- 2 tbsp. lemon juice
- ¼ cup pitted black olives
- 1 tbsp. Tahini
- 1 tbsp. fresh thyme leaves

Instructions:
1. Press sauté on the pot and add the oil and eggplant to cook for 5 minutes. Press cancel.

2. Mix in the garlic, water, and salt then seal the lid and the valve.
3. Set to manual to cook for 3 minutes at high pressure.
4. Press the cancel button and natural-release the steam then remove most of the liquid from the pot.
5. Remove the garlic skin then add the garlic to the pot with lemon juice, olives, and Tahini.
6. Puree with a dipping blender. Serve with olive oil and thyme leaves.

Nutrition Facts per Serving
Calories: 175 g; Fat: 14 g; Carbs: 13.1 g; Protein: 12.7

Spicy Eggplant Curry with Tomatoes

Prep + cook time: 8 minutes; serves: 4

Ingredients:
- 1 tbsp. olive oil
- 1 cup chopped' onion
- 2 tsp. minced' garlic
- ½ tsp. chopped' green chili
- ¼ cup chopped' bell peppers
- ½ tsp. ginger
- ½ tsp. garam masala
- 1½ cups chopped' eggplants
- ½ tsp. cumin
- ½ tsp. turmeric
- ¼ cup chopped' tomatoes
- 1 tsp. cayenne pepper
- ½ tsp. coriander
- ¼ tsp. salt

- ¼ cup water

Instructions:
1. Press sauté on the pot and add the oil and onions and garlic to cook until fragrant.
2. Mix in the green chili, bell peppers, ginger, and garam masala then press the cancel button.
3. Add the rest of the ingredients. Do not mix. Seal the lid and set to manual to cook for 3 minutes.
4. Quick-release the steam and stir. Serve.

Nutrition Facts per Serving
Calories: 108; Net Carbs: 6.8g; Fat: 7.6g; Carbs: 10.5g; Protein: 1.7g.

Creamy Cheesy Macaroni

Prep + cook time: 20 minutes; serves: 3

Ingredients:
- 1lb. uncooked macaroni
- 4 cups of water
- 2 tbsp. flour
- 2 tbsp. butter
- 3 cups whole milk
- 1 cup shredded Cheddar cheese
- ½ tsp. black pepper
- ½ tsp. salt

Instructions:
1. Mix the macaroni and water in the pot then cook for 4 minutes at high pressure.
2. Quick-release the pressure and drain the pasta.
3. Wipe the pot and press sauté then add the butter and the flour to cook until it is bubbling.
4. Add the milk and cook until thick then add the cheese to cook until it has melted. Add the salt and pepper then mix in the pasta. Cook through and serve.

Nutrition Facts per Serving

Calories: 713; Fat: 23.06 g; Carbs: 97.02 g; Fiber: 3.8 g; Protein: 27.85 g

Cheesy Lemony Zoodles

Prep + cook time: 12 minutes; serves: 4

Ingredients:
- 2 tbsp. olive oil
- 3 garlic cloves; diced
- zest of half lemon
- 2 large zucchinis; spiralized
- juice of a half lemon
- 2 tbsp. water
- Salt and pepper
- ¼ cup Parmesan cheese; grated

Instructions:
1. Press sauté on the pot and add the oil and garlic with the lemon zest to cook for 30 seconds while stirring.
2. Add the zucchini, water, and lemon juice then cook for 30 to 45 seconds. Press cancel then season with salt and pepper and add the cheese.
3. Mix and serve.

Nutrition Facts per Serving

Calories: 273 g; Fat: 20.6 g; Carbs: 14.7 g; Protein: 13.4

Cheesy Vegetable Jumble

Prep + cook time: 25 minutes; serves: 6

Ingredients:
- 3 tbsp. olive oil
- ½ cup chopped onion
- 1 tbsp. minced garlic
- ½ cup chopped carrots
- ½ cup chopped celery
- ½ cup chopped bell peppers
- 2 cup chopped fresh mushrooms
- 3 tbsp. chopped parsley
- 1 can crushed tomatoes
- 1 tsp. dried oregano
- 1 tsp. salt
- 1 tbsp. balsamic vinegar
- 1 tsp. sugar
- 1oz.chopped dried porcini mushrooms
- ½ tbsp. black pepper
- ¼ tsp. dried thyme
- 1 tbsp. tomato paste
- 12oz.rigatoni pasta
- ½ tsp. crushed red pepper flakes
- 1 tsp. dried basil
- 1 cup of water
- 1 cup whole milk
- 1 cup red wine
- 4 oz. mascarpone cheese
- ¼ cup grated parmesan cheese

Instructions:
1. Press sauté on the pot then add the onion, garlic, carrots, celery, and bell peppers to cook for 3 minutes while stirring.

2. Mix in the fresh mushrooms to cook for 2 minutes.
3. Press cancel then remove any stuck buts with some water. Mix in the rest of the ingredients except the cheese.
4. Seal the lid and the valve and set it to manual to cook for 7 minutes.

5. Quick-release the pressure and add the mascarpone cheese. Rest for some minutes till it thickens then serve topped with parmesan.

Nutrition Facts per Serving
Calories: 293, Fat: 14g, Carbs: 27g, Protein: 10g

Cheesy Garlic Spinach in Sauce

Prep + cook time: 10 minutes; serves: 4
Ingredients:
- 2 tbsp. butter
- 1 tbsp. flour
- ¼ cup diced' onion
- 1 tsp. minced' garlic
- ¼ cup half and half
- ½ cup water
- 1 cup chopped' spinach
- 2 tbsp. grated cheddar cheese
- ¼ tsp. pepper
- ¼ tsp. salt
- ½ tsp. nutmeg
- 1½ tbsp. lemon juice

Instructions:

1. Press sauté on the pot and add the butter and flour to cook for some minutes then add the onion and garlic to cook.
2. Mix in the half and half to cook for 2 minutes. Press the cancel button.
3. Pour water into the pot and add the spinach, cheese, pepper, salt, and nutmeg.
4. Seal the lid and the valve and set it to manual to cook for 3 minutes.
5. Quick-release the pressure and open the lid. Mix in the lemon juice and serve with sauce.

Nutrition Facts per Serving
Calories: 201; Net Carbs: 6.4g; Fat: 17.8g; Carbs: 7.4g; Protein: 4g

Sweet Quinoa with Mixed Veggies

Prep + cook time: 7 minutes; serves: 3
Ingredients:
- 8 oz. bag mixed vegetables; frozen
- 2 cups quinoa
- 2 tbsp. soy sauce
- 2 tbsp. rice vinegar
- 1 thumb grated ginger
- 2 tbsp. of sugar
- 4 cups of water

Instructions:

1. Mix all the ingredients in the pot except the vegetable then seal the lid and the valve.
2. Set to manual to cook for 1 minute.
3. Press the cancel button and natural-release the pressure for 10 minutes.
4. Open the lid and mix in the vegetables.

Nutrition Facts per Serving
Calories: 456; Fat: 7g; Carbs: 42.3g; Protein 18g; Fiber: 9.2g

Sweet Apple Sauce with Cabbage

Prep + cook time: 15 minutes; serves: 4
Ingredients:
- 1 tsp. olive oil
- 1 onion; chopped
- 3 cups red cabbage; chopped
- 1 tsp. apple cider vinegar
- 1 cup of water
- 1 tbsp. honey

- ½ cup unsweetened apple sauce
- Salt and pepper

Instructions:

1. Press sauté on the pot and add the onions to cook for 3 to 4 minutes.
2. Press the cancel button. Mix in the rest of the ingredients then seal the lid and the valve.

3. Set to manual to cook for 3 minutes at high pressure.
4. Press cancel and quick release the steam. Open the lid and serve.

Nutrition Facts per Serving
Calories: 85 g; Fat: 1.7 g; Carbs: 17.9 g; Protein: 1.4

Sweet Lentil Curry

Prep + cook time: 10 minutes; serves: 3

Ingredients:
- 1 tsp. coconut oil
- 1 tbsp. ginger; minced
- 3 garlic cloves; minced
- ½ tbsp. curry powder
- ½ onion; chopped
- ½ tsp. turmeric; ground
- 1 tsp. brown sugar
- 1 tbsp. lemon juice
- Salt
- a pinch of cayenne pepper
- ½ (14 oz) can coconut milk
- 1 cup lentils
- 1 cup of water

Instructions:

1. Press sauté on the pot then add the oil. Mix in the ginger, garlic, and onion to cook for 2 to 3 minutes.
2. Mix in the curry, turmeric, sugar, lemon juice, salt, and cayenne pepper. Press the cancel button.
3. Rinse the lentils with water then mix in the milk, water, and lentils then seal the lid and the valve. Set to manual to cook for 15 minutes at high pressure.
4. Press the cancel button. Natural-release the pressure for 10 minutes. Mix in the lemon juice and serve.

Nutrition Facts per Serving
Calories: 538 g; Fat: 18.1 g; Carbs: 39.9 g; Protein: 27.3

Spicy Black Beans with Vegetables

Prep + cook time: 45 minutes; serves: 4

Ingredients:
Chopped mixed vegetables
- 1 bay leaf
- ½ diced onion
- 1 ½ tsp. oregano
- ½ tsp. coriander powder
- 3 minced garlic cloves
- ½ tsp. smoked paprika
- 2 tsp. cumin
- 1 tsp. chili powder
- 3 cup vegetable broth
- 1 cup dry black beans
- ¼ tsp. kosher salt

For Garnishing
- Cilantro
- Hot sauce
- Cheese
- Sour cream
- Salsa

Instructions:
1. Press sauté on the pot and add the vegetables. When they are almost wilted, add the onions to cook.
2. Add the bay leaf, oregano, coriander, garlic, paprika, cumin, and chili powder then stir as it is cooking so that the garlic is not burning.
3. Mix in the broth and beans then seal the lid and the valve. Press the cancel button then set to manual to cook for 25 minutes.
4. Natural-release the steam for 15 minutes.
5. Open the lid and season as desired. Serve garnished with cilantro, hot sauce, cheese, sour cream, or salsa.

Nutrition Facts per Serving
Calories: 232, Fat: 0.8g, Carbs: 35.7g, Protein: 13.3g

Chili Potatoes with Beans and Carrots

Prep + cook time: 14 minutes; serves: 4

Ingredients:

- 2 chopped celery stalks
- 1 chopped carrot
- 1 chopped onion
- 1 diced sweet potato
- 1 can diced tomatoes
- 1 can chili beans
- 1 chopped red pepper
- ½ tsp. smoked paprika
- 2 tsp. cumin
- ½ cup of corn
- 2 tsp. olive oil
- 1 tbsp. chili powder
- 1 cup vegetable broth
- ¼ tsp. cinnamon
- Salt and Pepper
- Crushed tortilla chips
- Sliced jalapeño

Instructions:

1. Press sauté on the pot and add the oil and the vegetables to cook till soft.
2. Mix in the beans, potato, and stock then add the tomatoes when it starts to boil. Mix in the rest of the ingredients except the tortilla chips and jalapeno.
3. Set to manual to cook for 3 minutes at high pressure. Quick-release the steam then open the lid.
4. Check the corn and adjust the seasoning as desired. Serve topped with tortilla chips and jalapeno.

Nutrition Facts per Serving

Calories: 199, Fat: 4g, Carbs: 34g, Protein: 8g

Garlic Broccoli with Chickpeas

Prep + cook time: 20 minutes; serves: 3

Ingredients:

- ½ tsp. olive oil
- 3 large cloves of garlic; chopped
- Crushed red pepper as needed
- 1/8 tsp. fennel seeds
- 1 (15 oz.) can chickpeas; drained
- 1 bunch broccoli rabe; halved
- ¼ cup vegetable broth
- Salt

Instructions:

1. Press sauté on the pot and add the oil and garlic to cook for 2 minutes.
2. Mix in the fennel seeds and red pepper to cook for 30 seconds. Add the broccoli, broth and chickpeas then seal the lid and the valve.
3. Set to manual to cook for 4 minutes at high pressure.
4. Press the cancel button then natural-release the steam for 8 to 10 minutes.
5. Open the lid and serve.

Nutrition Facts per Serving

Calories: 506; Fat: 10g; Carbs: 44.3g; Fiber: 12g; Protein 24.3g

Spicy Potatoes Dish

Prep + Cook time: 14 minutes; Serves: 4

Ingredients:

- 2 tsp. olive oil
- 1 chopped red pepper
- 1 chopped carrot
- ½ cup of corn
- 1 chopped onion
- 2 chopped celery stalks
- ½ tsp. smoked paprika
- 1 tbsp. chili powder
- 2 tsp. cumin
- ¼ tsp. cinnamon
- 1 can chili beans
- 1 diced sweet potato
- 1 cup vegetable broth
- 1 can diced tomatoes
- Salt and pepper
- Sliced jalapeño
- Crushed tortilla chips

Instructions:

1. Press "Sauté" on the Instant Pot and add the olive oil.
2. Mix in the vegetables and spices to cook until they soften.
3. Mix in the beans, potatoes, and broth and bring to a boil. Add the tomatoes and seal the lid.

4. Set to cook for 3 minutes at high pressure. Quick-release the steam and open the lid.
5. Cook the corn and season with some salt and pepper.
6. Serve the dish topped with jalapeno and tortilla chips.

Nutrition Facts per Serving
Calories 199, Fat 4g, Carbs 34g, Protein 8g

Cauliflower and Mushroom Soup

Prep + cook time: 25 minutes; Serves: 4
Ingredients:
- 2 tsp. olive oil
- 1 yellow onion; chopped
- 1 tbsp. garlic; minced
- 1 cup fresh baby Bella mushrooms; chopped
- 2 cups cauliflower; chopped
- 4 cups homemade vegetable broth
- Salt and pepper
- 1 tsp. dried thyme; crushed

Instructions:
1. Pour the oil into the Instant Pot and press "Sauté". Add the onion and garlic to cook for 2 to 3 minutes.

2. Mix in the mushrooms and let it cook for 4 to 5 minutes. "Cancel" the preset function and add the cauliflower and the veggie broth then season with salt, pepper, and thyme.
3. Seal the lid and venting valve.
4. Press "Manual" and set to cook for 5 minutes at high pressure.
5. Press "Cancel" and natural-release the pressure for 10 minutes.
6. Blend with a dipping blender and serve.

Nutrition Facts per Serving
Calories 86, Fat 12.2g, Carbs 7.5g, Protein 4.1g

Cheesy Ziti with Tomatoes

Prep + Cook time: 20 minutes; Serves: 3
Ingredients:
- 1 tbsp. olive oil
- 1 onion; chopped
- 2 garlic cloves; minced
- 2 cups whole peeled tomatoes with juice; crushed
- 1 lb. uncooked ziti pasta
- 2 cups shredded mozzarella cheese

Instructions:
1. Press "Sauté" on the Instant Pot and add the oil, onions, and garlic to cook until clear.

2. Mix in the crushed tomatoes and pasta and pour in water to cover the pasta. Seal the lid and set to cook at low pressure for 5 minutes. Quick-release the pressure and open the pot.
3. Spread cheese over the pasta and close the lid until the cheese melts on "Keep Warm".

Nutrition Facts per Serving
Calories 375, Fat 17.11g, Carbs 40.23g, Protein 16.83g, Fiber 6.4g

Lemon Mushrooms and Rice Dish

Prep + cook time: 20 minutes; Serves: 3
Ingredients:
- 2 tsp. vegan butter
- 1 ½ cups chopped Portobello mushrooms
- 1 ½ cups white mushrooms
- 1 tsp. olive oil
- 2 minced garlic cloves
- 1 cup diced white onions

- 1 ½ cup uncooked Arborio rice
- ½ cup white wine
- 3 cups veggie broth
- Salt and pepper
- 3 tsp. lemon juice

Instructions:

1. Press "Sauté" on the Instant Pot and add 1 tsp of butter and the two types of mushrooms to cook until soft. Remove and set aside.
2. Pour the olive oil into the pot and add the rest of the butter, garlic, and onion to cook for 4-5 minutes.
3. Mix in the rice and cook until translucent then pour in the wine and cook until the wine evaporates.
4. Pour in the veggie broth and mix well. Seal the lid and the venting valve.
5. Press "Manual" and set to cook for 5 minutes.
6. "Cancel" and natural-release the pressure for 8 to 10 then open the pot. Serve into containers and season with salt and pepper. Mix with the lemon juice and serve warm.

Nutrition Facts per Serving
Calories 339, Fat 3g, Carbs 38.6g, Protein 6.3g, Fiber 1g

Cheesy Lemon Zoodles

Prep + cook time: 12 minutes; Serves: 4
Ingredients:
- 3 diced garlic cloves
- Zest of half lemon
- 2 large zucchinis; spiralized
- 2 tbsp. water
- Juice of a half lemon
- 2 tbsp. olive oil
- Salt and pepper
- ¼ cup grated parmesan cheese

Instructions:
1. Press "Sauté" on the pot and add oil.
2. Mix in the garlic and lemon zest and cook for 30 seconds.
3. Mix in the zucchini noodles, water, and lemon juice and make sure it is well coated with the oil mixture. Cook for 30 to 45 seconds to 1 minute.
4. "Cancel" the pot and sprinkle with salt and pepper and mix with the parmesan cheese. Serve.

Nutrition Facts per Serving
Calories 273, Fat 20.6g, Carbs 14.7g, Protein 13.4g

Vegetable in Tomato Stew

Prep + cook time: 20 minutes; Serves: 2
Ingredients:
- 2 tbsp. olive oil
- 2 minced garlic cloves
- 1 sliced onion
- 1 eggplant; cubed with skin removed
- 1 green pepper; cut into strips and deseeded
- 1 zucchini; sliced
- 1 tbsp. tomato paste
- 1 tbsp. minced parsley
- ½ cup veggie stock
- ½ can (14 oz) diced tomatoes; chopped
- Salt and pepper

Instructions:
1. Press "Sauté" on the Instant Pot and add the oil, garlic and onions to cook for 2 to 3 minutes. Mix in the eggplant, pepper, and zucchini and cook until the veggies are soft. Mix in the tomato paste and press "Cancel".
2. Mix in the parsley, stock, and tomatoes and season with some salt and pepper then seal the lid and the venting valve.
3. Press "Manual" and set to cook for 6 minutes at high pressure.
4. "Cancel" the pot and natural-release the pressure.
5. Let it simmer for 2 minutes and serve.

Nutrition Facts per Serving
Calories 200, Fat 14.3g, Carbs 16.6g, Protein 3.9g

Lentils with Vegetable Jumble

Prep + cook time: 17 minutes; Serves: 6

Ingredients:

- 1 tbsp. olive oil
- 1 tsp. minced garlic cloves
- 1 cup chopped celery ribs
- 1 chopped red bell pepper
- ½ tsp. cayenne powder
- ½ tbsp. oregano
- 1 tsp. Cajun mix
- 1 tbsp. dried thyme
- Sea salt and pepper
- 1 cup chopped okra
- 3 cup veggie broth
- 1 can diced tomatoes
- 2 tbsp. apple cider vinegar
- 1 cup lentils
- Fresh cilantro
- 1 cauliflower; chopped
- 1 ½ chopped onions

Instructions:

1. Press "Sauté" on the pot and add the olive oil, garlic, celery, and bell peppers to cook for 5 minutes until soft.
2. Mix in the spices and cook for 1 minute then add the rest of the ingredients, keeping the salt and pepper for last.
3. Seal the lid and select "Manual" to cook for 12 minutes at high pressure.
4. Do not add some extra salt while cooking to preserve the texture of the lentils.
5. Serve into bowls garnished with red pepper flakes, fresh cilantro, or jalapeno.

Nutrition Facts per Serving

Calories 173, Fat 3.3g, Carbs 25g, Protein 8g

Quinoa with Black Beans

Prep + cook time: 25 minutes; Serves: 4

Ingredients:

- 1 tsp. extra-virgin olive oil
- 1 diced red bell pepper
- ½ diced red onion
- ½ tsp. salt
- 1 tsp. cumin
- 1 cup of salsa
- 1 cup quinoa
- 1 cup of water
- 1 ½ cup cooked black beans

Instructions:

1. Press "Sauté" on the Instant Pot and add the oil. Add the red bell pepper and red onions to cook until softened.
2. Cook for 5 to 8 minutes then add the salt and cumin and reduce for 1 minute or until fragrant.
3. "Cancel" the "Sauté" function then add the salsa, water, quinoa, and black beans and seal the lid and the venting valve.
4. Cook on low for 12 minutes. Natural-release the pressure.
5. Open the lid and fluff the quinoa with a fork.
6. Serve as desired.

Nutrition Facts per Serving

Calories: 163, Fat: 7g, Carbs: 50g, Protein: 13g

Garlic Fusilli Pasta with Spinach and Pine Nuts

Prep + cook time: 20 minutes; Serves: 3

Ingredients:

- A drizzle of olive oil
- 2 garlic cloves; crushed
- 1 lb. spinach
- 1 lb. Fusilli pasta
- Salt and black pepper
- 2 garlic cloves; chopped
- ¼ cup chopped pine nuts

Instructions:

1. Press "Sauté" on the Instant Pot and add the oil, crushed garlic, and spinach to cook for 6 to 7 minutes until soft.
2. Mix in the pasta, salt, and pepper and add some water enough to cover the pasta. Seal the lid and the venting valve.

3. Set to cook at "Manual" for 6 minutes.
4. Press "Cancel" and quick-release the pressure. Mix in the chopped garlic and the pine nuts. Serve warm.

Nutrition Facts per Serving
Calories: 198; Fat: 1g; Carbs: 6.5g; Protein 7g, Fiber: 1g

Creamy Carrot and Tarragon Soup

Prep + cook time: 16 minutes; Serves: 4

Ingredients:

- 2 tbsp. butter
- 1 chopped onion
- 2 ½ cups raw carrots; chopped
- 4 cups veggie stock
- 2 sprigs fresh tarragon
- Salt and pepper
- 5 oz. Greek yogurt

Instructions:

1. Press "Sauté" on the Instant Pot and add the butter to melt.
2. Mix in the onions and let it cook for 2 to 3 minutes. Add the carrots, stock, tarragon, salt, and pepper. Press the "Cancel" button.
3. Select "Manual" and set to cook for 3 minutes at high pressure.
4. Press "Cancel" and quick-release the pot pressure.
5. Open the lid and remove some of the liquid. Puree the soup with a dipping blender until it is smooth.
6. Season with salt and pepper as needed. Serve topped with yogurt.

Nutrition Facts per Serving
Calories: 129 g; Fat: 8.4 g; Carbs: 11.2 g; Protein: 3.1

Eggplant and Black Olive Soup

Prep + cook time: 30 minutes; Serves: 2

Ingredients:

- 2 tbsp. olive oil
- 2 eggplants; peeled from one side only and chopped
- 2 garlic cloves
- 1 cup of water
- 1 tsp. salt
- 2 tbsp. fresh-squeezed lemon juice
- ¼ cup pitted black olives
- 1 tbsp. Tahini

Instructions:

1. Press "Sauté" on the Instant Pot and add the olive oil.
2. Add the eggplant and brown on all sides for 5 minutes then press "Cancel" on the pot.
3. Mix in the garlic, water, and salt and seal the lid and venting valve.
4. Press the "Manual" button and set to cook at high pressure for 3 minutes.
5. Press "Cancel" and natural-release the pot pressure.
6. Remove most of the liquid and remove the skin from the garlic cloves then return the garlic to the pot. Add the lemon juice, olives, and Tahini.
7. Puree the contents until smooth and serve in a bowl sprinkled with olive oil.

Nutrition Facts per Serving
Calories: 175; Fat: 14 g; Carbs: 13.1 g; Protein: 12.7

Spicy Green Beans with Tomatoes

Prep + cook time: 40 minutes; Serves: 4

Ingredients:

- ½ cup dry green beans
- 2 tbsp. olive oil
- ½ cup chopped red onion
- 4 garlic cloves
- 2 large tomatoes; chopped
- 1-inch ginger root; grated
- 1 tsp. ground coriander
- ½ tsp. garam masala

- ½ tsp. cayenne pepper
- ¼ tsp. black pepper
- 1 tsp. turmeric
- ½ tsp. cumin seeds
- 5 cups of water
- 1 tsp. lemon juice
- 1 tsp. salt

Instructions:
1. Soak the beans for 15 minutes. Blend the onions, garlic, ginger, 3 tsp of water and all the spices in a blender until smooth then set aside.
2. Press "Sauté" in the Instant Pot and add the oil. Mix in the cumin seeds to roast for 30 seconds.
3. Add the pureed onion spice mixture and cook until it is thick for 10 minutes then press the "Cancel" button.
4. Remove the beans from the liquid and add to the pot. Add the water, lemon juice, and salt and mix.
5. Seal the lid and set to "Manual" to cook for 15 minutes at high pressure.
6. Press "Cancel" and natural-release the pressure. Open the pot and serve.

Nutrition Facts per Serving
Calories: 45 g; Fat: 1.5 g; Carbs: 7.6 g; Protein: 1.6

Chicken with Celery and Mushroom Soup

Prep + cook time: 35 minutes; Serves: 4

Ingredients:
- 2 tbsp. olive oil
- 1 carrot; diced
- 1 onion; chopped
- 2 garlic cloves; chopped
- ½ celery; diced
- 7 oz. mushrooms; sliced
- ½ lb. chicken meat; cooked and shredded
- 5 cups chicken stock
- 1 tsp. thyme
- 1 tsp. rosemary
- 2 bay leaves
- Salt and pepper

Instructions:
1. Press "Sauté" on the Instant Pot and add the oil.
2. Mix in the carrots and onions to cook for 2 to 3 minutes then add the garlic, celery, and mushrooms to cook for 3 minutes.
3. Press "Cancel" and add the chicken, stock, thyme, rosemary, bay leaves, salt, and pepper.
4. Seal the lid and press the Soup/ Broth Button and set to less.
5. Press "Cancel" to stop the cooking and quick-release the pressure.

Nutrition Facts per Serving
Calories: 216 g; Fat: 11 g; Carbs: 5.4 g; Protein: 24

Beans and Potatoes with Tomatoes

Prep + cook time: 15 minutes; Serves: 3

Ingredients:
- ½ tbsp. whole cumin seeds
- 1 large onion; chopped
- 2 potatoes; peeled and cubed
- 1 tsp. turmeric
- 1 cup diced tomatoes
- ¼ tsp. ginger
- 1 tsp. coriander
- 1 cup garbanzo beans; cooked
- ½ tsp. salt
- Water

Instructions:
1. Press "Sauté" on the Instant Pot and pour ½ cup of water, cumin seeds, and onions into the pot to cook for 2 to 3 minutes.
2. Mix in the potatoes, turmeric, tomatoes, ginger, coriander, beans, and salt with a ¼ cup of water. Seal the lid and the venting valve.
3. Press "Manual" on the pot and set to cook for 5 minutes.

4. Press "Cancel" and natural-release the pot pressure for 8 to 10 minutes.
5. Open the pot and serve into containers. Serve with bread or rice.

Nutrition Facts per Serving
Calories: 236; Fat: 2g; Carbs: 42g; Protein 7g; Fiber 7.2g

Steamed Lemon Artichokes

Prep + cook time: 30 minutes; Serves: 2

Ingredients:
- 1 lemon wedge
- 2 medium-sized whole artichokes; rinsed, stem and top removed
- 2 cups of water

Instructions:
1. Rub the lemon wedge on the cut part of the artichokes to stop the browning.
2. Pour some water into the Instant Pot and put a steaming basket above the water. Put the artichokes in the basket and seal the lid.
3. Set to "Manual" to cook for 20 minutes at high pressure.
4. Press "Cancel" and natural-release the pressure.
5. Remove the artichokes and serve with dipping sauce.

Nutrition Facts per Serving
Calories: 64 g; Fat: 12.4 g; Carbs: 13 g; Protein: 13.5

Cheesy Rice Dish with Mushrooms

Prep + cook time: 20 minutes; Serves: 4

Ingredients:
- 1 tbsp. olive oil
- 2 minced garlic cloves
- ½ onion; diced
- 3 ½ oz. button mushrooms; sliced
- 1 cup risotto rice
- 2 cups veggie broth
- ½ tbsp. white wine
- Salt and pepper
- Grated parmesan cheese

Instructions:
1. Press "Sauté" on the pot and add the oil.
2. Mix in the garlic and onions to cook for 1 to 2 minutes. Mix in the mushrooms to cook for 3 to 4 minutes. Press "Cancel".
3. Mix in the rice, broth, white wine, salt, and pepper and seal the lid and venting valve.
4. Select the "Manual" button to cook for 6 minutes at high pressure.
5. Press "Cancel" and quick-release the pressure.
6. Open the pot and serve rice dish topped with parmesan.

Nutrition Facts per Serving
Calories: 428 g; Fat: 8.6 g; Carbs: 20.2 g; Protein: 12.9

Cheesy Rigatoni with Vegetables

Prep + cook time: 25 minutes; Serves: 6

Ingredients:
- 3 tbsp. olive oil
- ½ cup chopped carrots
- ½ cup chopped celery
- 1 tbsp. minced garlic
- ½ cup chopped bell peppers
- 1 oz. chopped porcini mushrooms
- 2 cup chopped mushrooms
- ½ tbsp. black pepper
- 1 can crushed tomatoes
- ¼ tsp. dried thyme
- 1 tsp. salt
- 1 tsp. dried oregano
- 1 tsp. dried basil
- 1 tbsp. balsamic vinegar
- 1 tsp. salt
- 1 tsp. sugar

- ½ tsp. crushed red pepper flakes
- 1 tbsp. tomato paste
- 1 cup whole milk
- 12 oz. rigatoni pasta
- 1 cup red wine
- 1 cup of water
- 4 oz. mascarpone cheese
- ¼ cup grated parmesan cheese
- 3 tbsp. chopped parsley

Instructions:
1. Press "Sauté" on the Instant Pot and add the olive oil.
2. Mix in the carrots, celery, garlic, and bell peppers to cook for 3 minutes.
3. Mix in the fresh mushrooms to cook for 2 minutes.
4. Put off the Instant Pot and remove any food stuck to the pot with 2 tbsp of water.
5. Add the dried porcini mushrooms, black pepper, crushed tomatoes, thyme, salt, oregano, basil, vinegar, sugar, tomato paste, milk, pasta, wine, and water.
6. Mix everything and seal the lid and venting valve.
7. Set to "Manual" to cook for 7 minutes.
8. Quick-release the pressure and add the mascarpone cheese then let it rest for some minutes until it is thick.
9. Serve pasta in a bowl sprinkled with cheese and parsley.

Nutrition Facts per Serving
Calories: 293, Fat: 14g, Carbs: 27g, Protein: 10g

Lemon Rice with Green Peas and Celery

Prep + cook time: 20 minutes; Serves: 2

Ingredients:
- 3 tbsp. olive oil
- 2 celery sticks; small cubes
- 1 diced brown onion
- ½ tsp. pepper
- ½ tsp. salt
- 2 cups veggie stock
- 2 cloves diced garlic
- 1 cup baby green peas
- 1 cup Arborio rice
- 2 tbsp. lemon juice

Instructions:

1. Press "Sauté" on the Instant Pot and add the oil, celery, onion, pepper, and salt to cool for 4 to 5 minutes.
2. Pour in the stock and add the garlic, peas, and rice, Mix well and seal the lid.
3. Set to "Manual" to cook for 5 minutes.
4. Press "Cancel" and quick-release the pressure then add the lemon juice and serve.

Nutrition Facts per Serving
Calories: 362; Fat: 13g; Carbs: 52.5g; Fiber: 3g; Protein 8g

Butternut Squash with Mushrooms and Beans

Prep + cook time: 23 minutes; Serves: 2

Ingredients:
- 1 tbsp. olive oil
- ¼ cup minced white onion
- 1 lb. butternut squash; cubed
- 1 cup mushrooms
- 1 cup unsalted veggie broth
- A pinch of white pepper
- ¼ tsp. kosher salt
- 1 lb. beans; sliced into 2-inch long slivers
- ½ cup almond slivers; toasted
- 1/8 cup minced chives

Instructions:

1. Press "Sauté" on the pot and add the olive oil and onions to cook for 4 minutes.
2. Mix in the squash, mushrooms, broth, white pepper, and salt and seal the lid.
3. Set to "Manual" to cook for 10 minutes.
4. Press "Cancel" and natural-release the pressure for 8 to 10 minutes.
5. Mix in the beans and close the lid for 2 minutes to warm. Season as needed and serve topped with almond and chives.

Nutritional Fact per Serving
Calories 406; Fat: 17g; Carbs: 43g; Fiber: 18.3g; Protein 28g

Farro with Mushrooms and Beans

Prep + cook time: 40 minutes; Serves: 3

Ingredients:
- 3 cups mushrooms; chopped
- 1 cup navy beans; dried
- 2 tbsp. onion powder
- 9 garlic cloves; minced
- 1 seeded jalapeno pepper; chopped
- 1 tbsp. shallot powder
- 2 tbsp. barley
- 1 tbsp. red curry paste
- 1/2 cup farro
- Pepper and salt as needed
- 2 tomatoes; diced

Instructions:
1. Mix all the ingredients in the Instant Pot and add water to cover them.
2. Seal the lid and the venting valve.
3. Set to "Manual" to cook for 30 minutes.
4. Press "Cancel" and natural-release the pressure for 8 to 10 minutes.
5. Mix in the tomatoes and serve.

Nutrition Facts per Serving

Calories: 238; Fat: 6.5g; Carbs: 38g; Protein 11g: Fiber 1.5g

Cheesy Penne with Broccoli and Spinach

Prep + cook time: 20 minutes; Serves: 3

Ingredients:
- 1 tbsp. olive oil
- ½ onion; chopped
- 3 ½ oz. cremini mushrooms
- 1 bell pepper; chopped
- 8 to 9 oz. penne pasta
- 1 cup broccoli florets
- 1 cup chopped fresh spinach
- ½ cup tomato sauce
- 2 cups of water
- Salt and pepper
- ½ cup grated mozzarella
- 1 tbsp. grated parmesan cheese

Instructions:
1. Press "Sauté" on the Instant Pot and add the oil.
2. Mix in the onions, mushrooms, and bell pepper to cook for 3 to 4 minutes.
3. Mix in the rest of the ingredients except the cheeses. Press the "Cancel" button and seal the lid and the venting valve.
4. Set to "Manual" to cook for 5 minutes at low pressure.
5. "Cancel" the pot and open it.
6. Mix in the mozzarella until melted and serve topped with parmesan.

Nutrition Facts per Serving

Calories: 322 g; Fat: 7.6 g; Carbs: 52.29 g; Protein: 13

Creamy Carrot Soup with Cilantro

Prep + cook time: 37 minutes; Serves: 2

Ingredients:
- 1 tbsp. unsalted butter
- 1 small onion; chopped
- ½ tsp. ginger; minced
- 1 garlic clove; minced
- ½ lb. carrots; peeled and chopped
- Salt and pepper
- 7 oz. canned unsweetened coconut milk
- 1 cup chicken broth
- ½ tbsp. Sriracha
- 1/8 tsp. brown sugar
- 1 tbsp. fresh cilantro; chopped

Instructions:
1. Press "Sauté" on the pot and open the lid then add the butter and onions to cook for 2 to 3 minutes.
2. Mix in the ginger and garlic to cook for 1 minute then add the carrots, salt, and pepper to cook for 2 minutes.
3. Mix in the milk, broth, and Sriracha and seal the lid and venting valve.

4. Set to "Manual" to cook for 6 minutes. Press "Cancel" and natural release the pressure for 8 to 10 minutes.
5. Mix in the sugar and puree with a dipping blender till smooth. Serve topped with cilantro.

Nutrition Facts per Serving
Calories 364; Fat: 30.5g; Carbs: 21.5g; Protein 6g; Fiber 5g

Creamy Potato with Zucchini and Tomatoes

Prep + cook time: 20 minutes; Serves: 3
Ingredients:
- 1 tbsp. olive oil
- 1 diced onion
- 1 minced garlic clove
- ½ tbsp. minced ginger
- 7 oz. coconut milk
- 7oz. diced tomatoes
- ½ diced bell pepper
- ½ diced zucchini
- 1 diced sweet potato
- 1 lime juice
- 1 tbsp. red curry paste
- ½ tsp. turmeric
- 1 tsp. curry powder
- ½ tsp. sea salt

Instructions:
1. Press "Sauté" on the Instant Pot and add the oil.
2. Add the onions to reduce until clear then add the garlic and ginger to cook for 1 minute.
3. Mix in the rest of the ingredients and seal the lid. Set to cook for 5 minutes at high pressure.
4. Quick-release the pressure and open the lid. Mix and serve.

Nutrition Facts per Serving
Calories: 251, Fat: 20.6g, Carbs: 16.7g, Protein: 3.5g

Beef with Potatoes and Mushrooms

Prep + cook time: 40 minutes; serves: 6
Ingredients:
- 2 tbsp. butter
- 1 diced yellow onions
- 1 lb. cubed beef
- Salt and pepper
- 2 sliced garlic cloves
- ½ cup dry red wine
- 3 sliced carrots
- 5 oz. mixed wild mushrooms
- 1 cup diced potatoes
- 4 cups beef broth
- 1 tbsp. red wine vinegar
- 4 cups of water
- 1 tbsp. red pepper flakes
- 1 can diced tomatoes
- 1 cup green beans

Instructions:

1. Press "Sauté" on the Instant Pot and add the butter to melt. When melted, add the onions to cook for 3 minutes.
2. Add the beef cubes and sprinkle with some salt and pepper. Brown on all sides for 5 to 7 minutes.
3. Mix in the garlic to cook for 1 minute then pour the red wine into the pot. Deglaze the pot by lifting the stuck bits with a spatula.
4. Press "Cancel" and add the remaining ingredients then seal the lid and set to "Manual" to cook for 15 minutes at high pressure.
5. Natural release the pressure and remove the bay leaf. Serve hot.

Nutrition Facts per Serving
Calories: 222, Fat: 10g, Carbs: 11.7g, Protein: 19.2g

Lemon Veggie Soup with Tomatoes

Prep + cook time: 25 minutes; Serves: 4

Ingredients:

- 1 chopped cabbage head
- 28 oz. chopped tomatoes
- 3 chopped celery stalks
- 3 chopped carrots
- 1 tbsp. lemon juice
- 3 tbsp. Apple cider vinegar
- 4 minced garlic cloves
- 3 cup chicken broth
- 1 chopped onion

Instructions:

1. Mix all the ingredients in the Instant Pot and seal the lid. Set to "Manual" to cook at high pressure for 15 minutes.
2. Quick-release the pressure and open the lid. Serve.

Nutrition Facts per Serving

Calories: 155, Fat: 1.3g, Carbs: 29.8g, Protein: 8.7g

Buttery Salmon Fillets

Prep + cook time: 15 minutes; Serves: 3

Ingredients:

- 1 lb. cubed salmon fillet
- 1 chopped onion
- 1 cup fish broth
- 1 tbsp. butter
- Salt and Pepper to taste

Instructions:

1. Mix all the ingredients in the Instant Pot and seal the lid. Set to cook at high pressure for 6 minutes.
2. Natural release the pressure for 8 minutes. Open the pot and mix the soup well and serve.

Nutrition Facts per Serving

Calories: 261, Fat: 13.7g, Carbs: 3.7g, Protein: 31.4g

Spicy Beef Stew with Kale and Potatoes

Prep + cook time: 55 minutes; Serves: 2

Ingredients:

- 1 tbsp. olive oil
- ½ lb. beef stew meat; cubed
- 1 tbsp. hot sauce
- 2 medium potatoes; chopped
- 1 small onion; chopped
- 1 celery stalk; chopped
- ½ tsp. garlic powder
- 2 carrots; peeled and chopped
- 1 cups kale leaves; trimmed and chopped
- 1 ½ cups beef broth
- Pepper and salt

Instructions:

1. Press "Sauté" on the Instant Pot and add the oil. Brown the beef on all sides for 4 to 5 minutes.
2. Mix in the rest of the ingredients then seal the lid and the valve.
3. Set to "Meat/Stew" for 40 minutes.
4. Press "Cancel" and quick release the pressure. Open and serve.

Nutrition Facts per Serving

Calories: 504; Fat: 15.5g; Carbs: 46.5g; Protein 42.5g; Fiber 8g

Tomato and Cashew Soup with Oats

Prep + cook time: 15 minutes; Serves: 3

Ingredients:

- 15 oz. diced tomatoes
- 15 oz. tomato puree
- 4 tbsp. cashew
- 1 ½ cup vegetable stock
- 1/2 tbsp. dried basil
- 1 ½ tbsp. quick oats

- 2 minced garlic cloves
- Salt and Pepper

Instructions:
1. Mix in the ingredients except for the pepper and salt in the Instant Pot and seal the lid.

2. Set to cook at high pressure for 4 minutes. Natural release the pressure and open the lid.
3. Blend smoothly with a dipping blender then sprinkle with salt and pepper.

Nutrition Facts per Serving
Calories: 166, Fat: 6.5g, Carbs: 26.8g, Protein: 5.9g

Cinnamon Chicken Soup

Prep + cook time: 20 minutes; Serves: 2

Ingredients:
- 1 tbsp. olive oil
- 2 tsp. minced garlic
- ¼ cup chopped onion
- 1lb. chopped chicken
- 1 tsp. ginger
- ½ cup chopped cilantro
- 1 tbsp. sugar
- 1 tsp. cinnamon
- 1 tsp. coriander
- 1 tbsp. fish sauce
- ¾ tsp. salt
- 3 cups low sodium chicken broth

Instructions:

1. Press "Sauté" on the Instant Pot and add the olive oil, garlic, and onions to cook for 2 to 3 minutes.
2. Add the chicken, ginger, cilantro, sugar, cinnamon, coriander, fish sauce, and salt to the pot and stir.
3. Pour in the chicken broth and stir again then seal the lid and the venting valve.
4. Set to "Manual" to cook for 15 minutes. Press "Cancel" and natural release the pressure for 8 to 10 minutes.
5. Open the pot and serve.

Nutrition Facts per Serving
Calories: 288; Fat: 14.5g; Carbs: 23g; Fiber; Protein 16.5g; Fiber 2.5g

Indian Black Bean soup

Prep + cook time: 47 minutes: serves: 2

Ingredients:
- 1 tbsp. olive oil
- 1 tsp. cumin seeds
- 1 medium onion; chopped
- 1 tbsp. garlic paste
- 1 tbsp. ginger paste
- 1 tsp. red chili powder
- ½ tsp. ground turmeric
- ½ tsp. garam masala
- 2 tsp. ground coriander
- Salt
- 1 cup black beans; soaked overnight and drained
- 2 cups of water

- 1 tsp. lemon juice

Instructions:
1. Press "Sauté" on the Instant Pot and add the oil, onion, garlic paste, ginger paste, and spices to cook for 3 to 4 minutes.
2. Mix in the beans and water and seal the lid and the venting valve.
3. Set to "beans/chili" to cook for 30 minutes.
4. Press "Cancel" and natural release the pressure for 8 to 10 minutes.
5. Mix in the lemon juice and serve.

Nutrition Facts per Serving
Calories: 437; Fat: 9g; Carbs: 68.5g; Protein 22g; Fiber 16.5g

Spicy Chicken and Lentils Soup

Prep + cook time: 45 minutes; Serves: 4

Ingredients:
- ½ lb. dried lentils
- 6 oz. skinless chicken thighs
- 1 diced tomato

- 2 tbsp. chopped cilantro
- 1/8 tsp. oregano
- ½ tsp. cumin

- 1 chopped scallion
- ½ chopped onion
- 3 ½ cup water
- ¼ tsp. paprika
- ½ tsp. garlic powder
- ¼ tsp. salt

Instructions:

1. Mix the lentils, chicken, tomato, cilantro, oregano, cumin, scallion, onion, water, paprika, garlic, and salt in the Instant Pot.
2. Seal the lid and set to cook for 30 minutes.
3. Natural release the pressure and open the lid.
4. Shred the chicken with a fork and mix it into the lentils. Serve.

Nutrition Facts per Serving
Calories: 293, Fat: 3.9g, Carbs: 36.5g, Protein: 27.5g

Creamy Curry Squash Soup

Prep + cook time: 40 minutes; Serves: 2

Ingredients:
- 1 tsp. olive oil
- ½ minced onion
- ½ tbsp. curry powder
- 1 minced garlic clove
- 1 ½ lb. cubed butternut squash
- 1 ½ cup of water
- ¼ cup of coconut milk

Instructions:
1. Press "Sauté" on the Instant Pot and add the oil and the onions to cook until soft.
2. Mix in the curry powder and the garlic to cook for 1 minute.
3. Add the butternut squash, water, and salt and seal the lid. Set to cook on "soup" for 25 minutes.
4. Quick-release the pressure and open the pot. Blend with a dipping blender and mix in the coconut milk.

Nutrition Facts per Serving
Calories: 260, Fat: 10.1g, Carbs: 45.4g, Protein: 4.7g

Pasta With White Beans Soup

Prep + cook time: 16 minutes; Serves: 2

Ingredients:
- 1 tbsp. olive oil
- 1 carrot; diced
- 1 diced onion
- 2 minced garlic cloves
- 1 tsp. dried oregano
- 1 tsp. dried basil
- Pepper and salt
- 14 oz. diced tomatoes
- ¼ cup fresh spinach
- 2 cups of chicken bone broth
- ½ cup elbow pasta
- 1 bay leaf

Instructions:
1. Press "Sauté" on the Instant Pot and add the oil, carrot, onion, and garlic to cook until soft.
2. Mix in the oregano, basil, pepper, and salt and add the tomatoes, spinach, broth, pasta, and bay leaf then seal the lid and the venting valve.
3. Set to "Manual" to cook for 6 minutes.
4. Press "Cancel" and natural release the pressure for 8 to 10 minutes. Open the pot and mix in the beans.

Nutrition Facts per Serving
Calories: 394; Fat: 3g; Carbs: 58g; Protein 20.5g; Fiber 9.5g

Pork with Cabbage and Ginger

Prep + cook time: 15 minutes; Serves: 2

Ingredients:
- 1 tbsp. olive oil
- ½ lb. ground pork
- 1 ½ cups cabbage; chopped
- ½ tsp. ground ginger
- 1 small onion; chopped
- 1 cup carrot; peeled and shredded

- 2 cups low-sodium chicken broth
- 1 tbsp. soy sauce
- Fresh pepper

Instructions:
1. Press "Sauté" on the Instant Pot and add the oil and the pork to brown for 4 to 5 minutes on all sides.

2. Mix in the rest of the ingredients and seal the lid and the venting valve.
3. Set to "Manual" to cook for 25 minutes.
4. "Cancel" the preset function and quick release the pressure. Open the pot and serve.

Nutrition Facts per Serving
Calories: 294; Fat: 11g; Carbs: 14.5g; Protein 34g; Fiber 3.5g

Spicy Carrot Soup

Prep + cook time: 15 minutes: serves: 3

Ingredients:
- 1 cup of water
- 1 lb. quartered carrots
- ¼ cup butter
- 3 cup chicken stock
- 1 tsp. paprika
- 1 tsp. ground cumin
- 2 tsp. minced garlic
- 2 tbsp. Dijon mustard
- Salt and pepper

Instructions:
1. Pour the water into the Instant Pot and put a steaming rack over it.
2. Place the carrots on the rack and seal the lid to cook at high pressure for 1 minute.

3. Quick-release the pressure and open the lid then place the carrots on a dish. Clean the pot and dry it with a paper towel.
4. Press "Sauté" on the pot and add the butter to melt.
5. Mix in the rest of the ingredients and add the carrots. Seal the lid to cook at high pressure for 4 minutes. Natural release the pressure and open the lid.
6. Use a dipping blender to puree the soup until smooth. Serve.

Nutrition Facts per Serving
Calories: 222, Fat: 16.6g, Carbs: 17.5g, Protein: 2.9g

Egg Noodles with Beef and Tomatoes

Prep + cook time: 20 minutes; Serves: 3

Ingredients:
- 1 tbsp. olive oil
- 1 tsp. minced garlic
- ½ chopped onion
- ½ lb. cubed beef
- 1 ½ tbsp. paprika
- 3 cup chicken broth
- 3 oz. egg noodles
- 7 oz. diced tomatoes
- 1/8 tsp. pepper
- ½ tsp. salt

Instructions:

1. Press "Sauté" on the Instant Pot and add the oil. Mix in the garlic, onion, and beef until it is brown.
2. Mix in the paprika, broth, noodles, tomatoes, salt, and pepper then seal the lid and set to cook for 5 minutes at high pressure.
3. Quick-release the pressure and open the lid. Stir and serve.

Nutrition Facts per Serving
Calories: 291, Fat: 11.8g, Carbs: 15.4g, Protein: 30.5g

Chapter 5 Poultry Recipes

Spicy Orange Chicken in Chili Sauce

Prep + cook time: 17 minutes; serves: 2

Ingredients:

- ½ lb. boneless chicken breast
- ½ tsp. cumin
- ½ tsp. grated orange zest
- 3 tsps. minced garlic
- 2 tbsps. chopped onion
- 1 bay leaf
- ¼ tsp. oregano
- ¼ tsp. salt
- ¼ tsp. pepper
- ¼ cup orange juice
- 2 tbsps. chicken broth
- 2 tbsps. mayonnaise
- 1 tbsp. tomato chili sauce - suracha
- ¼ tsp. salt
- ¼ tsp. garlic powder

Instructions:

1. Out the chicken in the Instant Pot and add the spices, orange zest, garlic, chopped onion, and bay leaf.
2. Pour in the chicken broth and orange juice over the chicken then seal the lid and valve.
3. Set to chicken to cook for 12 minutes at High Pressure.
4. In a bowl, mix the mayonnaise, tomato chili sauce, salt, and garlic powder until it is well mixed.
5. Natural-release the pressure and open the lid. Remove the chicken and put it on a chopping board. Shred the chicken and put it back in the pot and mix well.
6. Serve with the liquid drizzled with mayonnaise sauce.

Nutrition Facts per Serving

Calories: 352; Net Carbs: 7g; Fat: 24.7g; Carbs: 7.8g; Protein: 26.1g

Cheesy Turkey with Tomatoes and Olives

Prep + cook time: 10 minutes; serves: 3

Ingredients:

- 1 sliced turkey breast
- ½ minced Poblano pepper
- ½ tsp. chili flakes
- 2 tbsps. lemon juice
- 2 tbsps. olive oil
- 3 minced garlic cloves
- Rosemary
- Basil
- Salt and pepper
- 1 cup of water
- 3 tbsps. sliced olives
- ½ cup diced tomatoes
- ½ cup crumbled feta cheese
- Chopped parsley

Instructions:

1. Mix the Poblano pepper, chili flakes, lemon juice, olive oil, garlic cloves, rosemary, basil, salt and pepper in a bowl.
2. Put the turkey in the mixture, making sure to cover the turkey with the mix and cover the bowl with a plastic wrap and refrigerate for 3 hours.
3. Pour the water in the pot and place a rack above it. Put the turkey on the rack and pour the marinade over it.
4. Seal the lid and set to Manual to cook for 10 minutes at High Pressure.
5. Quick-release the steam and open the lid. Put a tomato slice, some olives, and cheese on each turkey then grill for 10 minutes in an oven. Serve garnished with parsley.

Nutrition Facts per Serving

Calories: 932, Fat: 32.2g, Carbs: 15.7g, Protein: 84.7g

Spicy Garlic Chicken with Tomatoes

Prep + cook time: 22 minutes; serves: 2

Ingredients:

- ½ lb. bone-in chicken
- 2 cloves garlic
- 2 shallots
- 2 red chilies
- ½ tsp. cayenne pepper
- ¼ tsp. salt
- ½ tsp. turmeric
- 1 lemongrass
- 1 bay leaf
- ¼ cup diced red tomatoes
- ½ cup of water

Instructions:

1. Put the garlic, shallots, red chilies, cayenne pepper, salt, and turmeric in a blender and puree till smooth.
2. Pour into a bowl and add the red tomatoes then mix well.
3. Cut the chicken into medium-sized pieces and rub it with the pureed mixture. Put the chicken on an aluminum foil then put the lemongrass and bay leaf on top of it then wrap the foil.
4. Pour the water into the pot and place a rack on it. Put the wrapped chicken on the rack and seal the lid.
5. Set to Manual to cook for 12 minutes at High Pressure.
6. Natural-release the pressure when the timer stops and open the lid. Remove the chicken and let it rest for some minutes.
7. Serve the chicken with some rice.

Nutrition Facts per Serving

Calories: 276; Net Carbs: 6.8 g; Fat: 17.4g; Carbs: 8g; Protein: 21.4g

Sweet and Spicy Chicken Wings

Prep + cook time: 16 minutes; serves: 2

Ingredients:

- ½ lb. chicken wings
- ¼ tsp. salt
- ¼ tsp. pepper
- ¾ cup chicken broth
- ½ tsp. brown sugar
- ½ tsp. honey
- ½ tsp. maple syrup
- ½ tsp. Tabasco
- ¼ tsp. ketchup
- ¼ tsp. BBQ sauce
- ¼ cup hot sauce
- 2 tbsps. butter
- ½ tsp. molasses

Instructions:

1. Rub the chicken wings with salt and pepper and set aside. Put a rack in the Instant Pot and pour the broth into the pot.
2. Put the wings on the rack and seal the lid.
3. Set to Manual to cook for 8 minutes at High Pressure.
4. Quick-release the pressure and remove the chicken and the rack. Set the chicken aside.
5. Mix the rest of the ingredients in the Instant Pot.
6. Press Sauté on the pot and cook for 2 to 3 minutes. Put the wings back into the pot and mix until the chicken is coated with the sauce.
7. Serve the chicken and the sauce on a dish.

Nutrition Facts per Serving

Calories: 338; Net Carbs: 5.8g; Fat: 24.4g; Carbs: 6g; Protein: 23.1g

Tamari Honey Chicken

Prep + cook time: 35 minutes; serves: 3

Ingredients:

- 2 lbs. boneless chicken thighs; fresh or frozen
- ¼ cup ghee
- ¼ cup honey
- 3 tbsps. tamari
- 3 tbsps. ketchup
- 2 tsps. garlic powder

- 1 ½ tsps. sea salt
- ½ tsp. black pepper

Instructions:

1. Mix all the ingredients in the Instant Pot and seal the lid and the valve.
2. Set to Manual to cook for 18 minutes for fresh chicken and 40 minutes for frozen chicken until the timer stops.
3. Press the Cancel button and Natural-release the pressure for 8 to 10 minutes.
4. Open the lid and serve into containers. Serve with vegetables and rice.

Nutrition Facts per Serving

Calories 544; Fat: 22g; Carbs: 48.2g; Protein 36.2g; Fiber: –4g

Sweet Garlic Chicken

Prep + cook time: 5 hours; serves: 2

Ingredients:

- ½ lb. chicken wings
- 1 tsp. minced garlic
- ¼ tsp. salt
- ¼ tsp. pepper
- ½ cup water
- 1¼ tsps. brown sugar

Instructions:

1. Coat the chicken with garlic, salt, and pepper and put it in the Instant Pot.
2. Pour the water into the Instant Pot and sprinkle the sugar on the chicken.
3. Seal the lid and set to Slow Cook to cook for 5 hours and move the valve to venting.
4. Natural-release the pressure and open the lid. Serve the chicken.

Nutrition Facts per Serving

Calories: 276; Net Carbs: 6.5g; Fat: 18g; Carbs: 6.5g; Protein: 21.1g

Lemon Garlic Chicken with Herbs

Prep + cook time: 25 minutes; serves: 3

Ingredients:

- 3 chicken breast halves; boneless and skinless
- Salt and pepper
- 2 tbsps. olive oil
- 1 tsp. rosemary
- 2 garlic cloves; peeled and sliced
- 1 cup chicken broth
- ½ cup white wine
- ¼ cup parsley; chopped
- ½ lemon; thinly sliced

Instructions:

1. Press Sauté on the Instant Pot and add the olive oil. Season the chicken with salt and pepper on each side.
2. Put the chicken in the oil to fry for 6 to 7 minutes on both sides.
3. Season the chicken with the rosemary and garlic then press the Cancel button.
4. Combine the broth, wine, and parsley in a bowl and pour it into the pot.
5. Seal the lid and the valve and set to Manual to cook for 8 minutes at High Pressure.
6. Press the Cancel button when the timer stops and Quick-release the pressure. Open the lid and serve with lemon slices on top.

Nutrition Facts per Serving

Calories: 192 g; Fat: 27.7 g; Carbs: 1.9 g; Protein: 14.4

Sweet and Spicy Ginger Honey Chicken

Prep + cook time: 20 minutes; serves: 4

Ingredients:

- 4 chicken breasts
- ½ sliced onion
- 3 tbsps. honey
- ¼ cup soy sauce
- 1 tsp. Worcestershire sauce
- 1 tbsp. sriracha sauce
- 2 green onions
- 1 tbsp. sesame seeds
- 1 tbsp. brown sugar
- 1 tbsp. minced garlic

- 1 ½ tbsps. minced ginger
- 2 tbsps. cornstarch

Instructions:
1. Cut the chicken and onions into chunks and put it in the Instant Pot.
2. Mix the rest of the ingredients in a bowl except the cornstarch and pour it into the Instant Pot.
3. Seal the lid and the valve and set to Manual to cook for 4 minutes at High Pressure.
4. Press the Cancel button and Quick-release the pressure then open the pot.
5. Take some of the sauce and pour it into a bowl and mix it with the cornstarch until when combined then pour it back into the pot.
6. Press Sauté on the pot and let it sauce thicken for some minutes.
7. Serve with plain rice.

Nutrition Facts per Serving
Calories: 155, Fat: 2g, Carbs: 15g, Protein: 17g

Pineapple Chicken with Zucchinis

Prep + cook time: 18 minutes; serves: 2

Ingredients:
- ½ lb. boneless chicken breast
- 2 tsps. minced garlic
- 1 tsp. curry powder
- ¼ tsp. brown sugar
- ¼ tsp. turmeric
- ¼ tsp. ginger
- ¼ tsp. salt
- ¼ tsp. pepper
- 2 tbsps. chopped onion
- ¼ cup pineapple chunks
- ½ cup water
- ¼ cup chopped zucchinis

Instructions:
1. Cut the chicken into cubes and put it in a bowl. Mix it with the garlic, curry, sugar, turmeric, ginger, salt, and pepper and put it in the Instant Pot.
2. Add the onion and the pineapple chunks to the pot and pour the water into the pot.
3. Seal the lid and the valve and set it to Manual to cook for 10 minutes.
4. Press the Cancel button and Natural-release the pressure for 8 to 10 minutes then open the pot.
5. Add the zucchinis and stir until soft. Serve into a dish with brown rice.

Nutrition Facts per Serving
Calories: 243; Net Carbs: 5.3g; Fat: 8.7g; Carbs: 6.5g; Protein: 33.6g

Jamaican Rice with Garlic Chicken

Prep + cook time: 18 minutes; serves: 2

Ingredients:
- ¾ cup long grain rice
- 2 tsps. olive oil
- ½ diced small onion
- 1 tbsp. Jamaican jerk seasoning
- 1 minced garlic clove
- 1 cup chicken broth

Instructions:
1. Rinse the rice in water until the water runs clear and set aside.
2. Press Sauté on the Instant Pot and add the oil.
3. Mix in the onions to cook for 1 to 2 minutes then mix in the rest of the ingredients.
4. Bring to a boil and add the rice and the chicken, making sure the broth covers them.
5. Seal the lid and the valve and set it to Manual to cook for 7 minutes. Press the Cancel button and Quick-release the pressure then open the lid.
6. Serve the chicken with the rice or shred it and mix it with the rice. Serve.

Nutrition Facts per Serving
Calories: 283, Fat: 2.5g, Carbs: 47g, Protein: 22g

Salsa Chicken

Prep + cook time: 4 hours; serves: 2

Ingredients:

- 1 tsp. avocado oil
- ½ lb. chicken thighs
- ¼ cup chipotle salsa
- ¼ tsp. salt
- ¼ tsp. pepper

Instructions:

1. Brush the pot with avocado oil then season the chicken with salt and pepper and put it in the pot.

2. Pour the salsa over the chicken and seal the lid and the valve. Set to Slow Cook to cook for 4 hours at High Pressure.

3. Natural-release the pressure when the timer stops, open the lid and serve.

Nutrition Facts per Serving
Calories: 239; Net Carbs: 4.1g; Fat: 8.7g; Carbs: 4.3g; Protein: 32.9g

Garlic Chicken in Tomato Sauce

Prep + cook time: 35 minutes; serves: 2

Ingredients:

- 1 tbsp. olive oil
- ¾ cup ketchup
- ¾ cup soy sauce
- ½ cup water or chicken stock
- 1 tsp. fresh basil; chopped
- ½ tsp. garlic cloves; minced
- 1 tsp. chili garlic sauce
- 1 tbsp. arrowroot starch; dissolved in 2 tbsp. of water

Instructions:

1. Press Sauté on the pot and add the oil and the chicken to cook for 6 to 7 minutes all both sides.

2. Press the Cancel button and mix in the rest of the ingredients except the dissolved arrowroot starch. Seal the lid and the valve and set to Manual to cook for 10 minutes at High Pressure.

3. Press the Cancel button when the timer stops and Quick-release the pressure.

4. Open the lid and remove the chicken. Mix in the dissolved arrowroot starch and press the Sauté button to cook on Low Pressure until the sauce thickens. Serve the sauce over the chicken.

Nutrition Facts per Serving
Calories: 532 g; Fat: 55.4 g; Carbs: 15.2 g; Protein: 30.2

Sweet BBQ Chicken Wings

Prep + cook time: 20 minutes; serves: 2

Ingredients:

- 2 lbs. chicken wings
- ½ cup barbecue sauce
- 1 cup of water
- ½ cup chopped onion
- 2 ½ tbsps. raw honey
- ½ tsp. pepper
- ¼ tsp. salt

Instructions:

1. Combine the BBQ sauce with water, onion, honey, pepper, and salt in a bowl and set aside.

2. Put the chicken in the pot and pour the sauce over it. Mix the ingredients and seal the lid and the valve.

3. Press the Cancel button when the timer stops and Quick-release the pressure.

4. Put a pan over medium heat and add the chicken sauce to the pan. Simmer until thick and serve.

Nutrition Facts per Serving
Calories 334; Fat: 10g; Carbs: 45g; Protein 10.5g; Fiber: 1.5g

Cheesy Spaghetti Squash with Chicken

Prep + cook time: 35 minutes; serves: 3

Ingredients:
- 1 spaghetti squash; cut in half and seeded
- 2 cups of water
- ½ cup marinara sauce
- 1 lb. cooked chicken; cubed
- 7 oz. mozzarella cheese

Instructions:
1. Pour the water into the pot and put the halves of the squash into pot on a rack. Seal the lid.
2. Set to manual to cook for 20 minutes at high pressure.
3. Press the cancel button and quick release the pressure. Shred the squash with a fork and pour the marinara sauce over it and mix.
4. Add the chicken cubes and top with cheese.

Nutrition Facts per Serving:
Calories: 300 g; Fat: 25.3 g; Carbs: 4 g; Protein: 14

Honey Garlic Chicken with Carrots

Prep + cook time: 18 minutes; serves: 2

Ingredients:
- 1 tbsp. soy sauce
- 2 tbsp. apple cider vinegar
- ½ tbsp. honey
- 1 tsp. mirin
- ½ lb. boneless chicken breast; cut into medium-sized cubes
- ¾ tbsp. olive oil
- 1 tsp. minced garlic
- ¼ tsp. salt
- ¼ tsp. pepper
- ¼ tsp. ginger
- 2 tbsp. sliced carrots

Instructions:
1. Mix the soy sauce, vinegar, honey, and mirin in a bowl and set aside.
2. Press sauté on the pot and add the olive oil in the Instant Pot and add the chicken breast.
3. Mix in the garlic to cook until the chicken is no longer pink and press the cancel button.
4. Pour half of the soy sauce mixture and water into the pot and season with salt, pepper, and ginger.
5. Seal the lid and set to manual to cook for 10 minutes at high pressure. Quick-release the pressure when the timer stops and open the lid.
6. Pour the rest of the sauce in the pot and add the carrot.
7. Press sauté and cooked with the lid open for 3 minutes.
8. Serve the chicken with gravy.

Nutrition Facts per Serving:
Calories: 201; Net Carbs: 6.7g; Fat: 8.3g; Carbs: 7g ; Protein: 25.2g

Lemon Chicken and Olives

Prep + cook time: 5 hours; serves: 2

Ingredients:
- ½ lb. chopped chicken
- ¼ tsp. salt
- ¼ tsp. pepper
- 1 tsp. avocado oil
- 1 tsp. minced garlic
- ¼ cup chicken broth
- 1 tbsp. red wine vinegar
- 1 tbsp. lemon juice
- 2 tsp. diced red pepper
- ½ cup Kalamata olives
- 2 tbsp. chopped onions
- ¼ tsp. thyme
- ¼ tsp. oregano

Instructions:
1. Coat the chicken with salt and pepper and keep aside. Press sauté on the pot and pour in the oil and add the garlic to cook for some minutes.
2. Add the chicken to cook for 2 minutes on each side then press the cancel button.

3. Mix the broth, wine, and lemon juice and pour t over the chicken then add the red pepper, olives, onion, oregano, and thyme.
4. Seal the lid and set to slow cook to cook for 5 hours at high pressure.
5. Natural-release the pressure and serve on a dish.

Nutrition Facts per Serving:
Calories: 271; Net Carbs: 3.9g; Fat: 4.5g; Carbs: 4.5g; Protein: 20g

Garlic Honey Chicken with Sesame Seeds

Prep + cook time: 20 minutes; Serves: 4
Ingredients:
- 4 chicken breasts
- ½ sliced onion
- 3 tbsp. honey
- 1 tsp. Worcestershire sauce
- 1 tbsp. Sriracha sauce
- 2 green onions
- 1 tbsp. sesame seeds
- 1 tbsp. brown sugar
- 1 tbsp. minced garlic
- 1 ½ tbsp. minced ginger
- 2 tbsp. cornstarch

Instructions:
1. Cut the chicken and onions into bite-sized chunks and put it inside the Instant Pot.
2. Mix the honey, Worcestershire sauce, Sriracha, green onions, seeds, sugar, garlic, and ginger in a bowl and pour it over the chicken.
3. Seal the lid and venting valve and set to "Manual" to cook for 4 minutes at high pressure.
4. Quick-release the pressure.
5. Scoop some of the hot liquid from the pot and mix it with the cornstarch in a bowl then pour it back in the pot.
6. Press "Sauté" on the pot and let it cook at Normal for a few minutes then stop cooking and let the chicken rest until the sauce thickens.
7. Serve with plain rice.

Nutrition Facts per Serving
Calories: 155, Fat: 2g, Carbs: 15g, Protein: 17g

Cornish Hens

Prep + cook time: 30 minutes; Serves: 2
Ingredients:
- 2 small Cornish hens
- ½ tsp. rosemary
- 1 cup chicken stock
- ½ tsp. black pepper
- 1 tsp. thyme
- 1 tsp. salt
- 2 tbsp. flour
- 2 tbsp. water

Instructions:
1. Coat the Cornish hens with rosemary, salt, pepper, and thyme and put it in the Instant Pot. Pour the stock over it and close the lid.
2. Set to cook for 20 minutes. Quick-release the steam and put the hens in a dish.
3. Press "Sauté" on the Instant Pot and boil the stock. Mix the flour and water in a small bowl and pour it in the stock. Mix continuously.
4. Serve chicken with the gravy.

Nutrition Facts per Serving
Calories: 316; Fat: 8.34 g; Carbs: 7.12 g; Protein: 49.6 g; Fiber 0.5g

Cheesy Spaghetti Squash with Chicken

Prep + cook time: 35 minutes; Serves: 3
Ingredients:
- 2 cups of water
- 1 spaghetti squash; split in half and seeded
- ½ cup marinara sauce
- 1 lb. chicken; cooked and chopped into cubes
- 7 oz. mozzarella cheese

Instructions:

Pour the water into the Instant Pot and place the steaming rack above the Instant Pot.

2. Put the halved squash on the steaming rack and seal the lid.
3. Select "Manual" and set to cook for 20 minutes at high pressure.
4. Select "Cancel" and quick-release the pot pressure.

5. Remove the spaghetti squash and pull apart with a fork. Pour the marinara sauce over the squash and mix.
6. Serve the chicken over the spaghetti squash and top with mozzarella cheese.

Nutrition Facts per Serving
Calories: 300 g; Fat: 25.3 g; Carbs: 4 g; Protein: 14

Garlic Chicken with Celery

Prep + cook time: 18 minutes; Serves: 2
Ingredients:
- 1 ½ tsp. olive oil
- 2 tbsp. minced garlic
- ½ cup chopped onion
- ¾ lb. chopped boneless chicken
- ½ tsp. salt
- ½ tsp. pepper
- 1 bay leaf
- 1 tbsp. chopped rosemary
- ¼ tsp. thyme
- 2 tbsp. chopped celery

Instructions:
1. Press "Sauté" on the Instant Pot and add the olive oil, the garlic, and the onions to cook for 2 minutes.

2. Add the cubed chicken to the pot then season with salt and pepper then add the bay leaf, chopped rosemary, and thyme then seal the lid.
3. Select the "Manual" button and set it to cook for 10 minutes.
4. "Cancel" the pot and natural release the pressure for 8 to 10 minutes.
5. Serve topped with celery.

Nutritional Fact per Serving
Calories: 176; Fat: 8g; Carbs: 7.5g; Protein 17g; Fiber 2g

Chicken with Basil

Prep + cook time: 35 minutes; Serves: 2
Ingredients:
- Olive oil
- 4 chicken thighs
- ¾ cup soy sauce
- 1 tsp. chili garlic sauce
- ½ tsp. minced garlic cloves
- ½ cup of water or chicken stock
- ¾ cup ketchup
- 1 tbsp. arrowroot starch; dissolved in 2 tbsp. of water

Instructions:
1. Press the "Sauté" button on the Instant Pot and add the chicken thighs to cook for 6 to 7 minutes until it is brown. "Cancel" the preset function.

2. Mix in the soy sauce, chili sauce, garlic, water or stock, and ketchup and seal the lid and venting valve.
3. Set to "Manual" to cook for 10 minutes at high pressure.
4. "Cancel" the preset function and quick release the pressure.
5. Remove the chicken and pour the arrowroot mixture into the pot. Press "Sauté" and let it cook at low pressure until the sauce is thick.
6. Pour the sauce over the meat and serve.

Nutrition Facts per Serving
Calories 532, Fat 55.4g, Carbs 15.2g, Protein 30.2g

Cola Chicken Wings

Prep + cook time: 30 minutes; Serves: 2

Ingredients:

- ½ tbsp. sesame oil
- 2 tsp. minced garlic
- 2 tbsp. chopped onion
- 1 lb. chicken wings
- 1 cup of your choice of cola
- 1 ½ tbsp. low sodium soy sauce
- ½ tbsp. rice wine

Instructions:

1. Press "Sauté" on the Instant Pot and add the oil, garlic, and onions to cook for 2 minutes.
2. Add the chicken wings to brown and mix in the cola, soy sauce, and rice wine.
3. Seal the lid and set it to "Manual" to cook for 20 minutes.
4. Press "Cancel" and natural release the pot pressure for 8 to 10 minutes. Open the pot and serve.

Nutrition Facts per Serving

Calories 228, Fat 8.5g, Carbs 32g, Protein 5.5g, Fiber 0.5g

Creamy Chicken with Zucchini

Prep + cook time: 20 minutes; Serves: 4

Ingredients:

- 1 tbsp. oil
- 1 chopped onion
- 1 chopped jalapeno
- 1 cup chicken breast; 1-inch slices
- 1 tbsp. curry paste
- 1 can full-fat coconut milk
- 1 tbsp. fish sauce
- 4 cups chicken broth
- Salt to taste
- 1 zucchini; spiralized
- ½ lime; juiced

Instructions:

1. Press "Sauté" on the Instant Pot and add the oil. Mix in the onions to cook for 2 to 3 minutes.
2. Add the jalapeno to cook for 1 to 2 minutes then mix in the chicken breasts, curry paste, and coconut milk to reduce for 2 to 3 minutes.
3. "Cancel" the pot and mix in the fish sauce, broth, and salt then seal the lid and set to "Manual" to cook for 5 minutes at high pressure.
4. Press "Cancel" and quick release the pot pressure.
5. Mix in the zoodles for 1 to 2 minutes and serve with soup and lime juice.

Nutrition Facts per Serving

Calories 319, Fat 22.8g, Carbs 10.8g, Protein 19.5g

Turkey Patty with Tomatoes and Eggs

Prep + cook time: 35 minutes; Serves: 4

Ingredients:

- 1 lb. ground turkey
- ¼ tsp. cayenne pepper
- Salt and pepper
- 1 tsp. Herbs de Provence
- 1 tbsp. olive oil
- 4 slices swiss cheese
- 4 slices turkey bacon
- 4 eggs
- 4 lettuce leaves
- 1 tomato; sliced

Instructions:

1. Mix the ground turkey, cayenne pepper, salt, herbs de Provence, and pepper in a bowl.
2. Mold 4 burger patties out of the mixture and set aside. Press "Sauté" on the Instant Pot and add the olive oil then brown the patties and set aside.
3. Pour 1 cup of water into the pot and place a steaming rack above the water. Put the patties on the steaming rack and put a slice of cheese on each patty. Put the turkey bacon on the steaming rack as well.

4. Seal the lid and set to "Manual" to cook for 5 minutes at high pressure.
5. Quick-release the pressure and layer a lettuce leaf with a tomato slice, turkey patty, bacon, and a fried egg.

Nutrition Facts per Serving
Calories 720, Fat 18.9g, Carbs 1.7g, Protein 122.3g

Garlic Tamari Chicken

Prep + cook time: 35 minutes; Serves: 3
Ingredients:
- 2-lb. boneless chicken thighs; fresh or frozen
- 1/4 cup ghee
- 1/4 cup honey
- 3 tbsp. tamari
- 3 tbsp. ketchup
- 2 tsp. garlic powder
- 1 ½ tsp. sea salt
- ½ tsp. black pepper

Instructions:

1. Mix all the ingredients in the Instant Pot and seal the lid and the venting valve.
2. Set to "Manual" to cook for 18 minutes, if cooking fresh chicken but for 40 minutes if cooking frozen chicken.
3. "Cancel" the preset function and natural release the pressure for 8 to 10 minutes.
4. Serve into containers with rice and veggies.

Nutritional Fact per Serving
Calories 544; Fat: 22g; Carbs: 48.2g; Protein 36.2g; Fiber 4g

Honey Barbeque Chicken

Prep + cook time: 20 minutes; Serves: 2
Ingredients:
- ½ cup bbq sauce
- 1 cup of water
- 2 ½ tbsp. raw honey
- ¼ tsp. salt
- ½ tsp. pepper
- 2 lb. Chicken wings

Instructions:
1. Combine the bbq sauce, water, honey, salt, and pepper in a bowl.
2. Put the chicken wings in the Instant Pot and mix in the sauce. Seal the lid and the venting valve.

3. Set to "Manual" to cook for 10 minutes.
4. Press "Cancel" on the pot and quick release the pot pressure.
5. Place a pan over medium heat for 1 minute then add the chicken mix to the pot. Let it cook on low heat for some minutes until the sauce has thickened. Serve.

Nutrition Facts per Serving
Calories 334; Fat: 10g; Carbs: 45g; Protein 10.5g; Fiber 1.5g

Creamy Apple Turkey

Prep + cook time: 30 minutes; Serves: 3
Ingredients:
- 1 cup onion; sliced
- 2 garlic cloves; minced
- 1 tsp. curry powder
- 1 lb. apple; cored and finely sliced
- 1 lb. cooked turkey breasts; chopped
- 1 cup of water
- Salt and pepper
- ½ cup full-fat yogurt

- 2 tbsp. lemon juice

Instructions:
1. Press "Sauté" on the Instant Pot and add the oil and onions to cook until golden brown then add the garlic to cook for 20 seconds.
2. Mix in the curry, apple, turkey, water, salt, and pepper then seal the lid.

3. Set to "Manual" to cook for 12 minutes at high pressure.
4. "Cancel" the preset function and quick release the pot pressure. Mix in the yogurt and the lemon juice.

5. Press "Sauté" and cook on low pressure for 5 minutes while stirring.

Nutrition Facts per Serving
Calories: 320 g; Fat: 28 g; Carbs: 5 g; Protein: 18

Dumplings with Carrots and Peas

Prep + cook time: 20 minutes; Serves: 4
Ingredients:
- 16 oz. refrigerated biscuits
- 1 tsp. olive oil
- 1 tsp. onion powder
- 2 tsp. oregano
- 1 ½ lb. cubed chicken breast
- 2 minced garlic cloves
- ½ tsp. salt
- ½ tsp. pepper
- 1 tsp. basil
- 1 cup of water
- 1 cup frozen peas
- 1 cup chopped carrots
- 2 cup chicken broth

Instructions:
1. Flatten the biscuits by pressing them then cut into 2-inch strips with a knife.

2. Mix the olive oil, onion powder, oregano, chicken, garlic, salt, pepper, and basil in the Instant Pot and seal the pot.
3. Press "Sauté" on the pot and cook until the chicken browns.
4. "Cancel" the function and pour in the water, peas, carrots, and broth. Add the biscuits then seal the lid.
5. Set to "Manual" to cook for 5 minutes.
6. Natural release the pressure for 10 minutes.
7. "Cancel" the pot and serve the chicken with biscuits in a bowl.

Nutrition Facts per Serving
Calories: 610, Fat: 12.1g, Carbs: 13.6g, Protein: 100.5g

Creamy Garlic Chicken with Tomatoes

Prep + cook time: 35 minutes; serves: 6
Ingredients:
- 4 tbsp. unsalted butter
- 3 chopped garlic cloves
- 1 chopped onion
- 1 chopped fresh ginger
- 1 tsp. ground turmeric
- 1 tsp. ground coriander
- 1 tbsp. garam masala
- 1 can diced tomatoes
- ½ cup coconut milk
- 2 lb. skinless chicken breasts
- 1 tsp. kosher salt

Instructions:
1. Press "Sauté" on the pot and add 2 tbsp. of the butter.
2. Mix in the garlic, onions, ginger, and the spices and cook them while stirring for 4 minutes.

3. Pour in the tomatoes and add the chicken breasts.
4. Seal the lid and set to "Manual" to cook for 10 to 12 minutes.
5. Remove the chicken and place it on a chopping board to cool.
6. Mix in the rest of the butter and add the coconut milk.
7. Cut the cooled chicken into 1-inch thick pieces and add them to the sauce in the pot. Mix it well and serve with quinoa, basmati, brown, or cauliflower rice.

Nutrition Facts per Serving
Calories: 537, Fat: 29.3g, Carbs: 14.5g, Protein: 54.2g

Turkey with Tomatoes and Vegetables

Prep + cook time: 30 minutes; Serves: 2

Ingredients:

- 1 tbsp. butter
- 2 lb. turkey breasts; ground
- 1 (15 oz.) can of diced tomatoes
- 2 cloves garlic; chopped
- 1 red onion; sliced
- 1 cup chicken stock
- 1 red bell pepper; chopped
- 1 green bell pepper; chopped

Instructions:

1. Press "Sauté" on the Instant Pot and add the butter and the turkey breast to cook for 5 minutes.
2. Mix in the tomatoes and their juice, garlic, onion, bell peppers, and chicken stock then seal the lid.
3. Set to "Manual" to cook for 15 minutes.
4. "Cancel" the preset function and quick release the pot pressure. Serve warm.

Nutrition Facts per Serving

Calories: 506; Fat: 19.5g; Carbs: 12g; Protein 62.5g; Fiber 2.5g

Orange Herb Turkey Breasts

Prep + cook time: 25 minutes; Serves: 2

Ingredients:

- 2 tbsp. oil
- 1 tsp. Dijon mustard
- 2 garlic cloves; minced
- 1 tsp. fresh sage; chopped
- 1 tsp. fresh thyme; chopped
- 1 tsp. fresh rosemary; chopped
- Salt and pepper
- 2 boneless turkey breasts; halved
- ½ orange; juiced
- 2 tbsp. lemon juice
- 1 cup chicken broth
- 1 orange; sliced

Instructions:

1. Mix 1 tbsp. of oil with the mustard, cloves, sage, thyme, and rosemary in a bowl and cover the turkey with the herb mixture. Sprinkle with some salt and pepper and set aside.
2. Pour the rest of the oil into the Instant Pot and press "Sauté" on the pot. Add the turkey breasts to the pot and seal the lid to cook for 3 to 4 minutes on each side.
3. "Cancel" the function and combine the orange and lemon juice with the broth in a bowl and pour it over the turkey.
4. Seal the lid and the venting valve.
5. Set to "Manual" to cook for 6 minutes at high pressure.
6. "Cancel" the function and quick release the pressure. Serve.

Nutrition Facts per Serving

Calories: 225 g; Fat: 8.8 g; Carbs: 4.1 g; Protein: 36.7

Cheesy Turkey with Tomatoes and Olives

Prep + cook time: 3 hours 10 minutes; Serves: 3

Ingredients:

- 2 tbsp. olive oil
- ½ minced poblano pepper
- 3 minced garlic cloves
- 2 tbsp. lemon juice
- ½ tsp. chili flakes
- Rosemary
- Basil
- 1 sliced turkey breast
- ½ cup tomato; diced
- 3 tbsp. sliced olives
- ½ cup crumbled feta cheese
- Chopped parsley
- Salt and pepper

Instructions:

1. Mix the olive oil, poblano pepper, garlic cloves, lemon juice, chili flakes, rosemary, basil, salt, and pepper in a bowl.
2. Put the turkey slices in the marinade and let it sit for some minutes then cover the bowl with a plastic wrap and place it in the refrigerator for 3 hours.
3. Pour the water into the Instant Pot and place the steamer rack inside it. Put the turkey pieces on the rack and pour the marinade on it.
4. Seal the lid and set to cook for 50 minutes at high pressure.
5. Quick-release the pressure and open the pot.
6. Place some tomatoes over each slice with some olives and the crumbled cheese then grill it for 10 minutes in an oven.
7. Serve garnished with parsley.

Nutrition Facts per Serving
Calories: 932, Fat: 32.2g, Carbs: 15.7g, Protein: 84.7g

Chicken Noodles with Carrots and Celery

Prep + cook time: 18 minutes: Serves: 3
Ingredients:
- 2 boneless chicken thighs; cubed
- 2 cups uncooked egg noodles
- 1 celery stalk; sliced
- 3 cups chicken stock
- 1 onion; diced
- 2 carrots; sliced
- 1 bay leaf
- 1/2 tsp. salt
- 1/2 tsp. black pepper

Instructions:
1. Mix all the ingredients in the Instant Pot and seal the lid. Set to cook for 8 minutes.
2. Remove the bay leaf and serve hot.

Nutrition Facts per Serving:
Calories: 311; Fat: 17.31 g; Carbs: 17.68 g; Protein: 20.21 g; Finer 1.3g

Creamy Lemongrass Chicken

Prep + cook time: 20 minutes; Serves: 2
Ingredients:
- 1 lemongrass
- 1 tsp. ginger
- 2 tsp. minced garlic
- 3 tsp. fish sauce
- 1 tbsp. lemon juice
- ¼ tsp. pepper
- ¾ coconut milk
- ½ tsp. coconut oil
- ¼ cup chopped onion
- 4 chicken drumsticks

Instructions:
1. Blend the lemongrass with a blender and add the ginger, garlic, fish sauce, lemon juice, and pepper.
2. Pour in the coconut milk and blend some more and set aside. Press "Sauté" on the Instant Pot.
3. Add the oil and onions to cook for 2 minutes until soft.
4. Put the chicken in the pot and pour the pureed lemongrass mixture over it then seal the lid and the venting valve.
5. Set to "Manual" to cook for 10 minutes.
6. "Cancel" the preset function and natural release the pressure for 8 to 10 minutes. Open and serve.

Nutrition Facts per Serving
Calories: 342; Fat: 28.5g; Carbs: 9.5g; Protein 13g; Fiber 2.5g

Spicy Garlic Chicken Breasts

Prep + cook time: 30 minutes; Serves: 3
Ingredients:
- ¼ tsp. garlic powder
- ½ tsp. salt
- 1/8 tsp. black pepper
- 1/8 tsp. oregano; dried
- 1/8 tsp. dried basil
- 3 boneless and skinless chicken breasts

- 1 tbsp. olive oil
- 1 cup of water

Instructions:
1. Mix the garlic powder, salt, black pepper, oregano, and basil together in a bowl. Pat dry the chicken with a paper towel to remove moisture then rub the chicken with half of the herb mix on one side.
2. Press "Sauté" on the pot and pour the oil into the pot and add the chicken with the seasoned side down. While cooking, season the other side of the chicken and cook for 3 to 4 minutes per side.

3. Remove the chicken from the pot and set aside. Pour the water into the pot and place a steaming rack in the pot. Put the chicken on the steaming rack and seal the lid and the venting valve.
4. Set to "Manual" to cook for 5 minutes.
5. "Cancel" the preset function and natural release the pressure for 8 to 10 minutes. Serve into containers.

Nutrition Facts per Serving
Calories 324; Fat: 9.3g; Carbs: 19.5g; Protein 42.3g; Fiber 2g

Pasta and Chicken with Tomatoes

Prep + cook time: 20 minutes; Serves: 2

Ingredients:
- ½ tsp. olive oil
- ½ cup chopped onions
- 1 ½ cup diced chicken
- ½ cup diced red bell pepper
- ½ cup diced tomatoes
- ¼ tsp. salt
- ½ tsp. pepper
- ½ tsp. oregano
- 1 bay leaf
- 2 tbsp. chopped parsley
- Cooked pasta of your choice

Instructions:

1. Press "Sauté" on the Instant Pot and add the oil and the onions to cook for 2 minutes.
2. Mix in the chicken, red pepper, and tomatoes then season with the salt, pepper, oregano, and bay leaf and seal the lid.
3. Set to "Manual" to cook for 10 minutes.
4. "Cancel" the preset function and natural release the pot pressure for 8 to 10 minutes.
5. Serve topped with parsley and with any pasta.

Nutrition Facts per Serving
Calories: 102; Fat: 2.5g; Carbs: 4g; Protein 15.5g; Fiber 1g

Garlic Lemon Chicken

Prep + cook time: 25 minutes; Serves: 3

Ingredients:
- 3 boneless and skinless chicken breast halves
- 1 tsp. rosemary
- 2 garlic cloves; peeled and sliced
- ½ cup white wine
- 1 cup chicken broth
- ¼ cup chopped parsley
- ½ lemon; thinly sliced
- Salt and pepper

Instructions:
1. Press "Sauté" on the Instant Pot and add the chicken breasts to cook for 6 to 7 minutes on both sides.

2. Sprinkle the chicken with the rosemary and add the garlic then "Cancel" the preset function.
3. In a bowl, mix the wine, broth, and parsley together and pour it into the pot.
4. Seal the lid and set to "Manual" to cook for 8 minutes at high pressure.
5. "Cancel" the preset function and quick release the pressure. Serve chicken with lemon slices.

Nutrition Facts per Serving
Calories: 192 g; Fat: 27.7 g; Carbs: 1.9 g; Protein: 14.4

Cheesy Turkey Meatballs in Marinara

Prep + cook time: 25 minutes; Serves: 6

Ingredients:
- 1.3 lb. ground turkey breast
- 1/4 cup grated Parmigiano–Reggiano cheese
- 1/4 cup chopped parsley.
- 1/4 Panko breadcrumbs
- 1 chopped onion
- 1 crushed garlic clove
- Salt and Pepper to taste
- 2 ½ cup marinara sauce

Instructions:
1. Mix the cheese, parsley, breadcrumbs, onions, garlic, salt, pepper, and turkey breasts in a bowl until turkey is well mixed in.
2. Mold 30 meatballs of 2-inch diameter out of the mix.
3. Pour the marinara sauce into the Instant Pot and press "Sauté" on the pot.
4. Let the sauce boil then add the meatballs to the pot.
5. Seal the lid and set to "Manual" to cook at high pressure for 20 minutes.
6. Natural release the pressure and serve sprinkled with herbs.

Nutrition Facts per Serving
Calories: 545, Carbs: 3.2g, Protein: 66.7g, Fat: 24.1g

Creamy Chicken with Tomatoes

Prep + cook time: 17 minutes; Serves: 2

Ingredients:
- ½ lb. boneless chicken breast; cut into small cubes
- 1 tbsp. olive oil
- 2 tbsp. minced onions
- 2 tsp. minced garlic
- ¾ tsp. turmeric
- ¾ tsp. smoked paprika
- ½ tsp. cumin
- ½ cup diced tomatoes
- ½ cup tomato chili sauce
- ¼ tsp. cayenne pepper
- ¼ cup chicken broth
- 2 tbsp. coconut milk

Instructions:
1. Press sauté on the Instant Pot and add the olive oil, onions, and garlic to cook until fragrant.
2. Mix in the chicken cubes to cook until it is no longer pink then press the cancel button.
3. Season the chicken with turmeric, paprika, cumin, diced tomatoes, tomato chili sauce, and cayenne pepper.
4. Pour the broth into the pot and stir. Seal the lid and the valve.
5. Set to manual to cook at high pressure. Quick-release the pressure when the timer stops.
6. Open the lid and add the coconut milk and stir then press sauté on the pot to cook on high pressure for 3 minutes.
7. Natural-release the pressure and serve the chicken with gravy with a warm bowl of rice.

Nutrition Facts per Serving:
Calories: 251; Net Carbs: 6.1g; Fat: 13.4g; Carbs: 8.3g Protein: 27.4g

Turkey with Tomatoes and Bell Peppers

Prep + cook time: 30 minutes; Serves: 2

Ingredients:
- 1 tbsp. butter
- 2 lb. Ground turkey breast
- 1 (15 oz. can) diced tomatoes
- 2 chopped garlic cloves
- 1 sliced red onion
- 1 chopped red bell pepper
- 1 chopped green bell pepper
- 1 cup chicken stock

Instructions:
1. Press sauté on the Instant Pot and add the butter and the turkey meat to the pot to cook for 5 minutes.

2. Pour in the tomatoes and the juice, garlic, onions, peppers, and stock. Seal the lid and the valve.
3. Set to manual to cook for 15 minutes until the timer stops.

4. Press the cancel button and quick release the pressure. Open the pot and serve.

Nutrition Facts per Serving:
Calories: 506; Fat: 19.5g; Carbs: 12g; Protein 62.5g; Fiber: 2.5g

Chicken Pasta with Tomatoes and Bell Peppers

Prep + cook time: 20 minutes; Serves: 2

Ingredients:
- ½ tsp. olive oil
- ½ cup chopped onion
- 1 bay leaf
- 1 ½ cup diced chicken
- ½ cup diced tomatoes
- ½ cup diced red bell pepper
- ½ tsp. oregano
- ¼ tsp. salt
- ½ tsp. pepper
- 2 tbsp. chopped parsley
- Cooked pasta of your choice

Instructions:

1. Press sauté on the Instant Pot and add the oil and the onions to cook for 2 minutes.
2. Mix in bay leaf, chicken, tomatoes, red bell pepper, oregano, salt, and pepper and seal the lid.
3. Set to manual to cook for 10 minutes until the timer stops.
4. Press the cancel button and natural-release the pressure for 8 to 10 minutes. Open and serve the pasta topped with parsley.

Nutrition Facts per Serving:
Calories: 102; Fat: 2.5g; Carbs: 4g; Protein 15.5g; Fiber: 1g

Sweet and Spicy Garlic Chicken

Prep + cook time: 21 minutes; serves: 2

Ingredients:
- ½ lb. boneless chicken breast; cut into small or medium cubes
- ¾ tbsp. soy sauce
- ½ tsp. Worcestershire sauce
- 1½ tbsp. chopped' onion
- ½ tsp. red chili flakes
- ½ tsp. brown sugar
- ½ tbsp. raw honey
- ½ tsp. minced' garlic
- ½ tsp. cayenne pepper
- ½ tsp. sesame seeds

Instructions:
1. Put the chicken inside the Instant Pot and add the rest of the ingredients minus the sesame seeds.
2. Seal the lid and the venting valve. Set to manual to cook for 12 minutes.
3. Quick-release the pressure and open the lid. Serve on a dish sprinkled with sesame seeds with warm brown rice.

Nutrition Facts per Serving:
Calories: 147; Net Carbs: 7g; Fat: 2g; Carbs: 7.6g; Protein: 25.5g

Jamaican Chicken with Rice

Prep + cook time:18 minutes; Serves: 2

Ingredients:
- ¾ cup long-grain white rice
- 2 tsp. olive oil
- ½ diced small onion
- 1 minced garlic clove
- 1 tbsp. Jamaican jerk seasoning
- 1 cup chicken broth
- 2 skinless chicken thighs

Instructions:

1. Rinse the rice with water until the water runs clear and set aside.
2. Press "Sauté" on the Instant Pot and add the olive oil and onions to cook for some minutes while stirring until they are translucent.
3. Mix in the garlic to cook for 20seconds then add the jerk seasoning while continuously stirring.

4. Pour in the chicken broth and add the chicken to the pot.
5. Seal the lid and set to cook at "Manual" for 7 minutes.
6. Let the pot sit for 5 minutes after the timer has stopped and open the venting valve to release the rest of the steam.
7. Open the pot and remove the chicken. Serve the chicken with some rice or shred the chicken and mix it with the rice then serve.

Nutrition Facts per Serving
Calories: 283, Fat: 2.5g, Carbs: 47g, Protein: 22g

Cheesy Chicken Rice Dish

Prep + cook time: 30 minutes; serves: 2

Ingredients:
- 1 tbsp. unsalted butter
- 1 tbsp. olive oil
- ½ onion; chopped
- 2 to 3 slices pancetta; diced
- ¾ lb. chicken meat; diced
- 2 chopped garlic cloves
- ¾ cup Arborio rice or risotto
- 1/3 cup white wine
- 3 ½ cups chicken stock
- 1 tsp. fresh thyme
- 1 tbsp. lemon zest
- Salt and pepper
- 2 tbsp. grated parmesan

Instructions:
1. Press "Sauté" on the Instant Pot and add the butter and olive oil.
2. Mix in the onions to cook for 1 to 2 minutes then add the diced pancetta, chicken, and garlic to cook for 2 to 3 minutes.
3. "Cancel" the preset function then mix in the stock, thyme, seat, salt, and pepper then seal the lid and set to "Manual" to cook for 6 minutes at high pressure.
4. "Cancel" the preset function and natural release the pot pressure.
5. Mix in the parmesan cheese and stir until it melts. Serve topped with lemon zest and extra parmesan.

Nutrition Facts per Serving
Calories: 586 g; Fat: 22.5 g; Carbs: 23.6 g; Protein: 45

Cinnamon Turkey with Raisins and Cranberry Sauce

Prep + cook time: 50 minutes; Serves: 2

Ingredients:
- 1 tbsp. olive oil
- 2 minced garlic cloves
- ¼ cup raisins
- 1 lb. turkey thighs or legs
- 1 small lemon; chopped with seeds removed
- ½ cup cranberries; fresh or frozen
- 1 cup apple cider
- 1 tsp. ground cinnamon
- 1 tsp. dried thyme
- ½ tbsp. dried parsley flakes
- 1 tsp. sea salt
- 1 tbsp. arrowroot starch dissolved in 1 tbsp. of water

Instructions:
1. Press "Sauté" on the Instant Pot and add the oil, garlic, and raisins to the pot to cook for 2 to 3 minutes.
2. Mix in the turkey and put the lemon and 1 cup of cranberries on the turkey then press the "Cancel" button.
3. Pour in the apple cider and add the cinnamon, thyme, parsley, and salt then seal the lid and press the " Stew/Meat" button.
4. Preheat the oven broiler while cooking then remove the turkey after the cooking has stopped in the pot and put it into the casserole to broil in the oven for 5 minutes.
5. Press "Sauté" on the pot and mix in the rest of the cranberries.
6. Add the arrowroot mix and let it cook on low heat until the sauce is thick.
7. Serve the turkey with cranberry sauce and steamed veggies.

Nutrition Facts per Serving
Calories: 287 g; Fat: 23.7 g; Carbs: 19 g; Protein: 21.7

Lemon Chicken and Potatoes

Prep + cook time: 30 minutes; Serves: 2

Ingredients:

- 1 lb. chopped chicken
- ½ tsp. salt
- ½ tsp. pepper
- 1lb. potatoes; peeled and make wedges
- 1 tbsp. Italian seasoning
- 2 tbsp. lemon juice
- ½ cup low sodium chicken broth
- 1 ½ tbsp. Dijon mustard
- 1 tsp. lemon zest

Instructions:

1. Sprinkle the salt and pepper on the chicken and set aside.
2. Put all the ingredients in the Instant Pot and stir them to combine.
3. Seal the lid and set it to "Manual" to cook for 15 minutes.
4. "Cancel" the preset function and natural release the pressure for 8 to 10 minutes. Serve warm.

Nutrition Facts per Serving

Calories: 256; Fat: 3.5g; Carbs: 34.5g; Protein 18.5g; Fiber 6g

Cajun Chicken with Rice

Prep + cook time: 30 minutes; Serves: 5

Ingredients:

- ½ cup white rice
- 1 lb. chicken breasts; sliced half lengthwise
- 1 diced onion
- 1 minced garlic clove
- 1 diced bell pepper
- 1 tbsp. tomato paste
- 1 tbsp. Cajun seasoning
- ¾ cup chicken broth

Instructions:

1. Rinse the rice continuously until the water runs clear.
2. Sprinkle1 tsp. of the Cajun seasoning on both sides of the chicken and set aside.
3. Press "Sauté" on the Instant Pot and add the onions and garlic to cook until soft.
4. Deglaze the pot with some water then mix in the rice, bell peppers, tomato paste, and 1 tsp. of Cajun seasoning and mix well.
5. Seal the lid and set to "Manual" to cook for 7 to 8 minutes at high pressure.
6. Natural release the pressure for 5 minutes then quick release the rest of the pressure.
7. Shred the chicken and mix it with the rice and season with some salt and pepper as desired.
8. Serve topped with chopped cilantro and a hint of lime.

Nutrition Facts per serving

Calories: 473, Fat: 7.4g, Carbs: 64.9g, Protein: 33.4g

Spicy Chicken with Mushrooms

Prep + cook time: 25 minutes; Serves: 4

Ingredients:

- 1 whole chicken
- 2 tsp. kosher salt
- ½ tsp. black pepper
- 1 tsp. paprika
- 2 tbsp. avocado oil
- 8 oz. sliced Cremini mushrooms
- 1 sliced yellow onions
- 1 chopped garlic clove
- 1 tbsp. tomato paste
- ½ tsp. dried oregano
- ½ tsp. thyme
- 1 cup low-sodium broth

Instructions:

1. Pat dry the chicken to remove the moisture then tuck the wings under the chicken and tie the drumsticks with a kitchen string.
2. Mix the salt, pepper, and paprika together in a bowl and rub the chicken with the mixture.
3. Press "Sauté" on the Instant Pot and add the oil to heat for 2 minutes.
4. Place the chicken in the pot with the breast side up to brown for 5 minutes. Then turn the chicken and brown for another 5 minutes then remove and set aside.
5. Mix in the mushrooms, onions, and garlic to cook until soft then add the tomato paste, oregano, and thyme to cook for 2 minutes.
6. Pour in the broth and mix with a wooden spoon, lifting the stuck bits with the spoon.
7. Place a rack into the pot and put the chicken into the pot with the breast side up then seal the lid and venting valve.
8. Press Poultry and set to cook for 20 minutes at high pressure.
9. Quick-release the pressure and remove the chicken to a chopping board and strain the liquid with a mesh strainer. Keep the mushrooms and onions in a bowl. Pour the liquid, with the fat removed, into the Instant Pot.
10. Press "Sauté" on the pot and cook until it thickens then sprinkle with some salt; as required.
11. Slice the chicken and place it on a platter then serve with the mushrooms and onions and with the sauce poured over it.

Nutrition Facts per Serving

Calories: 370, Fat: 21g, Carbs: 1.4g, Protein: 50.3g

Tomato Rice with Chicken and Bell Peppers

Prep + cook time: 30 minutes; serves: 3

Ingredients:

- 1 ½ cups white rice
- 1 lb. chicken breast
- 1 tbsp. Cajun seasoning
- 1 tbsp. olive oil
- 1 minced garlic clove
- 1 diced onion
- 1 diced bell pepper
- 1 tbsp. tomato paste
- 1 ¾ cups chicken broth
- 1 cup of water

Instructions:

1. Rinse the rice until the water runs clear then slice the chicken breasts in half lengthwise.
2. Rub the chicken with the Cajun seasoning then press the Sauté button and add the olive oil and the garlic and onion.
3. Lift the stuck bits with some water and a wooden spoon.
4. Mix in the rice, bell peppers, and tomato paste with 1 teaspoon of Cajun seasoning.
5. Pour the broth over the rice and put the chicken on it.
6. Seal the lid and the valve then set to Manual to cook for 7 to 8 minutes at High Pressure.
7. Natural-release the pressure for 5 minutes and open the lid. Shred the chicken and mix it with the rice. Season with some salt and pepper as required.
8. Serve topped with cilantro and a hint of lime.

Nutrition Facts per Serving

Calories: 473, Fat: 7.4g, Carbs: 64.9g, Protein: 33.4g

Cheesy Chili Chicken

Prep + cook time: 19 minutes; serves: 2

Ingredients:

- 1½ tsps. olive oil
- 3 tbsps. chopped onion
- 1 tsp. minced' garlic
- ½ lb. boneless chicken breast
- 1½ tsps. chili powder
- ¼ tsp. pepper
- ¼ tsp. salt
- ½ tsp. cumin
- ½ cup salsa
- ½ cup chicken broth
- ¼ cup grated cheddar cheese

Instructions:

1. Press Sauté on the pot and add the olive oil, onion, and garlic to cook until fragrant.
2. Press the Cancel button then add the chicken to the pot. Mix in the chili powder, pepper, salt, and cumin. Pour the salsa over the chicken and add the broth.
3. Seal the lid and the valve and set it to Manual to cook for 12 minutes at High Pressure.
4. Quick-release the pressure and open the lid then sprinkle the cheddar cheese over the chicken. Stir and serve the chicken over a bowl of brown rice.

Nutrition Facts per Serving

Calories: 241; Net Carbs: 5.6g; Fat: 10.6g; Carbs: 7.8g; Protein: 31.4g

Cheesy Rice with Pancetta and Chicken

Prep + cook time: 30 minutes; Serves: 2

Ingredients:

- 1 tbsp. olive oil
- 1 tbsp. unsalted butter
- ½ onion; chopped
- 2 to 3 slices diced pancetta
- ¾ lb. diced chicken meat
- 2 garlic cloves; chopped
- ¾ cup risotto or Arborio rice
- 1/3 cup white wine
- 3 ½ cups of chicken stock
- 1 tsp. fresh thyme
- 1 tbsp. lemon zest
- Salt and pepper
- 2 tbsp. parmesan; grated

Instructions:

1. Press sauté on the Instant Pot and add the oil and butter and the onion to cook for 1 to 2 minutes.
2. Mix in the pancetta, chicken, and garlic to cook for 2 to 3 minutes until the timer stops.
3. Press the cancel button then pour in the chicken stock, thyme, lemon zest, salt, and pepper. Seal the lid and the valve. Set to manual to cook for 6 minutes at high pressure.
4. Press the cancel button and natural- release the pressure for 8 to 10 minutes.
5. Open the pot and mix in the cheese until it melts. Serve topped with parmesan and lemon zest.

Nutrition Facts per Serving:

Calories: 489 g; Fat: 22.5 g; Carbs: 23.6 g; Protein: 45g

Spicy Sour Cream Chicken with Tomatoes

Prep + cook time: 40 minutes; Serves: 2

Ingredients:

- 1 tbsp. oil
- 2 chicken leg quarters
- 1 cup chicken broth
- 1 small onion; diced
- 2 tsp. hot paprika
- 1 medium tomato; skin removed and coarsely chopped
- 1 tsp. salt
- ½ cup sour cream

Instructions:

1. Press "Sauté" on the Instant Pot and add the oil. Add the chicken to brown for 4 to 5 minutes then pour in the broth, onion, and paprika.
2. Put the tomatoes on the chicken and season with some salt. Do not stir. Seal the lid and set to "Manual" to cook for 10 minutes at high pressure.
3. Press "Cancel" and natural release the pressure for 10 minutes.
4. Remove the chicken and set aside then press "Sauté" and reduce the pressure to low to cook for 15 minutes until the sauce thickens.
5. Remove ¼ cup of the cooking sauce and mix in the sour cream.
6. Pour in the sour cream mixture and add the chicken to the pot then cook on low heat for some minutes.
7. Serve the chicken topped with the sauce.

Nutrition Facts per serving
Calories: 260 g; Fat: 29 g; Carbs: 5.9 g; Protein: 16.3

Spicy BBQ Sliders

Prep +cook time: 26 minutes; Serves: 2

Ingredients:

- 4 lb. boneless chicken breasts
- ½ tsp. garlic powder
- ½ tsp. onion powder
- 3 cup coleslaw mix
- 2 tbsp. Dijon mustard
- 1 cup mayonnaise
- 2 tbsp. apple cider vinegar
- 1 tsp. celery salt
- 1 tsp. kosher salt
- ½ tsp. black pepper
- 12 sliders
- 1 ½ cup barbeque sauce

Instructions:

1. Mix the chicken with the seasoning in the Instant Pot then seal the lid and set to "Manual" to cook for 15 minutes but if the chicken is frozen, it will cook for 20 minutes at high pressure.
2. Quick-release the pressure then take out the chicken and place it on a cutting board. Shred the chicken with a fork then add it back into the sauce. Press "Sauté" or simmer then pour in the barbeque sauce.
3. Put the slaw mix into a bowl and set aside. Whisk the mustard, mayo, vinegar, black pepper, and celery salt in a bowl. Taste and season with some black pepper and kosher salt if required.
4. Mix the slaw mix with the dressing and use it on the sliders.
5. Cut the buns in half and layer the shredded chicken with coleslaw on it and add the top bun.
6. Serve.

Nutrition Facts per Serving
Calories: 403, Fat: 20g, Carbs: 19g, Protein: 35g

Chapter 6 Beef Recipes

Beef and Potatoes in Tomato Paste

Prep + cook time: 55 minutes; serves: 2

Ingredients:
- 1 lb. chuck beef
- 1 tsp. salt
- ½ tsp. black pepper
- 2 tbsps. butter
- 2 carrots; sliced
- 1 celery stalk; sliced
- 1 onion; chopped
- 1 tsp. thyme
- ½ tsp. rosemary
- 2 tbsps. flour
- 1 tbsps. tomato paste
- 2 cups beef broth
- ½ lb. potatoes; chopped

Instructions:
1. Rub the beef with salt and black pepper. Press Sauté on the pot and add the butter to melt then add the beef to brown then set aside.
2. Mix in the carrots, celery, and onion to cook until it is clear then mix in the thyme and rosemary then cook for 30 seconds. Mix in the flour until it is well coated.
3. Add the tomato paste and beef broth then scrape the stuck bits and add the potatoes. Return the beef to the pot and seal the lid and valve.
4. Set to cook for 35 minutes at High Pressure then season with salt and pepper. Serve.

Nutrition Facts per Serving
Calories: 570; Fat: 25.33 g; Carbs: 33.68 g; Protein: 53.64 g; Fiber: 4.5 g

Cheesy Pasta with Beef and Pork

Prep + cook time: 15 minutes; serves: 2

Ingredients:
- Cooking oil
- ¼ lb. ground beef
- ¼ lb. ground pork
- 1 cup of water
- 6 oz. ruffles pasta
- 1 cup pasta sauce
- 4 oz. ricotta cheese
- 4 oz. mozzarella cheese

Instructions:
1. Press Sauté on the pot and add the oil, pork, and beef to brown for 3 to 4 minutes.
2. Add the water, pasta, and sauce then seal the lid and the valve.
3. Set to Manual to cook for 5 minutes.
4. Press the Cancel button and Quick-release the pressure. Mix in the cheeses and serve warm.

Nutrition Facts per Serving
Calories: 588; Fat: 24g; Carbs: 52.5g; Protein 61g; Fiber: 4.5g

Spicy Cinnamon Beef Stew

Prep + cook time: 40 minutes; serves: 3

Ingredients:
- Cooking oil
- 1 tbsp. flour
- ½ tsp. black pepper
- ½ tsp. five-spice powder
- 2 cloves garlic; crushed and minced
- 1 tsp. fresh lemongrass; chopped
- 2 tbsps. rice vinegar
- ½ tbsp. soy sauce
- 1 tbsp. honey
- 1 lb. lean beef; cubed

- ½ cup red onion; chopped
- ½ cup carrots; chopped
- 1 jalapeno pepper; chopped
- ½ cup Poblano pepper; diced
- 1 cinnamon stick
- 2 cardamom pods
- 2 anise star pods
- 2 cups tomatoes; chopped
- 2 tbsps. tomato paste
- ½ cup acorn squash; cubed
- 2 cups beef broth

Instructions:
1. Combine the flour, black pepper, and five-spice powder in a bowl and coat the beef with the flour mixture.
2. Mix in the garlic, lemongrass, vinegar, soy sauce, and honey and refrigerate for 30 minutes.
3. Press Sauté on the Instant Pot and add the oil then add the beef, onions, and carrots to cook for 3 to 5 minutes. Mix in the Poblano pepper and jalapeno peppers then cook for 1 to 2 minutes.
4. Mix in the rest of the ingredients and cook for 3 to 5 minutes then press the Cancel button.
5. Pour in the beef broth then seal the lid and the valve then set to Manual to cook for 20 minutes at High Pressure.
6. Press the Cancel button and Quick-release the pressure then open the lid and serve with rice.

Nutrition Facts per Serving
Calories: 447 g; Fat: 15.5 g; Carbs: 29 g; Protein: 47.8

Creamy Potato and Beef

Prep + cook time: 15 minutes; serves: 4
Ingredients:
- 2 tbsps. olive oil
- ¾ lb. lean ground beef
- ¼ chopped onion
- 8 oz. cream of chicken soup
- 16 oz. frozen potato rounds

Instructions:
1. Press Sauté on the pot and add the oil. Add the beef and onion to cook for 5 minutes.
2. Mix in the chicken soup and add the potato rounds then seal the lid and set to Manual to cook for 25 minutes.
3. Natural-release the pressure for 5 minutes then open the lid and serve.

Nutrition Facts per Serving
Calories: 1100, Fat: 63.4g, Carbs: 92.7g, Protein: 35.2g

Cheesy Garlic Macaroni with Beef and Tomatoes

Prep + cook time: 20 minutes; serves: 3
Ingredients:
- 1 tbsp. olive oil
- ½ lb. ground beef
- 1 diced onion
- 2 cloves minced garlic
- 1 can whole tomatoes in their juice; crushed
- ½ cup beef stock
- 1 tbsp. Worcestershire sauce
- ½ tsp. salt
- ½ tsp. black pepper
- ½ lb. uncooked macaroni
- 1 cup shredded mozzarella cheese

Instructions:
1. Press Sauté on the pot and add the oil. Brown the beef then add the onion and garlic.
2. Mix in the tomatoes, stock, Worcestershire sauce, macaroni, salt, and pepper. Mix in the pasta and half of the cheese.
3. Seal the lid and the valve then set to cook for 8 minutes at High Pressure.
4. Spread the rest of the cheese over the pasta and close the lid until it has melted. Serve.

Nutrition Facts per Serving
Calories: 495; Fat: 19.89 g; Carbs: 48.74 g;; Protein: 29.07 g Fiber: 3.3 g

Spicy Lemon Beef

Prep + cook time: 30 minutes; serves: 2

Ingredients:

- ½ lb. beef tenderloin
- 1 tbsp. minced' garlic
- 2 Kaffir lime leaves
- ¼ cup water
- 2 tbsps. lemon juice
- ¼ tsp. salt
- 2 tbsps. red chili pepper
- 1 tbsp. vegetable oil

Instructions:

1. Cut the tenderloin in thin slices and put it in the pot.

2. Mix in the rest of the ingredients except the vegetable oil and seal the lid and the valve.

3. Set to Manual to cook for 20 minutes. Natural-release the pressure and open the lid.

4. Remove the gravy except for the beef then add the vegetable oil. Press the Sauté button and mix the oil with the beef. Serve.

Nutrition Facts per Serving

Calories: 268; Net Carbs: 5.5g; Fat: 15.1g; Carbs: 6.3g; Protein: 25.6g

Cheesy Beef

Prep + cook time: 20 minutes; serves: 2

Ingredients:

- ¼ lb. ground beef
- 1 tbsp. sesame oil
- ¼ cup cheddar cubes
- 2 tbsps. cornstarch
- 2 tsps. garlic powder
- 2 eggs
- ½ tsp. pepper

Instructions:

1. Mix all the ingredients in a bowl and spread the mix in a disposable aluminum pan.

2. Pour water into the Instant Pot and place a rack in it. Put the pan on the rack and seal the lid and valve.

3. Set to Steam to cook for 15 minutes at High Pressure.

4. Natural-release the pressure and open the lid. Remove the pan, let it sit for some minutes then serve.

Nutrition Facts per Serving

Calories: 368; Net Carbs: 3.4g; Fat: 30.7g; Carbs: 3.8g; Protein: 19.2g

Spicy Beef Brisket with Tomatoes

Prep + cook time: 30 minutes; serves: 2

Ingredients:

- ½ lb. beef brisket
- 3 tbsps. tamarind water
- 1 tsp. vegetable oil
- 2 tbsps. sliced shallots
- 2 tsps. minced' garlic
- ¼ cup diced' tomatoes
- 1 bay leaf
- ¼ tsp. salt
- ½ tsp. ginger
- 1½ tsps. red chilies

Instructions:

1. Cut the brisket into slices and rub it with the tamarind water. Pour the vegetable oil in the Instant Pot and press the Sauté button.

2. Mix in the shallots and garlic and cook till fragrant.

3. Mix in the brisket and add the tomatoes, bay leaf, salt, ginger, and red chilies then cook till fragrant.

4. Seal the lid and the valve then set to Manual to cook for 15 minutes. Natural-release the steam and open the lid.

5. Press Sauté and cook the beef uncovered for 3 minutes.

6. Serve the beef and gravy on a dish with a bowl of rice.

Nutrition Facts per Serving

Calories: 350; Net Carbs: 3.9g; Fat: 27.4g; Carbs: 4.5g; Protein: 21.7g

Beef with Peppercorns

Prep + cook time: 2 hours; serves: 2

Ingredients:

- 2 lbs. corned beef; flat cut
- 1 cup low–sodium chicken broth
- 1 tsp. dried thyme
- 4 whole peppercorns
- 2 large bay leaves
- ½ quartered onion
- ½ cup of water

Instructions:

1. Mix all the ingredients in the pot and seal the lid and the valve.
2. Set to Manual to cook at High Pressure for 90 minutes. Natural-release the pressure and serve.

Nutrition Facts per Serving

Calories: 797, Fat: 56.8g, Carbs: 4.9g, Protein: 62g

Creamy Spicy Garlic Beef

Prep + cook time: 25 minutes; serves: 2

Ingredients:

- 1 lemongrass
- 1 tbsp. red chili flakes
- 1 tsp. cayenne
- 2 shallots
- 2 cloves garlic
- ½ tsp. turmeric
- ¼ tsp. ginger
- 1 tsp. tamarind water
- ¼ tsp. salt
- ½ lb. beef tenderloin
- 4 tbsps. coconut milk
- 2 tbsps. of water

Instructions:

1. Put the lemongrass, chili flakes, cayenne, shallots, garlic, turmeric, ginger, tamarind water, and salt in the food processor and blend till smooth.
2. Cut the beef into slices and put it in the pot.
3. Pour the blended spices over it then add the coconut milk and water then stir well.
4. Seal the lid and the valve then set to Manual to cook for 20 minutes at High Pressure.
5. Natural-release the pressure and open the pot. Serve with gravy.

Nutrition Facts per Serving

Calories: 278; Net Carbs: 6.6g; Fat: 15.5g; Protein: 26.8g; Carbs: 8.1g;

Cheesy Beef Pot Pie

Prep + cook time: 50 minutes; serves: 2

Ingredients:

- 1 tbsp. olive oil
- ½ onion; chopped
- 2 garlic cloves; minced
- ½ lb. ground beef
- Salt and pepper
- 6 uncooked lasagna noodles
- 15 oz. marinara or Italian sauce
- 1 cup mozzarella cheese
- 1 cup ricotta cheese

Instructions:

1. Press Sauté on the pot and add the oil, onion, and garlic to cook for 2 minutes.
2. Add the beef, salt, and pepper to cook for 3 to 4 minutes. Remove from the pot and set aside.
3. Put a rack in the pot and prepare a spring form pan.
4. Put lasagna noodles on the bottom of the pan then layer it with 1/3 of the sauce. Spread 1/3 of the meat over the sauce then 1/3 of the cheeses.
5. Continue to layer the ingredients in the same way. Pour water into the pot and put the pan on the rack.
6. Seal the lid and set to Manual to cook for 20 minutes at High Pressure.
7. Press the Cancel button and Natural-release the pressure. Open the lid and serve.

Nutrition Facts per Serving

Calories: 712 g; Fat: 19.1 g; Carbs: 36.1 g; Protein: 56.7

Spicy Beef with Mushrooms

Prep + cook time: 35 minutes; serves: 2

Ingredients:
- 1 tbsp. oil
- ½ lb. beef stew meat; chopped
- Salt and pepper
- 6 oz. Portobello mushrooms
- 2 garlic cloves; chopped
- ½ onion; diced
- 2 sprigs fresh thyme
- 1 tbsp. flour
- 2 tbsps. dry sherry
- 1 cup beef broth
- 3 tbsps. sour cream
- 1 tbsp. chopped fresh parsley

Instructions:
1. Press Sauté on the pot and add the oil, beef, salt, and pepper to cook for 3 to 4 minutes.

2. Mix in the mushrooms, garlic, thyme, and onion to cook for 3 minutes. Then add the flour to cook for 1 minute.
3. Pour in the sherry, broth and add the meat then seal the lid and the valve and set to Manual to cook for 12 minutes at High Pressure.
4. Press the Cancel button and Quick-release the pressure.
5. Open the lid and press the Sauté button to cook on Low Pressure and mix in the sour cream and parsley. Season with salt as needed and cook for 2 to 3 minutes. Serve topped with parsley.

Nutrition Facts per Serving
Calories: 416 g; Fat: 20.4 g; Carbs: 9.9 g; Protein: 39.9

Sweet and spicy Beef Balls

Prep + cook time: 20 minutes; serves: 2

Ingredients:
- ½ lb. ground beef
- ½ tbsp. flour
- 1 egg white
- 1 tbsp. vegetable oil
- 1 tsp. minced garlic
- 1 tsp. sliced shallots
- 2 tbsps. red chili flakes
- ½ cup of water
- ½ tsp. brown sugar
- 1 bay leaf
- ¼ tsp. salt

Instructions:

1. Mix the beef with flour and egg then shape into small sized balls.
2. Press Sauté on the pot and add the oil, garlic, shallots, and chili flakes to cook until fragrant then press the Cancel button.
3. Put the balls in the pot and pour the water over it and add the bay leaf, sugar, and salt then seal the lid and the valve.
4. Set to Manual to cook for 15 minutes at High Pressure. Natural-release the pressure and serve.

Nutrition Facts per Serving
Calories: 381; Net Carbs: 6.5g; Fat: 29.4g; Protein: 21g; Carbs: 7.3g;

Chili Garlic Beef

Prep + cook time: 23 minutes; serves: 2

Ingredients:
- 1½ tsps. vegetable oil
- 3/4 lb. beef sirloin
- ¼ tsp. pepper
- ¼ tsp. salt
- ¼ cup chopped' onions
- 1 tsp. minced' garlic
- 1½ tsps. soy sauce
- 1½ tsps. black pepper
- 2 tbsps. diced' red pepper
- 2 tbsp. diced' green pepper
- 1½ tsps. fish sauce
- ¼ tsp. sugar
- ¼ cup beef broth
- 1 tsp. cornstarch

- 1 tbsp. water

Instructions:
1. Cut the beef into thin slices and rub with the pepper and salt. Press Sauté on the Instant Pot and add the oil.
2. Mix in the onion and garlic then cook till fragrant.
3. Mix in the beef and cook till it is no longer pink. Press the Cancel button.
4. Add the red pepper, green pepper, soy sauce fish sauce, sugar, and black pepper. Pour in the broth and seal the lid and the valve. Set to Manual to cook for 15 minutes at High Pressure.
5. Quick-release the pressure and open the lid then mix in the cornstarch and water.
6. Press Sauté and cook for 3 minutes then serve.

Nutrition Facts per Serving
Calories: 270; Net Carbs: 6.8g; Fat: 10.5g; Carbs: 10.2g; Protein: 37g;

Creamy Beef Curry

Prep + cook time: 60 minutes; serves: 3

Ingredients:
- 2 tbsps. oil
- ½ lb. beef stew chunks; chopped into small cubes
- 1 small onion; chopped
- 1 cup carrots; chopped
- 1 zucchini; chopped
- 1 tsp. ginger; chopped
- 1 cup beef broth
- 1 tsp. garlic power
- Salt and Pepper
- 1 tsp. turmeric powder
- ½ cup of coconut milk

Instructions:
1. Press Sauté on the Instant Pot and add the oil and beef to cook for 3 to 5 minutes then set aside.
2. Mix in the onions, carrots, zucchini, and ginger to cook for 2 to 3 minutes. Then add 2 tablespoons of broth to deglaze the pot.
3. Pour in the rest of the broth, add the beef, turmeric, garlic powder, salt, and pepper then mix well and seal the lid and the valve. Set to Meat to cook at High Pressure.
4. Press the Cancel button and Quick-release the pressure . open the lid and mix in the coconut milk.
5. Press Sauté and cook on Low Pressure for 2 to 3 minutes then stop the pot and serve.

Nutrition Facts per Serving
Calories: 180 g; Fat: 35 g; Carbs: 6 g; Protein: 20

Sweet Beef in Tomato Sauce

Prep + cook time: 26 minutes; serves: 2

Ingredients:
- ½ lb. beef tenderloin
- ¼ tsp. sugar
- ¼ cup chopped onion
- 2 tbsps. tomato sauce
- 1 tbsp. soy sauce
- ¼ tsp. salt
- ½ tsp. black pepper
- 2 tbsps. butter
- ½ cup water

Instructions:
1. Cut the beef into slices and rub with sugar, onion, tomato sauce, soy sauce, salt and pepper.
2. Press Sauté on the pot and add the butter to the pot. Put the beef slices into the pot and cook until wilted then press the Cancel button.
3. Pour the water over the beef and seal the lid and the valve.
4. Set to Manual to cook for 22 minutes at High Pressure.
5. Natural-release the pressure and open the lid.
6. Serve the beef with Sautéed carrots and fried potatoes.

Nutrition Facts per Serving
Calories: 299; Net Carbs: 2.9g; Fat: 19.6g; Carbs: 3.6g; Protein: 26g;

Beef and Bacon with Potatoes and Carrots

Prep + cook time: 50 minutes; Serves: 2

Ingredients:

- ½ tbsp. oil
- ½ lb. beef stew meat
- 2 bacon slices
- 1 medium onion; chopped
- 1 garlic clove; minced
- 1 large potato; cubed
- 1 tbsp. thyme
- ½ cup beef stock
- ½ cup red wine
- 2 medium carrots; chopped
- 1 tbsp. parsley
- ½ tbsp. honey

Instructions:

1. Press "Sauté" on the Instant Pot and add the oil and the beef to brown for 3 to 4 minutes.
2. Mix in the bacon and onions to reduce until clear then mix in the beef and the remaining ingredients.
3. Seal the lid and the venting valve.
4. Set to "Manual" to cook for 30 minutes.
5. Press "Cancel" and natural release the pressure for 8 to 10 minutes. Open the pot and serve.

Nutrition Facts per Serving

Calories: 558; Fat: 16.5g; Carbs: 46.5g; Protein 42g; Fiber 7g

Garlic Chuck Roast with Carrots

Prep + cook time: 55 minutes: serves: 3

Ingredients:

- 2 lb. beef chuck roast
- Salt and pepper
- 1 tbsp. fresh lemon juice
- 2 tbsp. unsalted butter
- 1 yellow onion; quartered
- 2 garlic cloves; minced
- 2 cups beef broth
- 2 carrots; peeled and cut into 1-inch pieces

Instructions:

1. Sprinkle the beef with salt and pepper and coat with the lemon juice.
2. Press sauté and add the oil and the onions to cook for 2 to 3 minutes. Mix in the garlic to cook for 1 minute.
3. Press cancel and add the beef and the broth then seal the lid. Set to manual to cook for 40 minutes at high pressure.
4. Press the cancel button and quick release the pressure. Open the lid and add the carrots.
5. Press sauté and cook on low pressure for 10 minutes. Season with salt; as needed.

Nutrition Facts per Serving:

Calories: 620 g; Fat: 50.6 g; Carbs: 5 g; Protein: 36.4

Beef with Carrots and Potatoes

Prep + cook time: 55 minutes; serves: 2

Ingredients:

- 1 lb. chuck beef
- 1 tsp. salt
- ½ tsp. black pepper
- 1 chopped onion
- 2 carrots; sliced
- 1 celery stalk; sliced
- 1 tsp. thyme
- ½ tsp. rosemary
- 2 tbsp. flour
- 1 tbsp. tomato paste
- 2 cups beef broth
- ½ lb. potatoes; chopped

Instructions:

1. Sprinkle the beef with salt and pepper. Press "Sauté" on the Instant Pot then add the butter to melt. Add the beef to brown then remove and set aside.
2. Mix in the onions, carrots, and celery to cook until the onion is clear then add the thyme and the rosemary to toast for 30 seconds. Mix in the flour until everything is coated.

3. Add the tomato paste and broth and scrape any stuck bits with a wooden spoon. Add the potatoes and the beef.
4. Seal the lid and set to cook for 35minutes at high pressure. Season with some salt and pepper and serve.

Nutrition Facts per Serving
Calories: 570; Fat: 25.33 g; Carbs: 33.68 g; Protein: 53.64 g; Fiber 4.5g

Cheesy Beef meatballs in Tomato Sauce

Prep + cook time: 30 minutes; Serves: 3
Ingredients:
- 1 tbsp. parmesan cheese
- 1 lb. ground beef
- ½ tsp. dried oregano
- ½ egg
- Salt and black pepper
- ½ tbsp. flaxseed meal
- ½ tbsp. olive oil
- 14 oz. tomato sauce

Instructions:
1. Mix the cheese, beef, oregano, egg, salt, pepper, and flaxseed meal in a bowl.
2. Mold 1-inch thick meatballs from the beef mixture.
3. Press "Sauté" on the Instant Pot and add the oil and the meatballs to brown.
4. Pour in the tomato sauce and add the water and seal the lid.
5. Set to "Manual" to cook at high pressure for 6 minutes. Natural release the pressure for 5 minutes. Serve.

Nutrition Facts per Serving
Calories: 358, Fat: 15g, Carbs: 3.1g, Protein: 50.6g

Beef with Broccoli and Carrots

Prep + cook time: 20 minutes; serves: 2
Ingredients:
- 1 tsp. olive oil
- ¼ cup chopped onion
- 2 tsp. minced garlic
- ½ lb. ground beef
- ½ cup broccoli florets
- ¼ cup carrots stick
- ¼ tsp. salt
- ¼ tsp. pepper
- ¼ tsp. nutmeg

Instructions:
1. Press sauté on the pot and add the oil, onion, garlic, and beef to cook until fragrant then cancel the pot.
2. Scoop the beef into a disposable aluminum pan and combine it with broccoli and carrots.
3. Sprinkle with salt, pepper, and nutmeg and mix well. Pour some water in the pot and add the rack over it. Place the aluminum pan on it and seal the lid and valve.
4. Set to steam to cook for 10 minutes at high pressure.
5. Natural-release the pressure and remove the pan.
6. Serve with veggies.

Nutrition Facts per Serving:
Calories: 374; Net Carbs: 3.8g; Fat: 30.5g; Carbs: 5.1g; Protein: 19.2g;

Flank Steak in Tomato Sauce Mix

Prep + cook time: 25 minutes; serves: 2
Ingredients:
- ½ lb. flank steak
- ¼ tsp. oregano
- ¼ tsp. cumin
- ¼ cup tomato sauce
- 1 tsp. vinegar
- ¼ tsp. pepper
- ¼ cup chopped onion
- ¼ tsp. salt

- 1½ tsp. minced garlic
- 1½ tbsp. canola oil
- ¼ cup dry red wine
- ½ cup water
- 1 bay leaf

Instructions:
1. Mix the oregano, cumin, tomato sauce, vinegar, pepper, onion, salt, and garlic in a bowl. Cut the flank steak into pieces and coat it with the spice mix then sit for 5 minutes.
2. Press Sauté on the pot and add the oil.
3. Mix in the steak and cook until it is not pink then press cancel.
4. Pour the water and wine on the steak and put the bay leaf on the steak.
5. Seal the lid and valve and set to manual to cook for 15 minutes at high pressure.
6. Natural-release the pressure and open the lid. Serve.

Nutrition Facts per Serving:
Calories: 130; Net Carbs: 3.8g; Fat: 12.2g; Carbs: 4.9g; Protein: 0.8g;

Cheesy beef Meatballs in Tomato Sauce

Prep + cook time: 30 minutes; serves: 3

Ingredients:
- 1 lb. ground beef
- ½ tsp. dried oregano
- ½ egg
- ½ tbsp. flaxseed meal
- 1 tbsp. grated Parmesan cheese
- Salt and Black pepper
- 14 oz. tomato sauce
- ½ tbsp. olive oil

Instructions:
1. Mix the beef, oregano, egg, flaxseed meal, cheese, salt and pepper in a bowl.
2. Mold 1-inch thick meatballs out of the mixture.
3. Press sauté on the pot and add the oil and the meatballs to brown then pour in the tomato sauce and water then seal the lid.
4. Set to manual to cook for 6 minutes at high pressure. Natural-release the steam for 5 minutes then open and serve.

Nutrition Facts per Serving:
Calories: 358, Fat: 15g, Carbs: 3.1g, Protein: 50.6g

Creamy Spicy Beef with Lemongrass

Prep + cook time: 25 minutes; serves: 2

Ingredients:
- ½ lb. beef tenderloin
- 2 shallots
- 2 garlic cloves
- ½ tsp. shrimp paste
- ¼ tsp. turmeric
- ½ tsp. vegetable oil
- ¼ cup of water
- 4 tbsp. coconut milk
- 2 cloves
- ¼ tsp. nutmeg
- 1 tbsp. fried sliced shallots
- 1 lemongrass
- 1 bay leaf
- ½ tsp. ginger
- ¼ cup water
- 1 kaffir lime leaf
- ¼ tsp. salt
- ¼ tsp. pepper

Instructions:
1. Cut the beef into slices and set aside.
2. Put the shallots, garlic cloves, shrimp paste, and turmeric in a blender and blend till smooth.
3. Pour in the oil and add the shallot mixture to cook until fragrant then add the beef and the rest of the ingredients. Seal the lid and the valve.
4. Set to manual to cook at high pressure for 20 minutes. Natural release the steam when the timer stops and open the lid.
5. Serve on a dish.

Nutrition Facts per Serving:
Calories: 275; Net Carbs: 6.5g; Fat: 15.4g; Carbs: 7.6g; Protein: 26.5g;

Beef and Gravy with Sesame Seeds

Prep + cook time: 25 minutes; serves: 2

Ingredients:

- ½ lb. beef sirloin; cut into thin slices
- 1 tsp. vegetable oil
- ¼ cup chopped onion
- ½ tsp. ginger
- ½ tsp. soy sauce
- ½ tsp. pepper
- 1 tsp. sugar
- ¼ cup water
- 1 tsp. cornstarch
- 1 tsp. sesame seeds

Instructions:

1. Press sauté on the pot and pour the oil into the pot. Add the onion to cook until soft then add the beef until it is no longer pink.
2. Press cancel then add the ginger, soy, pepper, and sugar. Seal the lid and the valve to cook at manual for 15 minutes.
3. Quick-release the pressure and open the lid. Take out 3 tablespoons of the liquid and add the cornstarch to it. Mix it well then pour it back into the pot.
4. Press sauté and cook for 2 minutes or until the liquid has thickened then serve with gravy and sprinkle with sesame seeds.

Nutrition Facts per Serving:
Calories: 181; Net Carbs: 6.3g; Fat: 6.9g; Carbs: 7.1g; Protein: 23.6g;

Spicy Tomato Beef Stew

Prep + cook time: 4 hours; serves: 2

Ingredients:

- 1 tsp. olive oil
- ¼ cup chopped onion
- 2 tsp. minced garlic
- ¾ lb. beef stew meat
- ¼ cup tomato puree
- ¾ cup water
- 3 tbsp. balsamic vinegar
- ¼ tsp. thyme
- ¼ tsp. oregano
- ¼ cup chopped onion
- ¼ tsp. rosemary

Instructions:

1. Press sauté on the pot and add the olive oil and the onion and garlic to the pot to cook until fragrant.
2. Add the beef stew meat and cook until it is not pink then press the cancel button.
3. Mix in the rest of the ingredients and seal the lid and the valve.
4. Set to slow cook to cook for 4 hours. Natural-release the pressure when the timer stops and serve on a dish.

Nutrition Facts per Serving:
Calories: 228; Net Carbs: 4.4g; Fat: 10g; Carbs: 5.6g; Protein: 27.9g;

Steamy Spicy Beef Loaf

Prep + cook time: 50 minutes; serves: 3

Ingredients:

- 1lb. ground beef
- 2 tbsp. tomato sauce
- ½ tsp. Italian seasoning
- 3 tbsp. onion; chopped
- 2 garlic cloves; minced
- 1/3 cup breadcrumbs
- 1 egg
- ½ tsp. paprika
- 1 tbsp. olive oil
- 1 cup of water
- 2 tbsp. ketchup

Instructions:

1. In a bowl, mix all the ingredients except the oil, water, and ketchup together and shape into a loaf.
2. Press sauté on the pot and add the oil. Put the loaf and cook for 2 to 3 minutes on each side.
3. Place 2 pieces of foil together and place the meatloaf on it. Fold the edges to form a pan for the loaf.

4. Pour the water into the pot and put the foil into the pot. Seal the lid and set to Meat/Stew to cook at normal.
5. Press the cancel button and quick release the pressure. Open the lid and serve.

Spicy Garlic Beef

Prep + cook time: 15 minutes; serves: 2

Ingredients:
- 1 tbsp. olive oil
- 2 tsp. garlic; minced
- 1 bunch green onion; sliced
- 2 cups vegetable broth
- ¼ tsp. cayenne pepper
- 1 tsp. oregano
- 1 tsp. cumin
- ½ tsp. smoked paprika
- 1 tbsp. chili powder
- ¼ cup cilantro; chopped
- 1 cup cornmeal
- 2 cups boiling water

Instructions:

1. Press sauté on the pot and add the garlic and onions to cook for 2 to 3 minutes.
2. Mix in the rest of the ingredients and seal the lid and the valve.
3. Set to manual to cook for 5 minutes until the timer stops.
4. Press the cancel button and natural-release the steam for 8 to 10 minutes then open the lid.
5. Serve into containers.

Nutrition Facts per Serving:
Calories 136; Fat: 1.2g; Carbs: 25.3g; Protein 3g; Fiber: 1.6g;

Nutrition Facts per Serving:
Calories: 380 g; Fat: 14 g; Carbs: 13.7 g; Protein: 53.3

Creamy Cinnamon Beef Ribs in Gravy

Prep + cook time: 25 minutes; serves: 2

Ingredients:
- ½ beef ribs; chopped
- 1 lemongrass
- 2 tsp. sliced shallots
- ¼ tsp. pepper
- 2 tsp. minced garlic
- ½ tsp. brown sugar
- 1 tbsp. soy sauce
- ¼ tsp. ginger
- ¼ tsp. cinnamon
- ¼ cup coconut milk
- ¼ cup water
- 1 bay leaf
- ¼ tsp. salt

Instructions:
1. Mix all the ingredients in the pot and seal the lid and the valve.
2. Set to manual to cook for 25 minutes at high pressure.
3. Natural release the pressure and open the lid. Serve with gravy on a dish.

Nutrition Facts per Serving:
Calories: 325; Net Carbs: 4.8g; Fat: 25.9g; Carbs: 5.9g; Protein: 17.7g

Spicy Lettuce-Wrapped Pork

Prep + cook time: 65 minutes; serves: 6

Ingredients:

- 3 lbs. bone-in pork shoulder
- ½ tsp. dried oregano
- 1 ¼ chopped onion.
- 1 ¼ pinches cayenne
- 1 ¼ tbsps. olive oil
- 1 ¼ orange
- 6 lettuce leaves
- 3/4 tsp. garlic powder
- 3/4 tsp. ground cumin
- ½ tsp. black pepper
- 3/4 tsp. sea salt

Instructions:

1. Mix all the ingredients except the oil and lettuce with the pork in a bowl and let it marinate overnight in the refrigerator.
2. Press Sauté on the pot and add the oil.
3. Put the pork in the oil to cook for 10 minutes.
4. Pour in 2 cups of water and seal the lid and the valve. Set to Manual to cook for 45 minutes.
5. Natural-release the pressure for 10 minutes and serve the pork on lettuce leaves.

Nutrition Facts per Serving

Calories: 514, Fat: 35.5g, Carbs: 7.6g, Protein: 39.2g

Ginger Rice with Pork and Eggs

Prep + cook time: 50 minutes; serves: 2

Ingredients:

- 1 lb. pork bones
- 1 lb. pork shank
- 2 thin slices ginger
- 1 cup jasmine rice
- 6 ½ cups cold running tap water
- Pork seasoning
- A dash of ground white pepper
- Salt to taste
- 3-century eggs; make small pieces
- ¼ tsp. sesame oil

Instructions:

1. Add the pork bones and shank, ginger, rice, and water to the pot and seal the lid and the valve.
2. Set to Manual to cook for 35 minutes then press the Cancel button.
3. Natural-release the pressure for 8 to 10 minutes and then open the pot.
4. Mix in the rest of the ingredients until you get the desired taste.
5. Serve and enjoy.

Nutrition Facts per Serving

Calories: 414; Fat: 18g; Carbs: 15.2g; Protein 47.3g; Fiber: 0.5g

Coconut Garlic Pork

Prep + cook time: 5 hours; serves: 2

Ingredients:

- 3/4 lb. pork tenderloin
- ½ cup coconut water
- ½ tsp. pepper
- ½ tsp. garlic powder
- 3 tsps. minced' garlic
- ¼ tsp. salt

Ingredients:

1. Mix all the ingredients in the pot then seal the lid and the valve.
2. Set to Slow Cook to cook for 5 hours.
3. Natural-release the pressure when the timer stops then open the lid.
4. Remove the pork and place on a chopping board then rest for 15 minutes. Pull the pork apart with two forks and serve on a dish.

Nutrition Facts per Serving

Calories: 265; Net Carbs: 3.5g; Fat: 6.1g; Carbs: 4.5g; Protein: 45.4g;

Sweet Garlic BBQ Pork

Prep + cook time: 30 minutes; serves: 2

Ingredients:

- ½ lb. pork butt
- 1 tbsp. apple cider vinegar
- 3/4 tsp. garlic powder
- 1 tbsp. honey
- ¼ cup water
- ½ tbsp. Worcestershire sauce
- ½ tsp. mustard
- 1 tbsp. ketchup
- ¼ tsp. salt

Instructions:

1. Mix all the ingredients together in a bowl except the water and rub coat the pork butt with the spice mixture.
2. Put it in the pot then pour water in the pot and sea; the lid and valve.
3. Set to Manual to cook for 25 minutes at High Pressure.
4. Natural-release the pressure and open the lid. Remove the pork and put it on a board then let it sit for 15 minutes.
5. Shred the pork and serve on a dish drizzled with the sauce.

Nutrition Facts per Serving

Calories: 152; Net Carbs: 6.1g; Fat: 15.1g; Protein: 13.8g; Carbs: 6.9g;

Cheesy Sweet Pork Roast

Prep + cook time: 40 minutes; serves: 2

Ingredients:

- 1lb. pork roast
- 2 tbsps. parmesan cheese; grated
- 1 tbsp. soy sauce
- 2 tbsps. raw honey
- ½ cup water
- ½ tbsp. garlic; minced
- ½ tbsp. dry basil
- ½ tbsp. cornstarch
- ½ tbsp. olive oil
- Salt

Instructions:

1. Mix all the ingredients in the pot and seal the lid and the valve.
2. Set to Meat to cook for 35 minutes until it stops.
3. Press the Cancel button and Natural-release the pressure for 10 minutes.
4. Open the pot and serve.

Nutrition Facts per Serving

Calories: 652; Fat: 29.5g; Carbs: 20g; Fiber: 0.5g; Protein 68g

Creamy Pork

Prep + cook time: 4 hours; serves: 2

Ingredients:

- ½ lb. pork shoulder
- 1 tsp. olive oil
- 2 tbsps. chopped' shallot
- 2 tsps. minced' garlic
- ¼ tsp. coriander
- ¼ tsp. candlenut
- 1 lemongrass
- ¼ cup of coconut milk
- 3/4 cup water

Instructions:

1. Cut the pork shoulder into cubes then set aside.
2. Press Sauté on the pot and add the oil, shallot, and garlic to cook till fragrant then add the pork cubes till it is no longer pink. Press the Cancel button.
3. Mix in the rest of the ingredients and seal the lid and the valve.
4. Set to Slow Cook for 4 hours until the timer stops. Natural-release the pressure and open the lid.
5. Serve.

Nutrition Facts per Serving

Calories: 377; Net Carbs: 3.9g; Fat: 30.8g; Protein: 20g; Carbs: 4.5g;

Spicy Garlic Pork

Prep + cook time: 25 minutes; serves: 2

Ingredients:

- ½ lb. pork tenderloin
- ¼ tsp. oregano
- 1½ tsps. minced' garlic
- ¼ tsp. black pepper
- ¼ tsp. salt
- 1½ tbsps. canola oil
- 1 bay leaf
- ¼ cup water

Instructions:

1. Cut the pork into pieces and set aside. Mix the oregano, garlic, black pepper, and salt in a bowl and rub the pork slices with the mixture then let it sit for 5 minutes.
2. Press Sauté on the pot and pour the oil into the pot then add the pork. To cook until it is no longer pink. Press the Cancel button.
3. Pour water over the pork and add the bay leaf then seal the lid and the valve.
4. Set to Manual to cook for 15 minutes.
5. Natural-release the pressure and open the lid. Serve on a dish.

Nutrition Facts per Serving

Calories: 186; Net Carbs: 0.7g; Fat: 9.6g; Carbs: 1g; Protein: 24.2g;

Spicy Cinnamon Pork Bites

Prep + cook time: 25 minutes; serves: 2

Ingredients:

- ½ lb. boneless pork shoulder
- ½ tsp. cayenne powder
- 1½ tsps. chili powder
- 3/4 tsp. cumin
- 3/4 tsp. coriander
- 1 tsp. paprika
- 3/4 tsp. oregano
- ½ tsp. salt
- 3 tbsps. lemon juice
- ¼ tsp. pepper
- 3/4 tbsp. olive oil
- ¼ cup chopped onion
- 2 tsps. minced garlic
- 1 bay leaf
- ¼ tsp. cinnamon

Instructions:

1. Cut the pork into bite sizes then set aside. Mix all the spices together in a bowl and rub the pork bites with the spice mixture.
2. Press Sauté on the pot and add the oil. Add the pork to cook until it is no longer pink. Remove the pork and set aside.
3. Mix in the onion and garlic and cook till fragrant then add the pork and pour the lemon juice over it. Add the cinnamon and bay leaf then seal the lid and the valve.
4. Set to Manual to cook for 20 minutes then Natural-release the pressure and open the lid. Serve.

Nutrition Facts per Serving

Calories: 368; Net Carbs: 3.7g; Fat: 29.3g; Carbs: 6g ; Protein: 20.2g;

Rice with Carrots and Ham

Prep + cook time: 8 minutes; serves: 2

Ingredients:

- 2 tbsps. scallions; sliced
- ½ cup matchstick carrots
- 1 ½ cups water
- 1 ½ cups brown rice
- 1 tbsp. soy sauce
- ½ cup ham; diced
- 1 tbsp. butter

Instructions:

1. Mix all the ingredients in the pot and seal the lid and the valve.
2. Set to Manual to cook for 6 minutes until the timer stops.
3. Press the Cancel button and Quick-release the pressure.
4. Loosen with a fork and serve.

Nutrition Facts per Serving

Calories: 116; Fat: 6g; Carbs: 12g; Fiber: 2.5g; Protein 4g

Spicy Pork with Tomatoes

Prep + cook time: 25 minutes; serves: 2

Ingredients:

- 1 tbsp. olive oil
- 2 tsps. minced garlic
- ¼ cup chopped onion
- ½ lb. ground pork
- ½ tsp. paprika
- ½ tsp. cumin
- ¼ tsp. coriander
- ½ tsp. oregano
- 2 tbsps. chili powder
- ½ cup vegetable broth
- 1 tbsp. tomato paste
- ½ tsp. salt
- ¼ cup diced tomatoes

Instructions:

1. Press Sauté on the pot and add the oil, garlic, and onions to cook until fragrant.
2. Add the pork to cook until it is no longer pink then press the Cancel button.
3. Add the spices and the broth to the pork and seal the lid and the valve.
4. Set to Manual to cook for 15 minutes then Quick-release the pressure when the timer stops.
5. Mix in the tomatoes and cook opened on Sauté for 2 minutes.
6. Serve into a dish.

Nutrition Facts per Serving
Calories: 281; Net Carbs: 5.8g; Fat: 12.9g; Carbs: 9.8g; Protein: 32.9g;

Spicy Garlic Pork Belly

Prep + cook time: 25 minutes; serves: 2

Ingredients:

- ¼ lb. pork belly
- ¼ cup water
- ¼ cup white wine
- 2 tsps. minced' garlic
- 1 tbsp. coconut oil
- ¼ tsp. thyme
- ¼ tsp. salt
- 1 tsp. paprika

Instructions:

1. Mix all the ingredients in the pot and seal the lid and the valve.
2. Set to Manual to cook for 15 minutes at High Pressure.
3. Natural-release the pressure and open the lid. Serve on a dish.

Nutrition Facts per Serving
Calories: 352; Net Carbs: 1.9g; Fat: 22.2g; Protein: 26.5g; Carbs: 2.4g;

Cinnamon Pineapple Pork

Prep + cook time: 35 minutes; serves: 2

Ingredients:

- ½ lb. pork tenderloin; sliced
- ½ cup tomato puree
- ½ tsp. nutmeg
- ½ tsp. cinnamon
- 1 cup unsweetened pineapple juice
- ½ cup pineapple chunks
- 2 cloves
- ¼ cup chopped onion
- ½ tsp. rosemary

Instructions:

1. Mix all the ingredients in the pot except the pineapple chunks.
2. Seal the lid and the valve then set to Manual to cook for 25 minutes until the timer stops.
3. Press the Cancel button and Quick-release the pressure. Serve the pork with pineapple chunks.

Nutrition Facts per Serving
Calories: 292; Fat: 5g; Carbs: 30g; Fiber: 3.5g; Protein 31.5g

Sweet Cinnamon Pork Tenderloin

Prep + cook time: 30 minutes; serves: 2

Ingredients:
- ½ lb. pork tenderloin; cubed
- 2 tsps. minced' garlic
- 2 tsps. sliced shallots
- 1 lemongrass
- ½ cup coconut water
- ¼ tsp. cinnamon
- ½ tsp. sugar
- 1 bay leaf
- ¼ tsp. ginger
- ¼ tsp. salt
- ¼ tsp. pepper

Instructions:
1. Put the pork cubes in the pot then mix in the rest of the ingredients. Seal the lid and the valve.
2. Set to Manual to cook for 25 minutes at High Pressure.
3. Natural-release the pressure and open the lid.
4. Serve the pork with the sauce.

Nutrition Facts per Serving
Calories: 188; Net Carbs: 4.7g; Fat: 4.2g; Protein: 30.5g; Carbs: 5.8g;

Chili Pork Ribs

Prep + cook time: 30 minutes; serves: 3

Ingredients:
- 1 tsp. paprika
- 1 tsp. garlic powder
- Salt and pepper
- 1 ½ lbs. pork spareribs
- ½ onion chopped
- ½ cup ketchup
- 2 tbsps. brown sugar
- ¼ cup chili sauce
- 1 cup beef broth

Instructions:
1. Mix the paprika, garlic, salt and pepper in a bowl and rub the pork with the spice mixture.
2. Combine the onion, ketchup, sugar and chili sauce in a bowl. Pour the broth inside the pot and add the pork then pour the ketchup mixture over the pork.
3. Seal the lid and the valve and set to cook for 20 minutes at High Pressure. For more tender pork, set to Cook for 30 minutes.
4. Press the Cancel button and Natural-release the pressure, open the lid, and serve.

Nutrition Facts per Serving
Calories: 606 g; Fat: 45.8 g; Carbs: 19.4 g; Protein: 32.9

Crunchy Pork Chops

Prep + cook time: 20 minutes; serves: 2

Ingredients:
- ¼ lb. pork chops
- 2 tbsps. flour
- 2 tbsps. butter
- ¼ cup chicken broth
- 1 tbsp. chopped onion
- ¼ tsp. salt
- ¼ tsp. black pepper

Instructions:
1. Coat the pork chops in flour and set aside. Press Sauté on the Instant Pot and add 1 tablespoon of the butter to melt.
2. Put the pork in the pot and sear for 4 minutes.
3. Remove the pork and set aside. Mix in the onion and the remaining butter to cook until fragrant then press the Cancel button.
4. Pour in the broth and season with salt and pepper. Add the pork to the pot and seal the lid and the valve.
5. Set to Manual to cook for 15 minutes. Natural-release the pressure for 10 minutes then serve.

Nutrition Facts per Serving
Calories: 231; Net Carbs: 6.8g; Fat: 17.2g; Protein: 12.1g; Carbs: 7.2g;

Pineapple Pork

Prep + cook time: 35 minutes; Serves: 2

Ingredients:

- ½ lb. pork tenderloin; sliced
- ½ cup tomato puree
- 1 cup unsweetened pineapple juice
- ½ cup pineapple chunks
- ½ tsp. nutmeg
- ½ tsp. cinnamon
- 2 cloves
- ¼ cup chopped onion
- ½ tsp. rosemary

Instructions:

1. Put the ingredients except for the pineapple into the Instant Pot and mix it well.
2. Seal the lid and set "Manual" to cook for 25 minutes.
3. Press the "Cancel" button and quick release the pot pressure then mix in the pineapple and serve.

Nutrition Facts per Serving
Calories: 292; Fat: 5g; Carbs: 30g; Protein 31.5g; Fiber 3.5g

Italian Meatloaf in Tomato Sauce

Prep + cook time: 50 minutes; Serves: 3

Ingredients:

- 1lb. ground beef
- 2 tbsp. tomato sauce
- ½ tsp. Italian seasoning
- 2 garlic cloves; minced
- 1/3 cup breadcrumbs
- ½ tsp. paprika
- 3 tbsp. onion; chopped
- 1 egg
- Salt and Pepper to taste
- 1 tbsp. olive oil
- 1 cup of water
- 2 tbsp. ketchup

Instructions:

1. Mix all the ingredients minus the oil, water, and ketchup in a bowl. Mold into a loaf and set aside.
2. Press "Sauté" on the Instant Pot and add the oil then add the meatloaf when hot to cook for 2 to 3 minutes on each side.
3. Place two pieces of foil over each other and put the meatloaf on it and bend the sides to form a pan.
4. Pour the water in the Instant Pot and place the meatloaf in the foil on a rack. Seal the lid and set to "Meat/Stew" to cook at normal pressure.
5. "Cancel" the function and quick release the pressure. Open the lid and serve.

Nutrition Facts per Serving
Calories: 364 g; Fat: 14 g; Carbs: 13.7 g; Protein: 53.3

Butter Pork with Celery

Prep + cook time: 1 hour 10 minutes; Serves: 3

Ingredients:

- 2 tbsp. olive oil
- 2 tbsp. lemon juice
- 2 garlic cloves; minced
- 2 tsp. dried rosemary
- Salt and pepper
- 1 cup chicken stock
- 1 (3/4 lb.) pork tenderloin
- 1 diced red onion
- 1 sliced celery stalk
- 2 carrots; sliced or cubed
- ¼ cup softened unsalted butter
- 1 tbsp. fresh herbs (sage, thyme, and chives); chopped

Instructions:

1. In a bowl, mix the oil, lemon juice, garlic, rosemary, salt, and pepper together. Pour the stock into the Instant Pot and add the pork tenderloin.
2. Pour the garlic mixture into the pot and seal the lid and the venting valve.

3. Set to "Manual" to cook for 30 minutes at high pressure.
4. Press "Cancel" to stop the preset function and quick release the pot pressure.
5. Open the pot and mix in the onion, celery, and carrots and seal the lid and set to "Manual" to cook for 6 minutes at high pressure.

6. "Cancel" the function and quick release the pressure.
7. Open the lid. Mix the butter with the herbs. Serve sliced pork with butter on it and veggies.

Nutrition Facts per Serving
Calories: 450 g; Fat: 39 g; Carbs: 7.5 g; Protein: 20.3

Smokey BBQ Ribs

Prep + cook time: 45 minutes; Serves: 2

Ingredients:
- 2 lb. rack of baby back ribs
- 2 tbsp. BBQ rub
- Salt and pepper
- 1 tbsp. liquid smoke
- ½ onion
- 2 cups of water
- 1 cup bbq sauce

Instructions:
1. Season the ribs with bbq rub, salt, and pepper and both sides with liquid smoke.
2. Pour the water into the Instant Pot and add place the ribs on a steamer rack with the onions.

3. Seal the lid and set to "Manual" to cook at high pressure for 25 minutes.
4. "Cancel" the preset function and natural release the pressure for 10 minutes.
5. Open the pot and pour the bbq sauce on the ribs and place it on a baking sheet.
6. Heat the oven to 375°F and cook the ribs for 5 to 10 minutes. Serve with bbq sauce.

Nutrition Facts per Serving
Calories: 559 g; Fat: 37.1 g; Carbs: 23.9 g; Protein: 30.1

Cheesy Sausage and Mushrooms in Marinara Sauce

Prep+ cook time: 55 minutes; Serves: 2

Ingredients:
- 2 large Portobello mushrooms
- 6 oz. pork sausages
- ½ cup whole milk ricotta cheese
- ½ cup marinara sauce
- ½ cup shredded mozzarella cheese

Instructions:
1. Fill each mushroom with some pork sausage then put the ricotta cheese over the sausage and dig a well in the middle of it.

2. Pour the marinara sauce over the ricotta cheese then cover it with mozzarella cheese and put it in the Instant Pot.
3. Seal the lid and set to "Manual" to cook at high pressure for 35 minutes. Natural release the pressure and serve.

Nutrition Facts per Serving
Calories: 624, Fat: 41.7g, Carbs: 27.2g, Protein: 34.9g

Chili Sweet Pork Ribs

Prep + cook time: 30 minutes; Serves: 3

Ingredients:
- 1 tsp. paprika
- 1 tsp. garlic powder
- Salt and pepper
- 1 ½ lb. pork spareribs
- ½ onion; chopped
- ½ cup ketchup

- ¼ cup chili sauce
- 2 tbsp. brown sugar
- 1 cup beef broth

Instructions:

1. In a bowl, mix the paprika, garlic powder, salt, and pepper in a bowl and rub the pork spareribs with the mixture and all sides.
2. In another bowl, mix the onion, ketchup, chili sauce, and brown sugar. pour the broth into the Instant Pot and add the pork to it. Pour the ketchup sauce over the into the pot and seal the lid and the venting valve.

3. Set to "Manual" to cook at high pressure for 20 minutes. For more tender ribs that fall off the bone, cook for 30 minutes.
4. "Cancel" the pot and natural release the pressure for 10 minutes. Serve.

Nutrition Facts per Serving
Calories: 606 g; Fat: 45.8 g; Carbs: 19.4 g; Protein: 32.9

Spicy Pork with Lettuce and Oranges

Prep + cook time: 65 minutes; Serves: 6

Ingredients:
- 3 lb. bone-in pork shoulder
- ½ tsp. dried oregano
- 1 ¼ chopped onion.
- 1 ¼ orange
- 6 lettuce leaves
- ¾ tsp. garlic powder
- ¾ tsp. ground cumin
- 1 ¼ pinches cayenne
- 1 ¼ tbsp. olive oil
- ½ tsp. black pepper
- ¾ tsp. sea salt

Instructions:

1. Mix all the ingredients except the olive oil and lettuce leaves and put it in the refrigerator overnight.
2. Press "Sauté" on the Instant Pot and add the olive oil.
3. Put the spicy pork in the oil to cook for 10 minutes.
4. Pour 2 cups of water into the pot and seal the lid. Set to "Manual" to cook for 45 minutes at medium pressure.
5. Natural release the pressure for 10 minutes and serve the pork on lettuce leaves.

Nutrition Facts per Serving
Calories: 514, Fat: 35.5g, Carbs: 7.6g, Protein: 39.2g

Creamy Pork Meatballs

Prep + cook time: 35 minutes; Serves: 2

Ingredients:
- ¾ lb. ground pork
- 1 organic egg
- 1 tbsp. breadcrumb
- ¼ cup coconut milk
- ¾ tsp. brown sugar
- ¼ cup chopped onion

Instructions:
1. Mix the pork with the egg and breadcrumbs then mold into balls.

2. Put the meatballs and milk in the pot then add the sugar and the onions.
3. Mix them together and seal the lid and venting valve.
4. Set to "Manual" to cook for 25 minutes.
5. "Cancel" the preset function and natural release the pressure for 8 to 10 minutes. Open the pot and serve.

Nutrition Facts per Serving
Calories: 272; Fat: 21g; Carbs: 6.5g; Protein 13.5g; Fiber 1.5g

Chili Pork with Carrots

Prep + cook time: 35 minutes; Serves: 3

Ingredients:
- ½ lb. pork ribs
- Salt and pepper
- 1 onion; chopped
- 2 garlic cloves; chopped
- 3 cups beef broth
- 1 carrot; chopped

- 1 can green chili; diced
- 1 tbsp. apple cider vinegar
- 1 tbsp. honey

Instructions:
1. Sprinkle salt and pepper on pork ribs and press "Sauté" on the Instant Pot and add the oil.
2. Mix in the onions and garlic to cook for 2 to 3 minutes while stirring continuously. Add the pork ribs to cook for 3 to 4 minutes until it is slightly brown then press the "Cancel" button.
3. Pour in the broth, carrot, green chili, vinegar, honey, salt, and pepper.
4. Seal the lid and venting valve and set to "Meat/Stew" to cook on low pressure.
5. Quick-release the pressure, open the lid and serve.

Nutrition Facts per Serving
Calories: 390 g; Fat: 23.9 g; Carbs: 16.1 g; Protein: 25.6

Butter Rosemary Pork with Vegetables

Prep + cook time: 25 minutes; serves: 2
Ingredients:
- ½ lb. pork roast; cut into small pieces
- 1 ½ tbsp. butter
- 1½ tsp. brown sugar
- ¼ cup chopped onion
- ½ tsp. mustard
- 1 tbsp. rosemary
- 2 tsp. minced garlic
- ½ cup chopped carrots
- 2 tbsp. chopped celeries
- ¼ cup apple juice
- 2 tsp. Worcestershire sauce
- ½ tsp. salt
- ¼ tsp. pepper

Instructions:
1. Press sauté on the pot and add the butter to melt.
2. Mix in the pork and cook until soft then press the cancel button.
3. Mix in the remaining ingredients and seal the lid and the valve. Set to manual to cook for 25 minutes at high pressure.
4. Natural release the pressure and open the lid. Serve.

Nutrition Facts per Serving:
Calories: 137; Net Carbs: 5.6g; Fat: 5.2g; Carbs: 6.7g; Protein: 17.8g;

Spice-in Fused Pork

Prep + cook time: 55 minutes; serves: 3
Ingredients:
- 2 lb. pork ribs
- ½ tsp. garlic powder
- ¼ tsp. coriander powder
- ¼ tsp. black pepper
- ½ tsp. onion powder
- ¾ tsp. Erythritol
- ½ tsp. allspice
- ½ tsp. salt
- ¼ tsp. liquid smoke
- 3/4 tbsp. red wine vinegar
- ½ tsp. ground mustard
- ¼ cup tomato ketchup

Instructions:
1. Mix all the dry spices together in a bowl and coat the pork with the spices to marinate for 1 hour.
2. Combine the mustard, vinegar, ketchup, and liquid smoke in another bowl. Put the pork ribs in the Instant Pot and pour the mustard mix over it.
3. Seal the lid and set to manual to cook for 35 minutes at high pressure.
4. Natural release the pressure for 5 minutes and open the lid.
5. Serve ribs on a platter. Press sauté on the pot to cook the sauce for 5 minutes then drizzle over the ribs.

Nutrition Facts per Serving:
Calories: 852, Fat: 53.8g, Carbs: 7.3g, Protein: 80.7g

Garlic Cinnamon Pork

Prep + cook time: 25 minutes; serves: 2

Ingredients:

- ¾ lb. pork ribs
- ½ tsp. garlic powder
- ½ tsp. salt
- ½ tsp. pepper
- ¼ cup red wine vinegar
- ½ tsp. onion powder
- ¼ tsp. paprika
- ¼ tsp. mustard
- ¼ tsp. cinnamon
- ½ tsp. chili powder
- ½ cup water
- 2 tbsp. tomato sauce
- 2 tbsp. ketchup
- 2 tbsp. brown sugar

Instructions:

1. Pour water into the Instant Pot and add the rack.

2. Rub the pork with garlic powder, salt, and pepper then put it on the rack and seal the lid and the valve.

3. Set to manual to cook for 10 minutes at high pressure.

4. Mix in the rest of the ingredients in a bowl and set aside. Remove the pork when it is done and pour the mixed sauce over it.

5. Wrap the pork in aluminum foil and put it on the rack. Seal the lid and set it to manual to cook for 10 minutes. Natural release the steam and open the lid.

6. Remove the pork, cut into thick slices, and serve on a dish.

Nutrition Facts per Serving:

Calories: 354; Net Carbs: 6.7g; Fat: 19.9g; Carbs: 7.8g; Protein: 35.4g

Soy Pork

Prep + cook time: 20 minutes; serves: 2

Ingredients:

- ½ lb. pork rinds
- ¼ tsp. ginger
- 3 tsp. minced garlic
- 3 tbsp. soy sauce
- ¼ tsp. salt
- ½ tsp. pepper
- ½ cup water

Instructions:

1. Cut the pork into medium-sized cubes and mix it with the rest of the ingredients and let it sit for 10 minutes.

2. Pour the water into the pot and add the pork rinds. Seal the lid and the valve and set it to manual to cook for 15 minutes.

3. Natural release the pressure and serve on a dish.

Nutrition Facts per Serving:

Calories: 621; Net Carbs: 3.2g; Fat: 37.6g; Carbs: 3.7g; Protein: 69.4g

Sticky Pulled Pork

Prep + cook time: 50 minutes; serves: 2

Ingredients:

- 1lb. pork belly; make cubes
- 1 ½ tsp. black pepper
- 1 tbsp. cornstarch
- ½ cup beef broth
- ½ cup chopped onion
- 3 tbsp. water
- 1 tsp. thyme
- ¼ tsp. salt

Instructions:

1. Open the pot and put all the ingredients in the pot except the water and the cornstarch.

2. Seal the lid and the valve and set it to manual to cook for 35 minutes.

3. Press the cancel button and quick release the pressure.

4. Mix the cornstarch and water together and add it to the pot. Serve the liquid over the pork.

Nutrition Facts per Serving:
Calories: 188; Fat: 15g; Carbs: 8g; Protein 4.5g; Fiber: 1.5g

Cinnamon Apple Pork Chops

Prep + cook time: 25 minutes; serves: 2
Ingredients:
- ½ lb. pork chops
- ¼ tsp. salt
- ¼ tsp. pepper
- ½ apple; sliced
- 1 tsp. brown sugar
- ¼ tsp. cinnamon
- ¼ tsp. nutmeg
- ½ cup of water

Instructions:
1. Season the pork with salt and pepper and set aside. Put the apple slices in a bowl and sprinkle it with brown sugar, cinnamon, and nutmeg then toss to coat.
2. Pour the water into the Instant Pot and put the apple slices in the pot and place the pork on the apple slices then seal the lid and the valve.
3. Set to manual to cook for 20 minutes at high pressure.
4. Natural release the steam and open the lid. Place the pork on a dish and garnish with cinnamon apples.

Nutrition Facts per Serving:
Calories: 267; Net Carbs: 7g; Fat: 16.6g; Carbs: 8.5g; Protein: 21.1g;

Pork Loaf with Mushrooms and Tomatoes

Prep + cook time: 25 minutes; serves: 2
Ingredients:
- ¾ lb. ground pork
- ½ tsp. ginger
- ¼ tsp. nutmeg
- ½ cup chopped mushrooms
- ¾ tsp. Worcestershire sauce
- ¼ tsp. salt
- ¼ cup diced tomatoes
- 1 egg white
- 2 tbsp. diced onion
- ½ tbsp. flour
- ¼ tsp. pepper

Instructions:
1. Mix all the ingredients together in a bowl.
2. Put the beef mixture into a pan and spread it evenly. Pour water in the Instant Pot and put a rack above it.
3. Put the pan on the rack and seal the lid and valve.
4. Set to steam to cook for 20 minutes at high pressure. Natural release the pressure when the timer stops then remove the pan from the pot.
5. Cut the loaf into slices and serve on a dish.

Nutrition Facts per Serving:
Calories: 378; Net Carbs: 4.5g; Fat: 24.3g; Carbs: 5g; Protein: 33g;

Cheesy Pork Sausages in Marinara Sauce

Prep + cook time: 55 minutes; serves: 2
Ingredients:
- 2 large Portobello mushrooms
- 6 oz. pork sausages
- ½ cup whole milk ricotta cheese
- ½ cup marinara sauce
- ½ cup shredded mozzarella cheese
- ¼ cup chopped parsley

Instructions:
1. Stuff the mushrooms with the pork sausages then place the ricotta cheese on each mushroom and dig a well in the middle of the mushrooms.
2. Pour the marinara sauce over the mushrooms and cover with the mozzarella cheese. Put the

stuffed mushrooms in the Instant Pot and seal the lid.
3. Set to manual to cook for 35 minutes at high pressure.

4. Natural release the steam and serve with parsley.

Nutrition Facts per Serving:

Calories: 624, Fat: 41.7g, Carbs: 27.2g, Protein: 34.9g

Honey Pork with Pineapple

Prep + cook time: 20 minutes; serves: 2

Ingredients:

- ½ lb. pork sirloin; cut into slices
- ¼ tsp. oregano
- 1 tbsp. soy sauce
- ½ cup water
- ½ cup chopped pineapple
- ½ tsp. ginger
- 2 tbsp. chopped onion
- 1 tsp. red chili
- ¼ tsp. salt
- ¼ tsp. pepper
- ¼ tbsp. honey

Instructions:

1. Put the pork slices in the Instant Pot and pour water over it.
2. Add the rest of the ingredients except the honey and seal the lid and the valve.
3. Set to manual to cook for 15 minutes at high pressure.
4. Natural release the pressure and open the lid. Serve the dish drizzled with honey.

Nutrition Facts per Serving:

Calories: 250; Net Carbs: 5.9g; Fat: 10.1g; Carbs: 6.7g; Protein: 23.4g

Sweet Apple BBQ Pork Ribs

Prep + cook time: 1 hour 45 minutes; serves: 4

Ingredients:

- 1 tsp. salt
- ½ tsp. black pepper
- ½ tsp. ground cumin
- ½ tsp. brown sugar
- ½ tsp. garlic powder
- 2 lb. baby back pork ribs
- 2 tbsp. apple cider vinegar
- 2 cup apple juice
- 1 tbsp. liquid smoke
- ¼ cup BBQ sauce
- ¼ cup tomato ketchup
- 1 tbsp. Worcestershire sauce

Instructions:

1. Mix the salt, pepper, cumin, garlic, brown sugar and pork together in a bowl and put it in the Instant Pot.
2. Add the vinegar, apple juice, and liquid smoke to the pot and seal the lid and set to Meat/Stew to cook for 20 minutes at high pressure.
3. Natural release the steam and remove the lid. Mix in the BBQ sauce, ketchup, and Worcestershire sauce. Cool before serving.

Nutrition Facts per Serving:

Calories: 746, Fat: 54.5g, Carbs: 25.2g, Protein: 36.6g

Chapter 8 Fish and Seafood

Mahi Mahi with Tomatoes

Prep + cook time: 25 minutes; serves: 4

Ingredients:
- 3 tbsp. butter
- 1 sliced onion
- 6 mahi-mahi fillets
- 28 oz. diced tomatoes
- 2 tbsp. lemon juice
- 1 tsp. dried oregano
- Salt and pepper

Instructions:
1. Press sauté on the pot and add the butter and onions to cook for 2 minutes.
2. Mix in the remaining ingredients except for the fillets and cook for 3 minutes.
3. Mix in the fillets and seal the lid and the valve. Set to cook at high pressure for 8 minutes.
4. Quick-release the pressure and open the lid. Serve.

Nutrition Facts per Serving

Calories: 268, Fat: 8.8g, Carbs: 13.1g, Protein: 33.8g

Sweet-fish Chunks

Prep + cook time: 20 minutes; serves: 3

Ingredients:
- 1 tbsp. olive oil
- 1lb.fish chunks
- ½ tbsp. sugar
- 1 tbsp. vinegar
- 1 tbsp. soy sauce
- Salt and pepper

Instructions:
1. Press sauté on the pot and add the oil.
2. Add the fish chunks to cook for 3 minutes then add the rest of the ingredients to cook for 6 minutes at high pressure.
3. Natural-release the pressure and serve.

Nutrition Facts per Serving

Calories: 402, Fat: 23.3g, Carbs: 28.1g, Protein: 22.5g

Lemon Ginger Fish with Horseradish

Prep + cook time: 15 minutes; serves: 2

Ingredients:
- 2 big whitefish fillets
- ½ tsp. salt
- 2 tbsp. Dijon mustard
- 1 tsp. horseradish; grated
- 1 tbsp. fresh lemon juice
- ½ tsp. black pepper
- 1 tsp. fresh ginger; grated
- 1 lemon; sliced
- 1 cup of water

Instructions:
1. Season the fish with salt and pepper and set aside.
2. Mix the mustard, horseradish, and lemon juice in a bowl and add the fish to it to marinate for 20 minutes.
3. Pour water into the pot and put a rack in it. Put the fish on the rack and seal the lid and the valve.
4. Set to manual to cook for 4 minutes at high pressure.
5. Cancel the pot then natural-release the pressure. Open the lid and serve topped with lemon slices.

Nutrition Facts per Serving

Calories: 176 g; Fat: 14.4 g; Carbs: 7 g; Protein: 1.2

Cheesy Shrimp with Tomatoes

Prep + cook time: 17 minutes; serves: 3

Ingredients:
- 2 garlic cloves; minced
- 1 onion; diced
- 14.5-ounce can diced tomatoes
- 2 tbsp. grass-fed butter
- 1 tbsp. salt-free Italian seasoning
- ½ tsp. cayenne pepper
- Salt;
- ½ lb. shrimps; peeled and deveined
- 4 tbsp. ricotta cheese

Instructions:

1. Press sauté on the pot and add the butter and garlic to cook for 3 minutes.
2. Mix in the rest of the ingredients except the cheese the seal the lid and set to manual to cook for 5 minutes.
3. Press the cancel button and quick release the pressure. Open the lid and serve with cheese over noodles.

Nutrition Facts per Serving

Calories: 260 g; Fat: 19.7 g; Carbs: 11.9 g; Protein: 20.4

Spicy Mussels and Tomatoes

Prep + cook time: 10 minutes; serves: 3

Ingredients:
- 2 tbsp. olive oil
- ½ tsp. red pepper flakes
- 1 yellow onion; chopped
- 2 garlic cloves; minced
- 2 lb. mussels; scrubbed
- 14 oz. tomatoes; chopped
- ½ cup chicken stock
- 2 tsp. dried oregano

Instructions:

1. Press sauté on the pot and add the oil, pepper, onion, and garlic to cook for 2 to 3 minutes.
2. Mix in the remaining ingredients then seal the lid and the valve. Set to manual to cook for 2 minutes.
3. Press the cancel button and natural-release the pressure. Serve.

Nutrition Facts per Serving

Calories: 291; Fat: 10g; Carbs: 11.2g; Fiber: 2g; Protein 38.7g

Spicy Garlic Swordfish

Prep + cook time: 15 minutes; serves: 2

Ingredients:
- 1lb. swordfish steaks
- ½ tsp. red pepper flakes
- 4 garlic cloves; minced
- ½ tsp. black pepper
- 1 can whole peeled tomatoes; crushed
- 2 tbsp. olive oil
- ½ tsp. salt

Instructions:

1. Press sauté and add the oil, pepper, garlic, and cook till fragrant. Mix in the rest of the ingredients then turn to coat.
2. Seal the lid and set to cook for 3 minutes.
3. Quick-release the pressure then serve.

Nutrition Facts per Serving

Calories: 427; Fat: 28.88 g; Carbs: 5.81 g; Protein: 45.81 g; Fiber: 2.1 g;

Creamy Scallops Curry

Prep + cook time: 25 minutes; serves: 4

Ingredients:
- 1 tbsp. olive oil
- 1lb. scallops
- 1 cup of coconut milk
- 1 ½ cup chicken broth
- 1 tsp. curry powder
- 1 tsp. vinegar

- 1 tsp. soy sauce
- ½ tsp. nutmeg powder
- ½ cup Thai red curry paste
- ½ tsp. salt

Instructions:
1. Press sauté and add the oil and scallops to cook for 3 minutes.

2. Mix in the rest of the ingredients and seal the lid and the valve. Ser to cook at high pressure for 6 minutes.
3. Quick-release the pressure then serve.

Nutrition Facts per Serving
Calories: 405, Fat: 28.2g, Carbs: 12.7g, Protein: 22.4g

Raspberry Salmon

Prep + cook time: 15 minutes; serves: 2

Ingredients:
- 1 cup red raspberries; minced
- 1 tbsp. cider vinegar
- 1 tbsp. olive oil
- 1 leek; chopped
- 1 cup clam juice
- 1 tbsp. parsley; chopped
- 1 tbsp. lemon juice
- black pepper; to taste
- 1/3 cup dill; chopped
- 1 tsp. sherry
- 2 salmon steaks
- 2 garlic cloves; minced
- a pinch of sea salt

Instructions:

1. Combine the raspberries and vinegar in a bowl then add the salmon. Marinate for 2 hours in the refrigerator.
2. Press sauté on the pot and add the oil then mix in the rest of the ingredients to cook for 2 minutes.
3. Add the salmon and the marinade then seal the lid and the valve.
4. Set to manual to cook for 4 minutes at high pressure.
5. Press the cancel button and quick release the pressure. Open the lid and serve with rice and veggies.

Nutrition Facts per Serving
Calories: 160 g; Fat: 25 g; Carbs: 5 g; Protein: 12

Lemon Tilapia with Dill

Prep + cook time: 13 minutes; serves: 2

Ingredients:
- 3 sprigs fresh dill
- 4 tilapia fillets
- ½ tsp. black pepper
- Juice of 1 lemon
- ½ tbsp. olive oil
- ½ tsp. salt
- 4 garlic cloves

Instructions:
1. Put the fish on an aluminum foil and season with lemon, oil, salt, and pepper.

2. Put the garlic and dill on the fish then cover it with another foil and fold the edges to seal.
3. Pour 2 cups of water into the pot and put the foil inside the pot. Seal the lid and ser to cook for 3 minutes at high pressure.
4. Quick-release the steam and serve.

Nutrition Facts per Serving
Calories: 269; Fat: 7.46 g; Carbs: 4.14 g; Protein: 47.14 g; Fiber: 0.4 g

Cinnamon Salmon with Broccoli and Carrots

Prep + cook time: 16 minutes; serves: 2

Ingredients:
- 2 salmon fillets; skin on
- 1 cinnamon stick
- 1 cup of water
- 1 bay leaf
- 3 cloves
- 1 cup baby carrots
- 2 cups broccoli florets
- Some lime wedges for serving

- 1 tbsp. canola oil
- pepper and salt

Instructions:
1. Put the cinnamon, water, bay leaf, and cloves in the pot then set a rack over the water.
2. Brush the salmon with oil then season with salt and pepper. Put it on the rack then add the carrots and broccoli. Seal the lid and the valve.
3. Set to manual to cook for 6 minutes. Press cancel and natural-release the pressure.
4. Serve with lime wedges.

Nutrition Facts per Serving
Calories: 421; Fat: 18g; Carbs: 42.3g; Fiber: 16.2g; Protein 32.4g

Sweet Lemon Salmon

Prep + cook time: 20 minutes: serves: 2
Ingredients:
- ¾ lb. salmon fillets
- ¼ tsp. pepper
- salt
- ½ tsp. ginger
- 1 tbsp. fish sauce
- 2 tbsp. soy sauce
- 2 tbsp. brown sugar
- 1 tsp. vegetable oil
- ¼ tsp. lemon zest
- 1 tbsp. lemon juice

Instructions:
1. Sprinkle salt and pepper on the salmon then set aside. Mix the remaining ingredients in a bowl.
2. Press sauté on the pot and add the oil mix to cook for 2 minutes. Add the salmon and seal the lid and the valve.
3. Set to manual to cook for 5 minutes.
4. Press cancel and natural-release the pressure for 10 minutes. Open the pot and serve.

Nutrition Facts per Serving
Calories: 294; Fat: 12.5g; Carbs: 11g; Fiber: 0.5g; Protein 34g

Lemon Fish with Potatoes and Celery

Prep + cook time: 19 minutes; serves: 3
Ingredients:
- 1 lb. small red potatoes; halved
- 2 carrots; sliced
- ½ tsp. pepper
- 2 stalks celery; sliced
- 1 lemon; halved
- 1 large onion; diced
- 4 cups of water
- 1 tsp. salt
- 2 lb. whitefish

Instructions:
1. Mix all the ingredients except the fish in the pot, seal the lid and the valve and ser to cook for 7 minutes.
2. Quick-release the steam and add the fish then seal the lid and set to 2 minutes.
3. Quick-release the steam and serve with rolls.

Nutrition Facts per Serving
Calories: 405; Fat: 13.54 g; Carbs: 23.29 g; Fiber: 2.9 g; Protein: 46.08 g

Lemon Salmon with Broccoli

Prep + cook time: 15 minutes; serves: 2
Ingredients:
- 2 tbsp. coconut aminos
- 2 tbsp. lemon juice
- 2 salmon fillets; boneless
- 1 tsp. sesame seeds
- 8 oz. broccoli
- 8 oz. cauliflower florets
- 1 cup of water
- a pinch of sea salt and black pepper

Instructions:
1. Mix the aminos and lemon juice in a bowl.
2. Season the salmon with salt and pepper and put it on a plate with the broccoli and

cauliflower. Pour the lemon juice mixture on it then let it marinate for 10 to 15 minutes.

3. Pour water into the pot and add a rack. Put the fish and vegetables on the rack then seal the lid and the valve.

4. Set to manual to cook for 5 minutes at high pressure.

5. Cancel the pot and quick release the steam then serve.

Nutrition Facts per Serving
Calories: 315 g; Fat: 22.3 g; Carbs: 14.2 g; Protein: 30.4

Sweet Garlic Shrimps with Parsley

Prep + cook time: 16 minutes; serves: 2

Ingredients:
- ½ lb. large shrimps; peeled
- 1 garlic clove; minced
- 1 tsp. olive oil
- 2 tsp. parsley; dried
- 1 tbsp. honey
- 2 tbsp. lemon juice; freshly squeezed
- 2 tsp. soy sauce
- ½ cup water
- 2 tsp. Creole seasoning

Instructions:
1. Press sauté on the pot and add the shrimps and garlic to cook for 2 to 3 minutes then press cancel.

2. Mix the honey, creole seasoning, parsley, and soy sauce in a bowl.

3. Pour the water into the pot and pour the honey mixture on the shrimps. Seal the lid and the valve.

4. Set to manual to cook for 3 minutes at high pressure.

5. Cancel the pot and quick release the pressure. Serve with parsley.

Nutrition Facts per Serving
Calories: 152 g; Fat: 2.5 g; Carbs: 12 g; Protein: 21.9

Buttery Garlic Shrimp

Prep + cook time: 15 minutes; serves: 2

Ingredients:
- ¾ lb. jumbo shrimp
- 2 chopped garlic cloves
- 2 tbsp. dry white wine
- 1/8 tsp. black pepper
- 1 tsp. kosher salt
- 1 tsp. lemon juice
- 2 tbsp. chopped parsley
- 3 tbsp. butter

Instructions:

1. Put the shrimp, garlic, wine, pepper, and salt in the pot and seal the lid to cook at high pressure for 1 minute.

2. Quick-release the pressure and open the pot. Remove the shrimp and set aside.

3. Cook the liquid on sauté mode until it reduces by half then mix in the butter to melt. Add the shrimp, lemon juice, and parsley. Mix well and serve.

Nutrition Facts per Serving
Calories: 293, Fat: 17.4g, Carbs: 1.8g, Protein: 30.9g

Mussels in Tomato Sauce

Prep + cook time: 13 minutes; serves: 2

Ingredients:
- 2 lb. fresh mussels; cleaned and rinsed
- ½ tbsp. dried parsley
- ½ tbsp. pepper
- 1 cup diced tomatoes
- ½ cup white wine
- Salt as per taste preference

Instructions:

1. Mix all the ingredients in the pot except the mussels.
2. Put the mussels in a rack and put the rack into the liquid in the pot.
3. Seal the lid and the valve and set it to manual to cook for 3 minutes.
4. Press cancel and quick release the pressure. Serve.

Nutrition Facts per Serving
Calories: 446; Fat: 10.5g; Carbs: 22.5g; Fiber: 2g; Protein 55g

Buttery Clams

Prep + cook time: 15 minutes; serves: 3
Ingredients:
- ¼ cup lemon juice
- 2 tbsp. Melted butter
- 1 tsp. garlic powder
- ¼ cup white wine
- 1 lb. mushy shell clams

Instructions:
1. Mix the lemon juice, butter, garlic, and wine in the pot then set aside.
2. Put a rack in the pot and put the clams on the rack. Seal the lid to cook for 3 minutes at high pressure.
3. Natural-release the pressure and serve.

Nutrition Facts per Serving
Calories: 159, Fat: 7.9g, Carbs: 4.4g, Protein: 13.7g

Sweet Lemon Salmon

Prep + cook time: 20 minutes; Serves: 2
Ingredients:
- ¾ salmon
- ¼ tsp. pepper
- Salt
- 1 tsp. vegetable oil
- 2 tbsp. brown sugar
- 1 tbsp. fish sauce
- 2 tbsp. soy sauce
- ½ tsp. ginger
- ¼ tsp. lemon zest
- 1 tbsp. lemon juice

Instructions:
1. Sprinkle the salmon with salt and pepper and set aside. Mix the rest of the ingredients in a bowl and set aside.
2. Press "Sauté" on the Instant Pot and add some extra oil and the sugar mixture to the pot to caramelize for 2 minutes.
3. Add the salmon and seal the lid. Set to "Manual" to cook for 5 minutes.
4. Press "Cancel" on the pot and natural release the pressure for 8 to 10 minutes. Open and serve.

Nutrition Facts per Serving
Calories: 294; Fat: 12.5g; Carbs: 11g; Protein 34g; Fiber 0.5g

Buttery Shrimp with Tomatoes

Prep + cook time: 17 minutes; Serves: 3
Ingredients:
- 2 tbsp. grass-fed butter
- 1 minced garlic cloves
- 1 diced onion
- 14.5 oz. can diced tomatoes
- 1 tbsp. salt-free Italian seasoning
- ½ tsp. ½ tsp. cayenne pepper
- Salt
- ½ lb. shrimps; peeled and deveined
- 4 tbsp. ricotta cheese

Instructions:
1. Press "Sauté" on the Instant Pot and add the butter to melt.
2. Mix in the garlic to cook for 30 seconds to 1 minute then add the onions, tomatoes, Italian seasoning, cayenne pepper, salt, and shrimps.

3. Seal the lid and set to "Manual" to cook for 5 minutes at high pressure.
4. Press "Cancel" and quick release the pressure.

5. Open the pot and mix in the ricotta cheese. Serve on a bed of noodles.

Nutrition Facts per Serving
Calories: 260 g; Fat: 19.7 g; Carbs: 11.9 g; Protein: 20.4

Creamy Bacon and Clam with Celery

Prep + cook time: 11 minutes; serves: 2

Ingredients:
- 2 tbsp. butter
- 2 tbsp. diced' bacon
- 1 tsp. minced garlic
- ¼ cup chopped' onion
- 1 cup chopped' clams
- 1 tbsp. diced' celeries
- ¼ tsp. salt
- ½ tsp. thyme
- ½ cup clam juice
- ¼ cup half and half
- ¼ tsp. pepper

Instructions:

1. Press sauté on the pot and add the butter, bacon, garlic, and onion to cook until fragrant then press cancel.
2. Add the clams, celery, and thyme then season with salt and pepper. Seal the lid and set to manual to cook for 3 minutes.
3. Quick-release the steam and add the half and half.
4. Set to sauté to cook for 2 minutes then serve.

Nutrition Facts per Serving
Calories: 231; Net Carbs: 6.1g; Fat: 13.3g; Protein: 21.7; Carbs: 6.5g

Instant Pot Anchovies

Prep + cook time: 9 minutes; serves: 2

Ingredients:
- 1 tbsp. sugar
- 1 tbsp. water
- 1 cup anchovies; dried
- 2 garlic cloves; minced
- 1 tbsp. sesame seed oil
- ½ tbsp. vegetable oil
- Black sesame seeds to serve
- Roasted sesame seeds to serve

Instructions:
1. Mix the sugar and water with the garlic in a bowl.

2. Press sauté on the pot and add the anchovies to cook for 1 minute.
3. Mix in the oil and the sugar mix. Seal the lid and set to manual to cook for 2 minutes.
4. Press cancel and natural-release the pressure.
5. Serve into containers then add the sesame oil and seeds. Serve.

Nutrition Facts per Serving
Calories 232; Fat: 17g; Carbs: 7.4g;; Protein 10.6g; Fiber: 1.2g

Cheesy crab Egg Dish

Prep + cook time: 8 minutes; serves: 2

Ingredients:
- ½ tsp. paprika
- 2 eggs
- ½ cup half and half
- ¼ tsp. salt
- ½ tsp. pepper
- ¼ cup crabmeat
- ½ cup chopped onion

- ½ cup grated cheddar cheese

Instructions:
1. Mix the paprika, eggs, half and half, salt and pepper in a bowl.
2. Mix in the crabmeat and pour it into an aluminum pan. Sprinkle cheese on it.

3. Pour water into the pot and put a rack over it. Put the pan on it and seal the lid and the valve.
4. Set to manual to cook for 25 minutes at high pressure.

5. Natural-release the pressure and open the lid. Serve warm.

Nutrition Facts per Serving
Calories: 276; Net Carbs: 5.8g; Fat: 20.9g; Carbs: 6.8g; Protein: 15.7;

Buttery Garlic Mussels with Parsley

Prep + cook time: 11 minutes; serves: 2
Ingredients:
- 2 cups fresh mussels
- 1 tbsp. butter
- ¼ cup vegetable broth
- ¼ cup white wine
- 1 tsp. shallot
- 1 tsp. minced' garlic
- 1 tbsp. lemon juice
- 1 tbsp. chopped' parsley

Instructions:
1. Remove the mussels' shells and put it in the pot.

2. Mix in the butter, broth, wine, shallot, and garlic.
3. Seal the lid and the valve and set to manual to cook for 4 minutes at high pressure.
4. Quick-release the pressure and open the lid then add the lemon juice.
5. Serve topped with parsley.

Nutrition Facts per Serving
Calories: 201; Net Carbs: 6.9g; Fat: 9.4g; Carbs: 7g; Protein: 18.8;

Mayo Lobster

Prep + cook time: 15 minutes; serves: 2
Ingredients:
- ½ cup chicken broth
- 1 tsp. scallions
- 1 lb. lobster tails
- 2 cups of ice water
- ¼ cup mayonnaise
- 2 tbsp. lemon juice

Instructions:
1. Pour the broth into the pot and add the scallions then season with salt.

2. Put a rack in the pot and put the lobster tails on it. Seal the lid and the valve and set it to manual to cook for 5 minutes.
3. Quick-release the steam and remove the tails to ice water.
4. Remove the vertebrae of the lobster with shears and cut into chunks.
5. Pour mayonnaise and lemon juice over the tails and serve.

Nutrition Facts per Serving
Calories: 314; Net Carbs: 3g; Fat: 12.3g; Carbs: 3.1g; Protein: 44.7;

Crab Legs

Prep + cook time: 14 minutes; serves: 2
Ingredients:
- 3/4 lb. fresh crab legs
- ¼ tsp. salt

Instructions:
1. Pour water in the pot and put a rack on it. Put the crab on the rack and sprinkle it with salt.

2. Seal the lid and valve and set it to manual to cook for 4 minutes.
3. Natural-release the steam and serve crab legs.

Nutrition Facts per Serving
Calories: 195; Net Carbs: 1g; Fat: 11.5g; Carbs: 1g; Protein: 20.5;

Sweet Ginger Squids

Prep + cook time: 4 hours; serves: 2

Ingredients:

- ½ lb. fresh squids
- 3 tsp. oyster sauce
- 1 bay leaf
- 1½ tsp. brown sugar
- 3 tsp. soy sauce
- ¼ cup water
- ¼ tsp. ginger
- 1 tsp. minced' garlic

Instructions:

1. Wash the squids and remove the heads. Put it in the pot and add the ginger, garlic, bay leaf, and sugar.
2. Add the water, oyster sauce, and soy sauce to the pot then seal the lid and the valve.
3. Set to slow cook to cook for 4 hours.
4. Natural-release the pressure and serve on a dish.

Nutrition Facts per Serving

Calories: 140; Net Carbs: 7g; Fat: 1.8g; Protein: 20; Carbs: 7.1g;

Spicy Lemon Shrimp

Prep + cook time: 15 minutes; serves: 3

Ingredients:

- 1lb. large shrimp
- 3 tbsp. Butter
- 4 minced garlic cloves
- 1 tsp. paprika
- 2 sliced lemons

Instructions:

1. Press sauté on the pot and add the butter.
2. Mix in garlic to cook for 1 minute then add the shrimp, paprika, and lemon. Seal the lid and set to cook at high pressure for 4 minutes.
3. Natural-release the steam and open the lid. Serve.

Nutrition Facts per Serving

Calories: 231, Fat: 11.6g, Carbs: 4.4g, Protein: 28.8g

Creamy Scallops Curry

Prep + cook time: 25 minutes: Serves: 4

Ingredients:

- 1 tbsp. olive oil
- 1 lb. scallops
- 1 cup of coconut milk
- 1 tsp. soy sauce
- ½ tsp. nutmeg powder
- ½ cup Thai red curry paste
- 1 ½ cup chicken broth
- 1 tsp. curry powder
- 1 tsp. vinegar
- ½ tsp. salt

Instructions:

1. Press "Sauté" on the Instant Pot and add the olive oil.
2. Mix in the scallops to cook for 3 minutes then add the rest of the ingredients.
3. Seal the lid and set to cook at high pressure for 6 minutes.
4. Quick-release the pressure and open the lid. Serve.

Nutrition Facts per Serving

Calories: 405, Fat: 28.2g, Carbs: 12.7g, Protein: 22.4g

Spicy cod With Peas

Prep + cook time: 10 minutes; Serves: 2

Ingredients:

- 1 cup white wine
- 1 cup fresh parsley
- Pepper and salt as per taste preference
- 1 tsp. oregano
- 1 sprig fresh rosemary
- 2 garlic cloves; smashed

- 1 tsp. paprika
- 1 bag (10 oz.) frozen peas
- 1 lb. cut into 4 fillets

Instructions:
1. Mix the wine, herbs, spices, and salt in a bowl.
2. Pour the wine mixture into the Instant Pot and add the peas.

3. Place the fish into the steaming rack and place it into the pot.
4. Seal the lid and the valve. Set to "Manual" to cook for 5 minutes.
5. "Cancel" the pot and quick release the pressure. Serve.

Nutrition Facts per Serving
Calories: 234; Fat: 1.5g; Carbs: 13.5g; Protein 30g; Fiber 44g

Ginger Whitefish with Horseradish

Prep + cook time: 15 minutes; Serves: 2

Ingredients:
- 2 tbsp. Dijon mustard
- 1 tsp. grated horseradish
- 1 tbsp. fresh lemon juice
- 1 tsp. freshly grated ginger
- ½ tsp. salt
- ½ tsp. black pepper
- 2 big whitefish fillets
- 1 cup of water
- 2 big whitefish fillets
- 1 lemon; sliced

Instructions:
1. In a bowl, combine the mustard, horseradish, lemon juice, and ginger.

2. Sprinkle the whitefish with salt and black pepper and put it in the mustard mixture to marinate for 20 minutes.
3. Pour water into the Instant Pot and put a trivet in the pot. Place the fish on the trivet and pour the marinade on it.
4. Seal the lid and set to "Manual" to cook for 4 minutes at high pressure.
5. "Cancel" the pot and natural release the pressure. Open and serve topped with lemon slices.

Nutrition Facts per Serving
Calories: 176 g; Fat: 14.4 g; Carbs: 7 g; Protein: 1.2

Lemon Shrimp with Parsley

Prep + cook time: 15 minutes; Serves: 2

Ingredients:
- ¾ lb. jumbo shrimp
- 2 chopped garlic cloves
- 2 tbsp. dry white wine
- 1/8 tsp. black pepper
- 1 tsp. kosher salt
- 3 tbsp. butter
- 1 tsp. lemon juice
- 2 tbsp. chopped parsley

Instructions:
1. Put the shrimp, garlic, wine, pepper, and salt in the Instant Pot.

2. Seal the lid and set to cook for 1 minute at high pressure.
3. Quick-release the pressure and open the pot. Remove the shrimp.
4. Press "Sauté" on the Instant Pot and cook on low heat until the sauce has reduced by half.
5. Mix in the butter until it has melted and add the shrimp to the pot. Mix in the lemon juice and parsley. Serve.

Nutrition Facts per Serving
Calories: 293, Fat: 17.4g, Carbs: 1.8g, Protein: 30.9g

Buttery Rice with Shrimp and Parsley

Prep + cook time: 18 minutes; Serves: 2

Ingredients:
- 2 tbsp. butter
- 1 small chopped onions
- 2 minced garlic cloves

- A pinch of crushed red pepper
- A pinch of saffron
- Sea salt and black pepper

- 1 cup risotto rice
- 1 cup chicken broth
- ¼ cup white wine
- ½ lb. big shrimp; deveined
- ¼ cup chopped parsley
- 1 lemon; quartered

Instructions:
1. Press "Sauté" on the Instant Pot and add the butter.
2. Mix in the onion to cook until soft and add the garlic to cook for 1 minute.

3. Mix in the red pepper, saffron, salt, black pepper, and rice for 1 minute. Pour in the broth and the wine.
4. Press "Cancel" and put the shrimp in the pot. Seal the lid and set to "Manual" to cook for 5 minutes at high pressure.
5. Press "Cancel" and quick release the pressure.
6. Serve with parsley and lemon wedges.

Nutrition Facts per Serving
Calories: 603 g; Fat: 13 g; Carbs: 44.7 g; Protein: 31.3

Buttery Crab with Lemon Juice

Prep + cook time: 8 minutes; Serves: 2
Ingredients:
- 1 ½ lb. crabs
- ¼ tsp. salt
- ¼ cup minced garlic
- 2 tbsp. fish sauce
- ¼ cup melted butter
- ½ cup of water
- 1 tbsp. lemon juice

Instructions:
1. Put the crabs in the Instant Pot and season with salt and garlic. Add the fish sauce and

the butter to the crab then pour the water over it.
2. Mix the contents and seal the lid and the valve.
3. Set to "Manual" to cook for 3 minutes.
4. Press the "Cancel" button and quick release the steam. Open and serve topped with lemon juice.

Nutrition Facts per Serving
Calories: 264; Fat: 18g; Carbs: 6.5g; Protein 17g; Fiber 0.5g

Chili Salmon

Prep + cook time: 15 minutes; Serves: 3
Ingredients:
- 1 ½ cups of water
- 1 tsp. ground cumin
- 1 tsp. red chili powder
- 1 minced garlic clove
- Salt and Pepper to taste
- 1 lb. salmon fillet

Instructions:
1. Pour the water in the Instant Pot and place a steaming rack in the pot.

2. Combine the cumin, chili, garlic, salt, and pepper in a bowl and cover the salmon with the spice mix.
3. Put it on the rack and seal the lid to cook for 2 minutes.
4. Quick-release the pressure and serve.

Nutrition Facts per Serving
Calories: 207, Fat: 9.7g, Carbs: 1.1g, Protein: 29.6g

Lemon Mahi-Mahi with Tomatoes

Prep + cook time: 25 minutes; Serves: 4
Ingredients:
- 3 tbsp. butter
- 1 sliced onion
- 2 tbsp. lemon juice
- 1 tsp. dried oregano

- 28 oz. diced tomatoes
- Salt and pepper
- 6 mahi-mahi fillets

Instructions:

1. Press "Sauté" on the Instant Pot and add the butter to melt.
2. Mix in the onions to cook for 2 minutes.
3. Mix in the rest of the ingredients minus the fillets to cook for 3 minutes.

4. Add the fillets and seal the lid to cook for 8 minutes at high pressure.
5. Quick-release the pressure and serve.

Nutrition Facts per Serving
Calories: 268, Fat: 8.8g, Carbs: 13.1g, Protein: 33.8g

Whitefish with Potatoes and Carrots

Prep + cook time: 19 minutes: Serves: 3
Ingredients:
- 1 lb. small red potatoes; halved
- 2 carrots; sliced
- 2 stalks celery; sliced
- 1 lemon; halved
- 1 large onion; diced
- 4 cups water
- ½ tsp. pepper
- 1 tsp. salt
- 2 lb. Whitefish

Instructions:

1. Mix all the ingredients except the fish in the Instant Pot.
2. Seal the lid and set to cook for 7 minutes. Quick-release the steam after cooking.
3. Mix in the whitefish and seal the lid to cook for 2 minutes. Quick-release the pressure and serve with buttered rolls.

Nutrition Facts per Serving
Calories: 405; Fat: 13.54 g; Carbs: 23.29 g; Protein: 46.08 g; Fiber 2.9g

Sweet Creole Shrimp

Prep + cook time: 16 minutes; Serves: 2
Ingredients:
- 1 tsp. olive oil
- ½ lb. large shrimps peeled
- 1 minced garlic clove
- 1 tbsp. honey
- 2 tsp. Creole seasoning
- 2 tsp. dried parsley
- 2 tbsp. fresh-squeezed lemon juice
- 2 tsp. soy sauce
- ½ cup of water

Instructions:
1. Press "Sauté" on the Instant Pot and add the oil. When hot, mix in the shrimps and garlic to cook for 2 to 3 minutes.

2. Press the "Cancel" button. In a bowl, mix the honey, Creole seasoning, parsley, lemon juice, and soy sauce together.
3. Pour the water in the Instant Pot and add the honey mix to the shrimps in the pot. Seal the lid and the valve.
4. Set to "Manual" to cook for 3 minutes at high pressure.
5. "Cancel" the pot and quick release the pressure. Open and serve topped with parsley.

Nutrition Facts per Serving
Calories: 152 g; Fat: 2.5 g; Carbs: 12 g; Protein: 21.9

Salmon with Steamed Vegetables

Prep + cook time: 15 minutes; Serves: 2
Ingredients:
- 1 cup red raspberries; minced
- 1 tbsp. cider vinegar
- 2 salmon steaks
- 1 tbsp. olive oil
- 2 garlic cloves; minced
- 1 tbsp. parsley; chopped

- 1 leek; chopped
- 1 tbsp. lemon juice
- 1 cup clam juice
- a pinch of sea salt
- black pepper
- 1 tsp. sherry

- 1/3 cup chopped dill

Instructions:

1. In a bowl, mix the raspberries and vinegar together. Mix in the salmon, cover, and keep in the fridge for 2 hours.
2. Press "Sauté" on the pot and add the oil.
3. Mix in the garlic, parsley, and leek to cook for 2 minutes. Mix in the lemon juice, clam juice, salt, pepper, sherry, and dill to cook for 2 minutes.

4. Add in the salmon and the sauce and stir then seal the lid and the valve.
5. Set to "Manual" to cook for 4 minutes at high pressure.
6. Press "Cancel" and quick release the pressure. Open the lid and serve with steamed veggies.

Nutrition Facts per Serving

Calories: 160 g; Fat: 25 g; Carbs: 5 g; Protein: 12 g

Buttery Spicy Shrimp

Prep + cook time:15 minutes; Serves: 3

Ingredients:

- 3 tbsp. butter
- 1 lb. large shrimp
- 4 minced garlic cloves
- 1 tsp. paprika
- 2 sliced lemons

Instructions:

1. Press "Sauté" on the pot and add the butter.

2. Mix in the garlic and cook for 1 minute.
3. Mix in the rest of the ingredients and seal the lid to cook for 4 minutes at high pressure.
4. Natural release the pressure and serve.

Nutrition Facts per Serving

Calories: 231, Fat: 11.6g, Carbs: 4.4g, Protein: 28.8g

Lemon Salmon with Tomatoes

Prep + cook time: 20 minutes; serves: 2

Ingredients:

- 4 Roma tomatoes
- 2 lemons
- 4 salmon fillets
- Pepper and salt
- ½ cup chopped shallots
- 4 sprigs rosemary
- 2 cups of water

Instructions:

1. Slice the tomatoes and lemons. Make two foil pouches and add two pieces of salmon on each pouch.

2. Season the salmon with salt and pepper then share the rest of the ingredients equally between them.
3. Fold the foil to secure the pouch.
4. Pour water in the pot then place a rack inside the pot. Put the pouch on the rack.
5. Seal the lid and the valve and set it to manual to cook for 10 minutes. Press the cancel button then quick release the steam, open the pot and serve.

Nutrition Facts per Serving:

Calories 466; Fat: 22g; Carbs: 13g; Protein 54.5g; Fiber: 2g

Lemon Ginger Haddock

Prep + cook time: 16 minutes; serves: 2

Ingredients:

- 2 tbsp. Olive oil
- 4 haddock fillets
- Pepper and salt
- 2 lemons; juiced with one lemon zested
- 4 green onions
- 1 cup white wine

- 1-inch chopped fresh ginger

Instructions:

1. Coat the fillets with olive oil and season with salt and pepper.

2. Put the rest of the ingredients in the pot and mix it together. Place the fish on a rack and lower it into the liquid.
3. Seal the lid and the valve and set it to manual to cook for 8 minutes. Press the cancel button and quick release the pressure.

4. Serve with rice or vegetable salad.

Nutrition Facts per Serving:
Calories: 230; Fat: 8.5g; Carbs: 5.5g; Protein 32g; Fiber: 1.5g

Buttery Stuffed Squids

Prep + cook time: 14 minutes; serves: 2

Ingredients:
- ½ lb. fresh squids
- ½ lb. chopped mushrooms
- 2 eggs
- 1 tsp. garlic powder
- ¼ tsp. salt
- ¼ tsp. pepper
- ½ tbsp. butter; melted
- Water

Instructions:
1. Rinse the squids and throw the ink away. Put the mushrooms and eggs in a food processor then add the garlic powder, salt, and pepper to it.

2. Blend until smooth and fill the squid with the mushroom mixture. Prick the squids with a toothpick.
3. Pour water in the Instant Pot and place the rack in the pot. Put the squids on the rack and coat generously with the butter.
4. Seal the lid and the valve. Set to manual to cook for 15 minutes.
5. Natural release the pressure. Serve on a dish.

Nutrition Facts per Serving:
Calories: 253; Net Carbs: 5.7g; Fat: 9.5g; Carbs: 7g; Protein: 35.2;

Creamy Coconut Shrimp Curry

Prep + cook time: 10 minutes; serves: 2

Ingredients:
- 1 lb. frozen shrimp
- ¾ cup onion masala
- ½ tsp. garam masala
- 1/8 tsp. cayenne
- ½ cup water
- ½ tsp. salt
- 2 tbsp. coconut milk
- 2 tbsp. chopped cilantro

Instructions:
1. Mix all the ingredients in the pot except the milk and cilantro.
2. Seal the lid and set to high to cook for 1 minute.
3. Quick-release the pressure and mix in the milk and sprinkle with cilantro.

Nutrition Facts per Serving:
Calories: 276, Fat: 7.7g, Carbs: 3g, Protein: 46.7g

Chili Garlic Salmon

Prep + cook time: 15 minutes; serves: 3

Ingredients:
- 1 tsp. red chili powder
- 1 minced garlic clove
- 1 tsp. ground cumin
- Salt and Pepper
- 1 lb. salmon fillet
- 1 ½ cups of water

Instructions:
1. Pour 1 ½ cups of water into the pot and put the rack in it.

2. Mix the chili powder, garlic clove, cumin, salt, and pepper in a bowl.
3. Coat the salmon with the mix and put it in the rack.
4. Seal the pot and set to steam to cook for 2 minutes. Quick-release the pressure and open the lid. Serve hot.

Nutrition Facts per Serving::
Calories: 207, Fat: 9.7g, Carbs: 1.1g, Protein: 29.6g

Garlic Cod with Peas

Prep + cook time: 10 minutes; serves: 2

Ingredients:
- 1 cup white wine
- 1 tsp. oregano
- 1 sprig fresh rosemary
- 2 garlic cloves; smashed
- 1 cup fresh parsley
- Pepper and salt as per taste preference
- 1 tsp. paprika
- 1 bag (10 oz.) frozen peas
- 1 lb. cod; cut into 4 fillets

Instructions:

1. Mix the wine, herbs, salt, and spices together in a bowl.
2. Pour it into the Instant Pot and add the peas.
3. Put the fillets on a rack and lower it into the liquid. Seal the lid and the valve.
4. Set to manual to cook for 5 minutes. Press the cancel button when the timer stops and quick release the pressure. Open and serve.

Nutrition Facts per Serving:
Calories: 200; Fat: 1.5g; Carbs: 13.5g; Protein 30g; Fiber: 44g

Buttery Jasmine Rice with Salmon

Prep + cook time: 10 minutes; serves: 2

Ingredients:
- 2 wild salmon fillets
- ½ tsp. saffron
- ½ cup jasmine rice
- 1 tbsp. butter
- ½ cup veggie stock mix; dried
- 1 cup chicken stock
- Salt and black pepper

Instructions:

1. Open the pot and mix in all the ingredients except the salmon.
2. Put the steaming rack in the pot and put the salmon on it. Sprinkle the salmon with salt and pepper and seal the lid and the valve.
3. Set to manual to cook for 5 minutes.
4. Press the cancel button and natural release the pressure for 8 to 10 minutes. Open the lid and serve the rice with the salmon.

Nutrition Facts per Serving:
Calories: 286; Fat: 12.4g; Carbs: 0.7g; Protein 24.6g; 18g; Fiber

Sweet and Spicy Snapper

Prep + cook time: 37 minutes; serves: 2

Ingredients:
- 1 red snapper; cleaned
- A pinch of salt
- 2 cups of water
- 3 tbsp. chili paste
- 2 tsp. sugar
- 1 garlic clove; minced
- ½ tsp. ginger; grated
- 1 tbsp. soy sauce
- 1 green onion; chopped
- 2 tsp. sesame seeds; toasted
- 1 tsp. sesame oil

Instructions:

1. Cut some slits in the snapper and sprinkle it with the salt. Let it sit for 25 to 30 minutes.
2. Pour the water into a pot and place a rack in the pot. Put the fish on the rack. Rub the snapper with the chili paste then seal the lid and the valve.
3. Set to manual to cook for 12 minutes.
4. Press the cancel button then natural release the pressure for 8 to 10 minutes. Serve into containers.
5. Mix the rest of the ingredients in a bowl and then serve the fish with the sauce.

Nutrition Facts per Serving:
Calories: 200; Fat: 12g; Carbs: 23.5g; Protein 6.2g; Fiber: 1g

Squids with Anchovies and Tomatoes

Prep + cook time: 20 minutes; serves: 2

Ingredients:

- ½ lb. fresh squids
- ½ tsp. olive oil
- ½ tsp. minced garlic
- ¼ cup white wine
- ¼ cup diced tomatoes
- 3 tbsp. chopped parsley
- 2 anchovies
- ½ tsp. red chili flakes
- 1 tbsp. lemon juice
- ¼ tsp. salt
- ¼ tsp. pepper

Instructions:

1. Remove the head of the squid and throw away the ink. Wash them well and cut into rings.
2. Press the sauté button and pour the oil into the pot then add the garlic to cook until it is fragrant.
3. Press the cancel button and mix in the rest of the ingredients then seal the lid and the valve.
4. Set to pressure cook to cook for 15 minutes. Serve in a dish.

Nutrition Facts per Serving:

Calories: 170; Net Carbs: 6.8g; Fat: 4.8g; Carbs: 7.5g; Protein: 24.9g

Spicy Orange Scallops

Prep + cook time: 16 minutes; serves: 2

Ingredients:

- ½ jalapeno pepper; seedless and minced
- 3 tbsp. extra virgin olive oil
- ¼ tsp. mustard
- Salt and pepper
- 1 tbsp. rice vinegar
- ½ lb. sea scallops; cleaned
- A pinch of cayenne pepper
- 1/3 cup water or broth
- 2 oranges; sliced

Instructions:

1. Put the jalapeno with 2 tablespoons of the oil, mustard, salt, pepper, and vinegar in a blender and blend.
2. Rub the cayenne pepper with the scallops. Press sauté on the pot then add the scallops to cook for 3 minutes on each side.
3. Press the cancel button and pour in the broth or water, jalapeno sauce. Seal the lid and the valve.
4. Set to manual to cook for 6 minutes at high pressure. Press the cancel button and quick release the pressure. Serve.

Nutrition Facts per Serving:

Calories: 350 g; Fat: 27.1 g; Carbs: 13.8 g; Protein: 20

Lemon Pepper Sherry Cod

Prep + cook time: 25 minutes; serves: 2

Ingredients:

- ¼ sherry
- 2 tbsp. lemon-pepper seasoning
- ½ tbsp. soy sauce
- 1 tbsp. balsamic vinegar
- 2 cod steaks

Instructions:

1. Mix the sherry, lemon pepper seasoning, soy sauce, and vinegar in a bowl.
2. Put the cod steaks in it and let it marinate for 20 minutes.
3. Put the cod in the pour and seal the lid. Set to cook at high pressure for 6 minutes. Natural release the pressure and serve.

Nutrition Facts per Serving:

Calories: 60, Fat: 0.3g, Carbs: 4.5g, Protein: 10.5 g

Spicy Garlic Tuna

Prep + cook time: 15 minutes; serves: 2

Ingredients:

- 3 cloves garlic
- 4 shallots
- ½ tsp. turmeric
- ¼ cup cayenne pepper
- ½ lb. fresh tuna
- 1 bay leaf
- 1 kaffir lime leaf

Instructions:

1. Put the garlic, shallot, cayenne pepper, and turmeric in a blender to blend till smooth.
2. Coat the tuna with the spice mix then put it on an aluminum foil. Put the bay leaf and the lime leaf on the fish then wrap the tuna with the foil.
3. Pour the water into the rack and place the rack into the pot. Put the tuna in the pot and seal the lid.
4. Set to steam to cook for 10 minutes.
5. Natural release the pressure and open the lid. Open the lid and open the tuna then let it cool. Serve with s plate of brown rice.

Nutrition Facts per Serving:
Calories: 156; Net Carbs: 6.4g; Fat: 2.3g; Carbs: 8.3g; Protein: 26.7

Creamy Shrimp Curry

Prep + cook time: 8 minutes; serves: 2

Ingredients:

- ½ lb. fresh shrimps
- ½ cup chopped onion
- ¼ tsp. garam masala
- ¼ tsp. curry
- ¼ tsp. salt
- ¼ tsp. cayenne
- ¼ cup of water
- 2 tbsp. heavy cream

Instructions:

1. Remove the shrimp heads and put it in the Instant Pot then add the onion, garam masala, curry, salt, and cayenne in the pot.
2. Pour the water over the shrimp and seal the lid then set to manual to cook for 2 minutes.
3. Quick-release the pressure and open the lid. Press sauté on the pot and mix in the heavy cream. Cook for 1 minute.
4. Serve the shrimps on a dish.

Nutrition Facts per Serving:
Calories: 200; Net Carbs: 4.3g; Fat: 7.6g; Carbs: 5.1g; Protein: 26.5;

Spicy Seasoned Lemon Shrimp

Prep + cook time: 15 minutes; serves: 2

Ingredients:

- 1lb. frozen shrimp; peeled and deveined
- 1 lemon; juiced
- 1 tsp. cayenne pepper
- 2 cloves garlic; minced
- 1 sweet onion; minced
- 1 jalapeno pepper; minced
- 1 tsp. black pepper
- 1 tsp. white pepper
- 1 can diced tomatoes (15 oz.)

Instructions:

1. Let the shrimp thaw at room temperature for 15 minutes.
2. Mix all the ingredients in the Instant Pot and seal the lid and the valve. Set to manual to cook for 5 minutes at high pressure.
3. Quick-release the pressure and serve.

Nutrition Facts per Serving:
Calories: 172; Fat: 2.5g; Carbs: 10g; Fiber: 2.5g; Protein 26g

Buttery Rice Dish with Shrimp and Lemon

Prep + cook time: 18 minutes; serves: 2

Ingredients:

- 2 tbsp. butter
- 1 small onion; chopped
- 2 minced garlic cloves
- 1 pinch of crushed red pepper
- A pinch of saffron
- A pinch of sea salt
- Black pepper
- ½ lb. deveined bug shrimps
- 1 cup chicken broth
- ¼ cup white wine
- 1 cup risotto rice
- ¼ cup chopped parsley
- 1 lemon; quartered

Instructions:

1. Press sauté in the pot and add the butter, onions, and garlic to cook for 1 minute until soft.
2. Mix in the red pepper, saffron, salt, and pepper then add the rice and cook for 1 minute. Pour in the wine and broth then press the cancel button.
3. Add the shrimps then close the lid and the valve.
4. Set to manual to cook at high pressure for 5 minutes.
5. Press the cancel button and quick release the pressure. Open and serve topped with parsley and with the lemon wedges.

Nutrition Facts per Serving:
Calories: 420 g; Fat: 13 g; Carbs: 44.7 g; Protein: 31.3

Sea Bass and Shrimps with Avocado and Celery

Prep + cook time: 9 minutes; serves: 2

Ingredients:

- ½ lb. sea bass fillets
- ¼ tsp. salt
- ¼ tsp. pepper
- ¾ tbsp. avocado oil
- ¼ cup diced onions
- ¼ lb. fresh shrimps
- 2 tbsp. diced celery
- ½ cup diced tomatoes
- 1 tbsp. tomato paste
- ¾ tbsp. Cajun seasoning
- ½ cup of water

Instructions:

1. Season the sea bass with salt and pepper and set aside.
2. Pour the oil into the pot and add the sea bass to sear for 4 minutes on both sides. Remove the sea bass and set aside.
3. Add the onions to cook until fragrant then press the cancel button.
4. Mix in the shrimps, Cajun seasoning, celery, tomatoes, and tomato paste.
5. Pour the water over the ingredients in the pot and seal the lid and the valve. Set to manual to cook for 2 minutes. Quick-release the pressure and open the pot.
6. Serve sea bass with the shrimp and tomatoes over it.

Nutrition Facts per Serving:
Calories: 210; Net Carbs: 3.7g; Fat: 4.2g; Carbs: 5.3g; Protein: 36.9g

Instant Pot Crab Cakes with Chili Garlic Sauce

Prep + cook time: 20 minutes; serves: 2

Ingredients:

Crab cakes:

- ½ lb. crab meat; free of shells
- 1 egg
- ¼ cup breadcrumbs
- ½ tsp. salt
- ¼ tsp. white pepper
- 2 tbsp. fresh parsley; chopped
- 3 tbsp. flour
- ¼ tsp. paprika

- Sauce:
- ½ cup jarred roasted red pepper and garlic sauce
- 2 tbsp. butter
- ¼ cup mayonnaise
- 1 tbsp. lemon juice
- ¼ cup water

Instructions:
1. Combine the crab cakes ingredients in a bowl and mold into flat cakes.
2. Press sauté on the pot and add the butter. Brown the crab cakes for 3 minutes on each side.
3. Combine the red pepper and garlic sauce, mayo, and water in a bowl then pour it into the cooker.
4. Press the cancel button. Seal the lid and set to cook for 5 minutes at high pressure on manual.
5. Press the cancel button and quick release the pressure. Open the lid and serve.

Nutrition Facts per Serving:
Calories: 460 g; Fat: 27.4 g; Carbs: 31.9 g; Protein: 21.1

Creamy Cheesy Tilapia

Prep + cook time: 20 minutes; serves: 2

Ingredients:
- 2 tbsp. mayonnaise
- 2 tbsp. lemon juice
- Salt and pepper
- 2 tilapia fillets
- ½ cup grated parmesan cheese

Instructions:
1. Mix the mayonnaise, lemon juice, salt, and pepper together in a bowl then put the fillets inside it to marinate.
2. Put it in the Instant Pot then seal the lid and set to cook for 7 minutes at high pressure.
3. Natural release the pressure and sprinkle the parmesan over it. Press sauté on the pot and cook for 3 minutes until the cheese melts.
4. Serve.

Nutrition Facts per Serving:
Calories: 345, Fat: 16.6g, Carbs: 3.9g, Protein: 48.3g

Buttery Salmon Fillets

Prep + cook time: 10 minutes; serves: 2

Ingredients:
- ½ lb. salmon fillets
- ¼ tsp. salt
- ¼ tsp. pepper
- 3 fresh lemons
- 1 tbsp. dill

Instructions:
1. Sprinkle the salmon with salt and pepper and set aside.
2. Cut the lemon in half then squeeze the lemon. Pour the juice inside the Instant Pot.
3. Pour the water into the pot and place a rack in the pot. Put the seasoned salmon on the rack. Sprinkle the dill over the salmon.
4. Seal the lid and set to steam to cook for 5 minutes.
5. Natural release the pressure for 8 to 10 minutes and open the lid.
6. Remove the salmon and serve on a dish. Top with some dill and serve.

Nutrition Facts per Serving:
Calories: 261; Net Carbs: 6.5g; Fat: 17.1g; Carbs: 9.2g; Protein: 21.4;

Buttery Lemon Crabs

Prep + cook time: 8 minutes: serves: 2

Ingredients:
- 2 tbsp. fish sauce
- ¼ cup butter; melted
- ¼ tsp. salt
- 1 ½ lb. crabs
- ½ cup water
- ¼ cup minced garlic

- 1 tbsp. lemon juice

Instructions:
1. Mix all the ingredients in the pot except the lemon juice and seal the lid and the valve.
2. Set to manual to cook for 3 minutes.

3. Press the cancel button and quick release the steam. Open the pot, pour the lemon juice over the crabs and serve.

Nutrition Facts per Serving:
Calories: 264; Fat: 18g; Carbs: 6.5g; Protein 17g; Fiber: 0.5g;

Sweet Ginger Shrimps

Prep + cook time: 15 minutes; serves: 2

Ingredients:
- ½ lb. fresh shrimps
- ½ tsp. ginger
- 1 tsp. vegetable oil
- ½ tbsp. raw honey
- 1 tsp. minced garlic
- 4 tbsp. soy sauce

Instructions:
1. Remove the heads of the shrimp and throw away then put the shrimps in a plastic bag and add the rest of the ingredients. Allow to mix well then set aside for 5 minutes.
2. Pour the shrimp and marinade into the Instant Pot and seal the lid. Set to manual to cook for 4 minutes.
3. Quick-release the pressure and serve with the sauce.

Nutrition Facts per Serving:
Calories: 179; Net Carbs: 5g; Fat: 3.8g; Carbs: 5.1g; Protein: 27.1g;

Ginger Orange Salmon

Prep + cook time: 8 minutes; serves: 2

Ingredients:
- ½ tsp. minced garlic
- ¾ orange marmalade
- 1½ tsp. soy sauce
- ½ tsp. ginger
- ¼ tsp. salt
- ¼ tsp. pepper
- ½ lb. salmon fillets

Instructions:
1. Pour all the ingredients in a plastic bag and add the salmon to mix. Let it sit for 15 minutes.

2. Pour water into the pot and place a rack in it.
3. Put the salmon on the rack and seal the lid and the valve. Set to steam to cook for 3 minutes.
4. Natural release the pressure and open the lid.
5. Serve salmon on a dish with steamed veggies.

Nutrition Facts per Serving:
Calories: 294; Net Carbs: 5.8g; Fat: 16.5g; Carbs: 6g; Protein: 30.4;

Sweet and Creamy Scallops

Prep + cook time: 10 minutes; serves: 2

Ingredients:
- ¾ lb. jumbo scallops
- ¼ cup water
- ¼ tsp. salt
- ¼ tsp. ginger
- 2 tbsp. coconut milk
- ½ tbsp. maple syrup

Instructions:

1. Mix all the ingredients in the pot except the maple syrup then seal the lid and the valve.
2. Set to manual to cook for 5 minutes.
3. Natural release the pressure and open the lid. Serve on a dish drizzled with maple syrup.

Nutrition Facts per Serving:
Calories: 150; Net Carbs: 7g; Fat: 4.6g; Carbs: 7.4g; Protein: 21.8;

Creamy Lemony Fish Curry

Prep + cook time: 14 minutes; serves: 2

Ingredients:

- ½ lb. tuna fillet
- 2 tbsp. halved cherry tomatoes
- 1 tsp. green chili
- 2 tbsp. chopped onion
- ½ tsp. ginger
- ½ tsp. coriander
- ¾ tsp. curry powder
- ¼ cup coconut milk
- ¼ cup water
- 1 tsp. minced garlic
- ¼ tsp. salt
- 1 tbsp. lemon juice

Instructions:

1. Cut the fillets into cubes and put it in the Instant Pot.
2. Mix in the rest of the ingredients except the lemon juice and seal the lid and the valve.
3. Set to manual to cook for 5 minutes at high pressure. Quick-release the steam and open the pot.
4. Drizzle the lemon juice over the curry and serve.

Nutrition Facts per Serving:

Calories: 464; Net Carbs: 5.8g; Fat: 38.3g; Carbs: 8g; Protein: 23.1;

Creamy Spicy Shrimp with Tomatoes

Prep + cook time: 14 minutes; serves: 2

Ingredients:

- ½ lb. fresh shrimps
- 1 tbsp. yogurt
- ½ tsp. cumin
- ¼ tsp. ginger
- ¼ tsp. salt
- ½ tsp. paprika
- ½ tsp. garam masala
- ½ tsp. minced garlic
- 1 tsp. lemon juice
- 1 tbsp. butter
- 1 tbsp. diced onion
- ½ cup heavy cream
- ¼ tsp. red chili flakes
- ½ cup diced tomatoes

Instructions:

1. Remove the head of the shrimps and peel the shrimps. Put it in a Ziploc bag and add the yogurt, cumin, ginger, paprika, salt, garam masala, and garlic.
2. Mix well and coat the shrimps then set aside for 10 minutes.
3. Press sauté on the Instant Pot and add the butter and onions to cook until fragrant then cancel the pot.
4. Mix in the cream, chili flakes, and tomatoes then seal the lid and the valve and set to manual to cook for 6 minutes.
5. Quick-release the pressure and add the shrimps with the marinade to cook for 3 minutes on sauté mode.
6. Serve the shrimps with gravy.

Nutrition Facts per Serving:

Calories: 297; Net Carbs: 4.1g; Fat: 18.7g; Carbs: 5.1g; Protein: 28.9;

Chapter 9 Snacks and Appetizers

Maple Syrup Brussels Sprouts

Prep + cook time: 9 minutes: serves: 2

Ingredients:
- ½ lb. Brussels sprouts; trimmed
- 1 ½ tsp. maple syrup
- 3 tbsp. orange juice
- 1 tbsp. butter
- 1 tsp. orange zest
- Pinch of salt
- Pinch of pepper

Instructions:

1. Put all the ingredients in the Instant Pot and seal the lid and the venting valve.
2. Set to "Manual" to cook for 4 minutes.
3. Press the "Cancel" button and quick release the pressure. Open the pot and serve.

Nutrition Facts per Serving

Calories: 68; Fat: 4g; Carbs: 6g; Protein 2.5g; Fiber 1g

Spicy Mango Potatoes

Prep + cook time: 30 minutes; Serves: 2

Ingredients:
- 1 cup of water
- 3 large sweet potatoes; peeled and cut into wedges
- 1 tbsp. dry mango powder
- 2 tbsp. vegetable oil
- 1 tsp. paprika
- ½ tsp. salt
- Cooking oil as needed

Instructions:

1. Pour water into the pot and place the steaming rack in the pot. Lay the potatoes on the rack and seal the lid and the valve.
2. Set to "Manual" to cook for 15 minutes.
3. Press the "Cancel" button and quick release the pressure. Remove the water and set the potatoes aside.
4. Press "Sauté" on the Instant Pot and add the oil to cook for 2 minutes until it turns brown.
5. Mix the rest of the ingredients in a bowl and cover the wedges with the mango mix. Serve.

Nutrition Facts per Serving:

Calories: 164; Fat: 6.5g; Carbs: 25.5g; Protein 1.5g; Fiber 3g

Sweet Carrots

Prep + cook time: 20 minutes; Serves: 2

Ingredients:
- ½ lb. carrots
- 1 cup of water
- 1 tbsp. Dijon mustard
- 1 tbsp. honey
- Dash of hot sauce
- ¼ tsp. paprika
- 1 tsp. garlic; minced
- ½ tsp. ground cumin
- 1 tbsp. butter
- Pepper and salt

Instructions:

1. Cut the carrots into quarters lengthwise and cut each quarter in half.
2. Pour the water into the Instant Pot and place the steaming rack over it. Lay the carrots on the rack and seal the lid.
3. Set to "Manual" to cook for 2 minutes. When it stops, press "Cancel" and quick release the pressure.
4. Remove the carrots and set aside then clean the pot. Press "Sauté" and add the butter and the rest of the ingredients to cook for 30 seconds.
5. Press "Cancel" and mix in the carrots. Serve.

Nutrition Facts per Serving

Calories: 138; Fat: 6g; Carbs: 21g; Protein 1.5g; Fiber 3.5g

Prosciutto Asparagus

Prep + cook time: 13 minutes: serves: 2

Ingredients:

- 5 oz. sliced prosciutto
- ½ lb. asparagus spears

Instructions:

1. Wrap the prosciutto slices around each asparagus spears.
2. Pour 2 cups of water into the Instant Pot and place a rack above it.
3. Lay the wrapped asparagus on the rack and seal the lid and the valve.
4. Set to "Manual" to cook for 3 minutes.
5. Press the "Cancel" button and natural release the pressure for 8 to 10 minutes. Open and serve.

Nutrition Facts per Serving

Calories: 124; Fat: 4g; Carbs: 5.5g; Protein 17g; Fiber 2g

Lemon Asparagus

Prep + cook time: 7 minutes; Serves: 2

Ingredients:

- ¼ lb. Asparagus
- 2 tbsp. lemon juice
- 1 tsp. olive oil
- 1 cup of water

Instructions:

1. Remove the woody parts of the asparagus and trim them then add the lemon juice and olive oil and mix well.
2. Pour the water into the Instant Pot and place a rack over it. Put the lemon asparagus on the rack and seal the lid and the valve.
3. Set to "Manual" to cook for 2 minutes.
4. Press the "Cancel" button and natural release the pressure for 8 to 10 minutes. Open and serve.

Nutrition Facts per Serving

Calories 38; Fat: 2.5g; Carbs: 2.8g; Protein 2g ; Fiber 1g

Cheesy Bacon and Eggs

Prep + cook time: 20 minutes; Serves: 3

Ingredients:

- 4 eggs
- ¼ tsp. lemon-pepper seasoning
- 4 slices precooked bacon; crumbled
- 1 diced green onions
- 4 tbsp. shredded cheddar cheese

Instructions:

1. Put the rack in the Instant Pot and pour 1 ½ cups of water into the pot.
2. Whisk the eggs and lemon pepper in a bowl and set aside.
3. Put the bacon, green onions, and cheese into 4 muffin cups and pour the egg mixture into it.
4. Put the muffin cups on the steaming rack and seal the lid.
5. Set to "Manual" to cook for 8 minutes.
6. Press "Cancel" and quick release the pressure then serve.

Nutrition Facts per Serving

Calories: 170; Fat: 13g; Carbs: 1g; Protein 12g

Sweet and Spicy Tofu

Prep + cook time: 2 hours 35 minutes: serves: 2

Ingredients:

- 1 container extra firm tofu; cut to make 1-inch cubes
- ¼ tsp. garlic powder
- ½ tbsp. red pepper flakes
- 1 ½ tbsp. brown sugar
- ¾ cup ketchup
- ½ tbsp. apple cider vinegar
- 1 tbsp. soy sauce

- ¼ tsp. salt

Instructions:

1. Mix all the ingredients in the Instant Pot and seal the lid and the valve.
2. Set to slow cook to cook for 2 hours 35 minutes.

3. Press the "Cancel" button when it stops timing and natural release the pressure for 8 to 10 minutes.
4. Open and serve.

Nutrition Facts per Serving

Calories 433; Fat: 5.3g; Carbs: 27.2g; Protein 15g; Fiber 4g

Green Beans and Eggplant Dish

Prep + cook time: 10 minutes; Serves: 2

Ingredients:

- ½ tsp. olive oil
- 2 tsp. minced garlic
- 1 cup chopped green beans
- 1 cup chopped eggplant
- 1 tbsp. fish sauce
- 2 tbsp. soy sauce
- 1 tbsp. oyster sauce

Instructions:

1. Press "Sauté" on the Instant Pot and add the oil and garlic to cook for 2 minutes. Mix in the beans and eggplant, soy sauce, oyster sauce, and fish sauce.
2. Pour some water into the pot and seal the lid and the venting valve.
3. Set to "Manual" to cook for 3 minutes.
4. Press "Cancel" and quick release the pressure. Open the lid and serve.

Nutrition Facts per Serving

Calories: 46; Fat: 0.5g; Carbs: 9g; Protein 3g; Fiber 3.5g

Garlic Eggplant with Tomatoes

Prep + cook time: 18 minutes; serves: 3

Ingredients:

- 3 tbsp. olive oil
- 1 cup chopped yellow onions
- 2 minced garlic cloves
- 1 cup sweet bell pepper; chopped
- 2 cups chopped eggplant
- ¼ cup minced sun-dried tomatoes
- ¼ cup vegetable stock
- Salt and pepper
- 2 tbsp. tomato paste

Instructions:

1. Press "Sauté" on the Instant Pot and add the oil and onions to cook for 2 to 3 minutes.
2. Add the garlic, bell pepper, and eggplant and cook for 2 minutes. Mix in the tomatoes, stock, salt, and pepper, and tomato paste.
3. Seal the lid and the valve and set it to "Manual" to cook for 5 minutes.
4. Press "Cancel" and quick release the pressure. Serve on toasted bread.

Nutrition Facts per Serving

Calories: 162; Fat: 4g; Carbs: 7.5g; Protein 8g; fiber 3g

Instant Pot Hummus

Prep + cook time: 45 minutes; Serves: 2

Ingredients:

- 1 cup dry chickpeas
- ½ cup Tahini
- 3 garlic cloves; minced
- Juice of 1 lemon
- ¼ tsp. cumin
- 2 cups of water
- ½ tsp. black pepper

- ½ tsp. salt

Instructions:

1. Put the chickpeas in the pot and add some water. Seal the lid and cook for 35 minutes at high pressure.
2. Remove the chickpeas and put them in a food processor. Mix in the Tahini, garlic, lemon

juice, cumin, salt, and pepper. Blend until it is smooth.
3. Sprinkle with some salt, pepper, and lemon. Serve with bread or chips.

Nutrition Facts per Serving
Calories: 375; Fat: 19.23 g; Carbs: 39.7 g; Protein: 15.58 g; Fiber 9.1g

Spicy Jalapeno Dip

Prep + cook time: 40 minutes; Serves: 2
Ingredients:
- 1 jalapeno; seeded
- 1 cup dried pinto beans; rinsed
- 1 medium onion; quartered
- ¼ tsp. black pepper
- ¼ cup salsa
- ½ tsp. paprika
- 1 ½ cups water
- 2 cloves garlic; chopped
- ½ tsp. chili powder
- ½ tsp. cumin
- ½ tsp. salt

Instructions:
1. Put all the ingredients in the Instant Pot and seal the lid and the venting valve.
2. Set to "Manual" to cook for 28 minutes.
3. Press the "Cancel" button and quick release the pressure.
4. Blend the contents with a dipping blender till smooth. Serve with crackers or tortilla chips.

Nutrition Facts per Serving
Calories: 288; Fat: 2g; Carbs: 26.5g; Protein 21g; Fiber 11g

Cheesy Artichokes Cannellini Dip

Prep + cook time: 80 minutes; Serves: 2
Ingredients:
- 8 medium-sized artichokes; halved
- 2 minced garlic cloves
- ½ lemon
- 1 cup vegetable broth
- ½ cup cannellini beans; soaked for 4 hours
- ¾ cup plain yogurt
- ¼ tsp. ground pepper
- ¾ tsp. salt
- ½ cup grated ricotta cheese
- Nachos

Instructions:

1. Boil the artichokes in a pot of water for 30 minutes. Remove the leaves and throw the chokes away.
2. Put the garlic, lemon, broth, artichoke leaves, and beans in the Instant Pot then seal the lid. Set to "Manual" to cook for 20 minutes.
3. Press the "Cancel" button and natural release the pot pressure for 8 to 10 minutes.
4. Mix in the yogurt, pepper, salt, and cheese.
5. Put all the mix in a blender and puree till smooth. Serve with nachos.

Nutrition Facts per Serving
Calories: 188; Fat: 2.5g; Carbs: 29.5g; Protein 14g; Fiber 13g

Spicy Mushrooms with Beans and Tomatoes

Prep + cook time: 40 minutes; serves: 3
Ingredients:
- 3 cups mushrooms; chopped
- 1 cup navy beans; dried
- 2 tbsp. onion powder
- 1 tbsp. shallot powder
- 2 tbsp. barley
- 1 tbsp. red curry paste
- ½ cup farro
- 9 garlic cloves; minced
- 2 tomatoes; diced
- 1 seeded jalapeno pepper; chopped
- Pepper and salt as needed

Instructions:
1. Mix all the ingredients in the pot except the tomatoes and seal the lid and the valve.

2. Set to manual to cook for 30 minutes.
3. Press the cancel button when the timer stops then natural release the pressure for 8 to 10 minutes.

4. Open the lid and mix in the tomatoes and serve sprinkled with scallions and cilantro.

Nutrition Facts per Serving:
Calories: 238; Fat: 6.5g; Carbs: 38g; Protein 11g; Fiber: 1.5g;

Cheesy Pasta with Broccoli and Spinach

Prep + cook time: 20 minutes; serves: 3

Ingredients:
- 1 tbsp. olive oil
- ½ onion; chopped
- 3 ½ oz. Cremini mushrooms
- 1 bell pepper; chopped
- Salt and Pepper
- 8 oz. penne pasta (any other pasta will also work well)
- 1 cup fresh spinach; chopped
- 1 cup broccoli florets
- 2 cups of water
- ½ cup tomato sauce
- 1 tbsp. parmesan cheese; grated
- ½ cup mozzarella; grated

Instructions:

1. Press sauté on the pot and add the oil, onions, mushrooms, and bell pepper to cook for 3 to 4 minutes.
2. Mix in the salt, pepper, pasta, spinach, broccoli, water, and tomato paste then press the cancel button.
3. Set to manual to cook for 5 minutes at low pressure.
4. Press the cancel button and quick release the pressure. Open the lid.
5. Spread the mozzarella on the top and let it melt then serve sprinkled with parmesan.

Nutrition Facts per Serving:
Calories: 322 g; Fat: 7.6 g; Carbs: 52.29 g; Protein: 13

Chili Cabbage with Carrots

Prep + cook time: 10 minutes; serves: 4

Ingredients:
- 1 tsp. sesame oil
- ¾ lb. cabbage
- ¼ cup grated carrots
- ½ tsp. sugar
- ½ tsp. cayenne pepper
- ½ cup of water

Instructions:
1. Cut the cabbage into wedges. Press sauté on the pot and add the oil.

2. Brown the cabbage for 3 minutes on one side. Press the cancel button.
3. Add the carrots, sugar, and cayenne over the cabbage and pour the water over it.
4. Seal the lid and set to cook for 5 minutes at pressure cook.
5. Natural release the pressure and open the lid. Serve.

Nutrition Facts per Serving:
Calories: 70; Net Carbs: 7g; Fat: 2.5g; Carbs: 11.6g; Protein: 2.3g;

Creamy Artichoke and Beans Dip

Prep + cook time: 80 minutes; serves: 2

Ingredients:
- 8 medium-sized artichokes; halved
- ½ cup cannellini beans; soaked for about 4 hours
- 1 cup vegetable broth
- ½ lemon
- 2 garlic cloves; minced
- ¼ tsp. ground pepper
- ½ cup grated ricotta cheese
- ¾ cup plain yogurt
- ¾ tsp. salt

- Nachos to serve

Instructions:
1. Put the artichokes in water and boil for 30 minutes then remove the leaves and throw the chokes away.
2. Put the beans, broth, lemon, and garlic in the Instant Pot and seal the lid. Set to manual to cook for 20 minutes at high pressure.

3. Press the cancel button and natural release the pressure for 8 to 10 minutes.
4. Mix in the rest of the ingredients then pour it into a blender and puree till smooth.
5. Serve with nachos.

Nutrition Facts per Serving:
Calories: 188; Fat: 2.5g; Carbs: 29.5g; Protein 14g; Fiber: 13g

Chewy Asparagus

Prep + cook time: 13 minutes; serves: 2

Ingredients:
- ½ lb. asparagus spears
- 5 oz. sliced prosciutto

Instructions:
1. Wrap the asparagus with the prosciutto.
2. Pour the water into the pot then put a rack in the pot. Put the wrapped asparagus on the rack and seal the lid.

3. Set to manual to cook for 3 minutes at high pressure then press the cancel button when the timer stops.
4. Natural release the pressure for 8 to 10 minutes then open the lid and serve.

Nutrition Facts per Serving:
Calories: 124; Fat: 4g; Carbs: 5.5g; Protein 17g; Fiber: 2g;

Sweet and Spicy Carrots

Prep + cook time: 20 minutes; serves: 2

Ingredients:
- ½ lb. carrots
- 1 tbsp. Dijon mustard
- ¼ tsp. paprika
- 1 tsp. garlic; minced
- ½ tsp. ground cumin
- 1 tbsp. butter
- 1 tbsp. honey
- Dash of hot sauce
- Pepper and salt

Instructions:
1. Cut the carrots in quarters lengthwise then cut the quarters in half.

2. Pour water into the pot and put a rack above the water. Put the carrots on the rack and seal the lid and the valve.
3. Set to manual to cook for 2 minutes at high pressure. Press the cancel button and quick release the pressure.
4. Remove the carrots and pour out the water from the pot and dry the pot.
5. Press sauté on the pot and add the butter and the rest of the ingredients to cook for 30 seconds then cancel the pot and add the carrots. Toss and serve.

Nutrition Facts per Serving:
Calories: 138; Fat: 6g; Carbs: 21g; Protein 1.5g; Fiber: 3.5g

Sweet and Spicy Tofu

Prep + cook time: 2 hours 35 minutes; serves: 2

Ingredients:
- 1 container extra firm tofu; cut to make 1-inch cubes
- 1 ½ tbsp. brown sugar
- ¾ cup ketchup
- ½ tbsp. apple cider vinegar

- 1 tbsp. soy sauce
- ¼ tsp. garlic powder
- ½ tbsp. red pepper flakes
- ¼ tsp. salt

Instructions:

1.   Put all the ingredients in the pot and mix well. Seal the lid and the valve.
2.   Set to slow cook to cook for 2 hours 30 minutes. Press the cancel button and natural release the pressure for 8 to 10 minutes.
3.   Open the lid and serve.

Nutrition Facts per Serving:
Calories 433; Fat: 5.3g; Carbs: 27.2g; Protein 15g; Fiber: 4g;

Lemon Garlic Hummus

Prep + cook time: 45 minutes; serves: 2
Ingredients:
- 1 cup dry chickpeas
- 2 cups of water
- ½ cup tahini
- Juice of 1 lemon
- ¼ tsp. cumin
- ½ tsp. black pepper
- 3 garlic cloves; minced
- ½ tsp. salt

Instructions:

1.   Put the chickpeas in the pot with the water and seal the lid. Set to cook for 35 minutes at high pressure.
2.   Quick-release the steam and put it in a blender. Add the rest of the ingredients and puree till smooth.
3.   Season with salt and pepper and serve.

Nutrition Facts per Serving:
Calories: 375; Fat: 19.23 g; Carbs: 39.7 g; Protein: 15.58 g; Fiber: 9.1 g

Eggplants and Beans Dish

Prep + cook time: 10 minutes; serves: 2
Ingredients:
- ½ tsp. olive oil
- 2 tsp. minced garlic
- 1 cup chopped green beans
- 1 cup chopped eggplant
- 1 tbsp. fish sauce
- 2 tbsp. soy sauce
- ½ cup water
- 1 tbsp. oyster sauce

Instructions:

1.   Press sauté on the pot and add the oil and garlic to cook for 2 minutes until fragrant.
2.   Mix in the rest of the ingredients and seal the lid and the valve.
3.   Set to manual to cook for 3 minutes.
4.   Press the cancel button, quick release the pressure, and open the lid. Serve warm.

Nutrition Facts per Serving:
Calories: 46; Fat: 0.5g; Carbs: 9g; Protein 3g; Fiber: 3.5g

Garlic Lentils with Okra and Cauliflower

Prep + cook time: 17 minutes; serves: 6
Ingredients:
- 1 tbsp. olive oil
- 1 tsp. minced garlic
- 1 cup chopped celery ribs
- 1 chopped bell pepper
- 1 cup chopped okra
- 3 cup vegetable broth
- 1 can diced tomatoes
- 2 tbsp. apple cider vinegar
- ½ cup tomato sauce
- ½ tsp. cayenne powder
- ½ tbsp. oregano
- 1 cup lentils
- Fresh cilantro
- 1 chopped cauliflower
- 1 ½ chopped onions
- 1 tbsp. dried thyme
- 1 tsp. Cajun mix
- Sea salt and black pepper

Instructions:
1.   Press sauté on the Instant Pot and add the oil and garlic, celery, and bell peppers to cook for 5 minutes until it is soft.

2. Add the spices and the rest of the ingredients minus the salt and pepper.
3. Seal the lid and the valve and set it to manual to cook at high pressure for 12 minutes.
4. Season with ½ to 1 teaspoon of salt with the black pepper.

5. Mix well and keep warm. Serve into bowls and garnish with your favorite toppings.

Nutrition Facts per Serving:
Calories: 173, Fat: 3.3g, Carbs: 25g, Protein: 8g

Sour Spicy Green Beans

Prep + cook time: 40 minutes; serves: 4
Ingredients:
- ½ cup dry green beans
- 1 tsp. ground coriander
- ½ tsp. garam masala
- ½ cup red onion; chopped
- 2 large tomatoes; chopped
- 4 garlic cloves
- ½ tsp. cayenne pepper
- ¼ tsp. black pepper
- 5 cups of water
- 1 tsp. lemon juice
- 1-inch ginger root; grated
- 1 tsp. turmeric
- ½ tsp. cumin seeds
- 1 tsp. salt

Instructions:

1. Soak the beans in water for 15 minutes. Put the onions, garlic, tomato, ginger, pepper and spices with 3 teaspoons of water in a blender to puree till smooth.
2. Press sauté on the pot and add the cumin seeds to roast for 10 minutes.
3. Mix in the puree and cook till it thickens for 10 minutes then press the cancel button.
4. Remove the beans and put it in the pot then add the water and the lemon juice and salt.
5. Seal the lid and the valve and set it to manual to cook for 15 minutes at high pressure.
6. Press the cancel button and natural release the pressure then open the lid and serve.

Nutrition Facts per Serving:
Calories: 45 g; Fat: 1.5 g; Carbs: 7.6 g; Protein: 1.6

Buttery Garlic Asparagus

Prep + cook time: 7 minutes; serves: 4
Ingredients:
- 1 handful asparagus
- 3 tsp. minced garlic
- ¼ cup butter
- 3 tbsp. grated cheddar cheese

Instructions:
1. Cut off the ends of the asparagus then put it in a disposable aluminum pan.
2. Add the garlic to the tops of the asparagus then put the butter on top of the asparagus.

Pour the water in the pot and put a rack in the pot.
3. Put the asparagus on the rack and seal the lid and set to steam to cook for 4 minutes.
4. Natural release the pressure for 8 to 10 minutes then open the lid.
5. Remove the pan and serve on a dish and serve with cheese.

Nutrition Facts per Serving:
Calories: 265; Net Carbs: 2.6g; Fat: 26.6g; Carbs: 4g; Protein: 4.6g;

Garlic Green Beans

Prep + cook time: 9 minutes; serves: 4
Ingredients:
- ½ lb. chopped green beans
- ¾ tbsp. olive oil
- 2 tsp. minced garlic
- ¼ tsp. salt
- 1 tsp. fish sauce

Instructions:

1. Pour the water into the pot and put a rack above it.
2. Put the green beans on the rack then seal the lid and the valve.
3. Set to manual to cook on low pressure for 2 hours. Quick-release the pressure in the Instant Pot and open the lid.
4. Open the lid and remove the greens then pour out the water and dry the pot.

5. Pour in the oil and add the garlic to cook until fragrant then add the beans, salt, and fish sauce. Press the cancel button and serve on a dish.

Nutrition Facts per Serving:
Calories: 85; Net Carbs: 5.2g; Fat: 5.4g; Carbs: 9.1g; Protein: 2.4g;

Cumin Quinoa and Beans Bowls

Prep + cook time: 25 minutes; serves: 4

Ingredients:
- 1 tsp. olive oil
- ½ diced red onion
- 1 diced bell pepper
- 1 tsp. ground cumin
- ½ tsp. salt
- 1 cup of salsa
- 1 cup of water
- 1 cup of quinoa
- 1 ½ cup cooked black beans

Instructions:

1. Press sauté on the pot and add the olive oil, onions, and bell peppers to cook until soft for 5 to 8 minutes.
2. Mix in the salt and the cumin and cook for 1 minute then add the salsa, water, quinoa, and beans. Seal the lid and set to cook at low pressure for 10 to 15 minutes.
3. Open the lid and loosen the quinoa with a fork. Serve with desired toppings.

Nutrition Facts per Serving:
Calories: 320, Fat: 7g, Carbs: 50g, Protein: 13g

Lemon Garlic Rice With Peas and Celery

Prep + cook time: 20 minutes; serves: 2

Ingredients:
- 3 tbsp. olive oil
- 2 celery sticks; cubed
- 1 diced brown onion
- ½ tsp. salt
- ½ tsp. pepper
- 1 cup baby green peas
- 2 cups vegetable stock
- 1 cup Arborio rice
- 2 cloves garlic; diced
- 2 tbsp. lemon juice

Instructions:

1. Press sauté on the Instant Pot and add the oil, celery, onions, salt, and pepper to cook for 4 to 5 minutes until it is soft.
2. Mix in the peas, stock, rice, and garlic then seal the lid and the valve. Set to manual to cook for 5 minutes.
3. Press the cancel button when the timer stops and open the lid. Mix in the lemon juice and serve.

Nutrition Facts per Serving:
Calories: 362; Fat: 13g; Carbs: 52.5g; Protein 8g; Fiber: 3g;

Garlic Cauliflower with Mushroom Soup

Prep + cook time: 25 minutes; serves: 4

Ingredients:

- 2 tsp. olive oil
- 1 yellow onion; chopped
- 1 tbsp. minced garlic
- 1 cup fresh baby Bella mushrooms; chopped
- 2 cups chopped cauliflower
- 4 cups homemade vegetable broth
- Salt and pepper

Instructions:

1. Press sauté on the pot and add the oil, onion, and garlic to cook for 3 minutes until fragrant.

2. Add the mushrooms and cook for 4 to 5 minutes more. Press the cancel button and add the cauliflower and the broth. Sprinkle some salt and pepper.

3. Seal the lid and the valve then set to manual to cook at high pressure for 5 minutes.

4. Press the cancel button then natural release the pressure. Open the lid. Puree with a dipping blender and serve.

Nutrition Facts per Serving:

Calories: 86 g; Fat: 12.2 g; Carbs: 7.5 g; Protein: 4.1

Eggplant and Tomato Pot Pie

Prep + cook time: 8 minutes; serves: 4

Ingredients:

- ¾ cup diced tomatoes
- ¼ cup diced onion
- ½ tsp. garlic powder
- ¾ tsp. oregano
- Salt and pepper
- ¼ cup white wine
- 1 ½ cup chopped eggplant
- ½ cup grated mozzarella cheese

Instructions:

1. Put the tomatoes, tomato sauce, and onions in a bowl then season with garlic powder, oregano, salt, and pepper then mix in the white wine.

2. Place half of the eggplant on the bottom of the aluminum pan and pour half of the tomato mixture on the eggplant and spread.

3. Layer with the rest of the eggplant and with the tomato sauce then sprinkle the grated mozzarella cheese on it.

4. Pour water into the Instant Pot and put a rack in the pot. Place the pot pie on the rack then seal the lid and the valve.

5. Set to steam to cook for 3 minutes. Natural release the pressure and open the lid.

6. Remove the pot pie and serve warm.

Nutrition Facts per Serving:

Calories: 134; Net Carbs: 6.9g; Fat: 6.6g; Carbs: 11.1g; Protein: 7.9g;

Chapter 10 Desserts

Buttery Brussels Sprouts with Feta and Cashew

Prep + cook time: 15 minutes; serves: 3

Ingredients:

- 1 cup of water
- 1 lb. Brussels sprouts
- 2 tbsps. pomegranate seeds
- 1 cup crumbled feta cheese
- 2 tbsps. melted butter
- ¼ cup chopped cashew nuts

Instructions:

1. Pour the water into the Instant Pot and put a rack in the pot.
2. Put the sprouts on the rack and seal the lid and the valve then set to cook for 3 minutes at High Pressure.
3. Quick-release the pressure and open the lid.
4. Remove the sprouts and put it in a bowl then sprinkle it with melted butter and the rest of the ingredients then mix well. Serve.

Nutrition Facts per Serving
Calories: 379, Fat: 24.8g, Carbs: 20.2g, Protein: 14.8g

Creamy Cinnamon Buckwheat Dish

Prep + cook time: 8 minutes; serves: 2

Ingredients:

- 1 cup buckwheat groats; rinsed
- 2 tbsps. brown sugar; plus more for serving
- 3 cups milk; plus more for serving
- 1 tsp. ground cinnamon
- 1 ripe banana; sliced

Instructions:

1. Mix all the ingredients together in the Instant Pot and seal the lid.
2. Seal the lid and set to cook for 6 minutes at High Pressure.
3. Serve with some more milk and brown sugar.

Nutrition Facts per Serving
Calories: 409; Fat: 12.7 g; Carbs: 62.26 g; Protein: 15.08 g; Fiber: 4.5 g

Creamy Lemon Tapioca

Prep + cook time: 16 minutes; serves: 2

Ingredients:

- ½ cup tapioca pearls; rinsed and drained
- 1 tbsp. lemon zest
- ½ lemon; sliced (for serving)
- ½ tsp. sweetener Stevia
- 1 ¼ cup milk
- 1 ½ cup water

Instructions:

1. Pour water into the pot and put a rack in it.
2. Mix all the ingredients in a baking dish until the sweetener dissolves. Then put it on the rack and seal the lid and the valve.
3. Set to manual to cook for 6 minutes at high pressure.
4. Press the cancel button and quick release the pressure.
5. Serve the pudding into 5 cups with lemon slices.

Nutrition Facts per Serving
Calories: 214 g; Fat: 3.2 g; Carbs: 41.8 g; Protein: 5.1

Orange Cardamom Panna Cotta

Prep + cook time: 26 minutes; serves: 2

Ingredients:

- 1 tsp. vanilla
- 1 tsp. unflavored gelatin
- ¼ cup sugar
- 1 cup Basic Yogurt
- 1 tbsp. hot water
- Juice of 1 orange with pulp

- ¼ tsp. cardamom
- ¼ cup honey

Instructions:

1. Whisk the yogurt, sugar, and vanilla in a bowl.
2. Put the gelatin over the hot water to soften until it dissolves while whisking then add to the yogurt mix.
3. Pour the mixture into 2 ramekins and chill for 2 hours.

4. Mix the honey, cardamom, ad orange in the pot then seal the lid and the valve. Seal the lid and set to cook for 1 minute. Quick-release the pressure and chill.
5. Run a knife around the edges of the ramekins then turn into a plate. Serve with sauce.

Nutrition Facts per Serving
Calories: 343; Fat: 4.1 g; Carbs: 75.25 g; Protein: 5.08 g; Fiber: 1.7 g

Banana Bread

Prep + cook time: 40 minutes; serves: 4

Ingredients:

- 1/3 cup milk
- 3 tsp. lemon juice or white vinegar
- 2 bananas; mashed
- 3/4 cup sugar
- 1/3 cup butter
- 1 egg
- 2 cups flour
- 1 tsp. baking soda
- ½ tsp. baking powder
- 2 cups of water
- a pinch of salt

Instructions:

1. Whisk the milk, lemon juice or vinegar in a bowl.
2. Mix the bananas, sugar, butter, and eggs in a bowl and set aside.

3. Mix the flour, baking soda, baking powder, and salt in another bowl then add it to the butter mixture then add the milk mixture.
4. Pour the dough into a greased pan and cover the pan with an aluminum foil.
5. Pour water into the pot and put a rack in it. Place the pan on the rack and seal the lid and the valve.
6. Set to manual to cook for 30 minutes at high pressure.
7. Press cancel then natural-release the pressure. Open the lid and remove the excess moisture.
8. Cool and serve.

Nutrition Facts per Serving
Calories: 267 g; Fat: 20.4 g; Carbs: 6.6 g; Protein: 13.7

Chocolate Dish

Prep + cook time: 18 minutes; serves: 2

Ingredients:

- 2 ounces' semi-sweet chocolate; chopped
- ¼ cup butter
- ½ cup confectioner's sugar
- 1 egg yolk
- 1 egg
- ½ tsp. instant coffee
- ½ tsp. vanilla extract
- 3 tbsp. all-purpose flour
- ⅛ tsp. salt
- ½ tbsp. powdered sugar

Instructions:

1. Coat two ramekins in butter then with sugar.

2. Mix the chocolate, sugar, and butter in a bowl. Add the egg, yolk, vanilla, and coffee. Then the flour and salt.
3. Share into the ramekins. Pour 2 cups of water into the pot and add a rack. Put the ramekins on the rack and seal the lid and valve.
4. Set to manual to cook for 9 minutes.
5. Press cancel then quick release the pressure.
6. Remove the ramekins and serve topped with sugar.

Nutrition Facts per Serving
Calories: 561; Fat: 32.5g; Carbs: 58g; Protein 7g; Fiber: 2.5g

Cinnamon Pumpkin Pot Pie

Prep + cook time: 45 minutes; serves: 3

Ingredients:
- 1 can pumpkin
- 1 prepared graham cracker pie crust in an aluminum pan
- ½ tsp. nutmeg
- ½ cup milk
- ½ cup brown sugar
- 1 tsp. cinnamon
- 1 egg

Instructions:

1. Mix all the ingredients together and pour it in the graham cracker crust pan.
2. Pour water into the pot and put a rack in it. Put the pan on the rack then seal the lid and the valve.
3. Set to cook for 35 minutes at high pressure. Cook then serve.

Nutrition Facts per Serving
Calories: 413; Fat: 13.85 g; Carbs: 68.5 g; Protein: 6.1 g; Fiber: 4.8 g

Sweet Brownies

Prep + cook time: 30 minutes; serves: 2

Ingredients:
- ½ cup butter
- 1 cup of sugar
- 2 eggs
- 1 tsp. vanilla
- 2/3 cup flour
- 1/3 cup cocoa powder
- ½ tsp. baking powder
- ½ tsp. salt

Instructions:

1. Whisk the butter and sugar together in a bowl then add the eggs one at a time. Mix in the vanilla.
2. Mix the flour, cocoa, baking powder, and salt in a bowl.
3. Mix the dry ingredients into the wet then pour it into an Instant Pot size pan.
4. Pour water into the pot and put a rack in it. Put the pan on the rack then seal the lid and the valve.
5. Set to cook for 20 minutes.
6. Serve brownies warm.

Nutrition Facts per Serving
Calories: 524; Fat: 26.25 g; Carbs: 70.72 g; Fiber: 2.7 g; Protein: 6.45 g

Sweet Pumpkin Cake

Prep + cook time: 45 minutes; serves: 4

Ingredients:
- 2 cups pumpkin puree
- 3 eggs
- ½ cup milk
- a pinch of salt
- 2 tbsp. pumpkin pie spice
- ½ cup honey
- 1 cup of water

Instructions:

1. Mix the pumpkin puree and eggs in a blender then add the milk, salt, spice, and honey.
2. Spray the pan with a coconut-based spray then pour in the cake batter.
3. Pour water into the pot and add a rack. Put the pan on the rack and seal the lid and the valve.
4. Set to manual to cook for 35 minutes at high pressure.
5. Cancel the pot and natural-release the pressure.
6. Cool in the refrigerator then serve.

Nutrition Facts per Serving
Calories: 237 g; Fat: 18.9 g; Carbs: 28.9 g; Protein: 15.2

Strawberry and Blackberry Cheesecake

Prep + cook time: 30 minutes: serves: 4

Ingredients:
- 1 tsp. butter
- 1 ½ pack (8 oz.) cream cheese
- 1 tsp. vanilla extract
- 6 tbsp. sugar
- 2 eggs
- ½ cup chopped strawberries
- ½ cup blackberries
- 1 cup of water

Instructions:
1. Coat a springform pan with butter and make sure it fits into the Instant Pot.
2. Whisk the cream cheese until it is soft and creamy and mix in the vanilla, sugar, eggs, strawberries, and blackberries.
3. Pour the cheesecake mix into the pan and cover the pan with a foil.
4. Pour the water into the Instant Pot and place a rack into the pot. Place the pan on the rack and seal the lid and the venting valve.
5. Set to "Manual" to cook for 20 minutes at high pressure.
6. Press "Cancel" and natural release the pressure for 8 to 10 minutes.
7. Remove the cheesecake and remove the foil. Use a knife to separate the cheesecake from the edges of the pan but do not remove it yet.
8. Use a plastic wrap to cover the pan and put it in the refrigerator for 1 hour. Serve with berries.

Nutrition Facts per Serving
Calories: 254 g; Fat: 23.9 g; Carbs: 3.7 g; Protein: 16.7

Sweet Pumpkin Cake

Prep + cook time: 45 minutes: serves: 4

Ingredients:
- 2 cups pumpkin puree
- 3 eggs
- ½ cup of milk
- ½ cup of honey
- 2 tbsp. pumpkin spice
- A pinch of salt
- 1 cup of water

Instructions:
1. Whisk the puree and eggs in a bowl then add the milk, honey, spice, and salt.
2. Spray a 6-inch round cake pan with a cooking spray and pour the mixture into the pan. Close with a foil.
3. Pour the water into the pot and place a steaming rack in the pot. Put the filled pan on the rack and seal the lid and valve and set to "Manual" cook for 35 minutes at high pressure.
4. Press the "Cancel" button and natural release the pressure for 10 minutes.
5. Cool and refrigerate for some hours.

Nutrition Facts per Serving
Calories: 237 g; Fat: 18.9 g; Carbs: 28.9 g; Protein: 15.2

Mini Chocolate Cupcakes

Prep + cook time: 18 minutes: serves: 2

Ingredients:
- ½ tbsp. sugar
- ¼ cup butter
- 2 oz. semi-sweet chocolate; chopped
- ½ cup confectioners' sugar
- 1 egg yolk
- 1 egg
- ½ tsp. vanilla extract
- ½ tsp. instant coffee
- 3 tbsp. all-purpose flour
- 1/8 tsp. salt

Instructions:
1. Coat two ramekins with some butter or cooking spray and cover with sugar.

2. Mix the butter and chocolate in a mixing bowl then add the confectioners' sugar and mix well.
3. Mix in the egg yolk, egg, vanilla, coffee, flour, and salt and share it into the ramekins.
4. Pour 2 cups of water into the Instant Pot and place a rack over the water. Put the ramekins on the rack and seal the lid and valve.

5. Set to "Manual" to cook for 9 minutes.
6. Press "Cancel" and quick release the steam then remove the cake from the ramekins and top with powdered sugar.

Nutritional Fact per Serving
Calories: 561; Fat: 32.5g; Carbs: 58g; Protein 7g; fiber 2.5g

Creamy Cardamom Panna Cotta

Prep + cook time: 26 minutes: serves: 2
Ingredients:
- 1 cup basic yogurt
- ¼ cup of sugar
- 1 tsp. vanilla
- 1 tsp. unflavored gelatin
- ¼ cup honey
- 1 orange; juiced with pulp
- ¼ tsp. cardamom

Instructions:
1. Whisk the yogurt, sugar, and vanilla in a bowl.

2. Spread the gelatin over some water to soften then whisk until the gelatin dissolves. Mix into the yogurt mixture.
3. Pour the mixture into 2 ramekins and chill for 2 hours in a fridge. Mix the honey, orange, and cardamom to make a sauce in the pot.
4. Seal the lid and set to cook for 1 minute. Then chill completely.
5. Run a knife around the sides of the ramekin and turn over on a plate. Top with sauce.

Nutrition Facts per Serving
Calories: 343; Fat: 4.1 g; Carbs: 75.25 g; Protein: 5.08 g; Fiber 1.7g

Cinnamon wine Pears

Prep + cook time: 17 minutes. Serves: 2
Ingredients:
- ¼ bottle of your choice of red wine
- 2 pears; peeled
- ½ cup of sugar
- 1 cinnamon stick
- 1 piece of ginger
- 1 clove

Instructions:
1. Mix all the ingredients in the Instant Pot and seal the lid and the venting valve.

2. Set to "Manual" to cook for some minutes. Quick-release the pressure and remove the pears.
3. Press "Sauté" on the pot and cook the liquid until it reduces by half. Serve hot sauce over pears.

Nutrition Facts per Serving
Calories: 328; Fat: 3g; Carbs: 38.5g; Protein 2g; Fiber 6g

Cinnamon Pumpkin Pie

Prep + cook time: 45 minutes; Serves: 3
Ingredients:
- 1 prepared graham cracker pie crust in an aluminum pan
- 1 can pumpkin
- ½ cup brown sugar
- 1 tsp. cinnamon
- ½ tsp. nutmeg
- ½ cup milk

- 1 egg

Instructions:
1. Mix all the ingredients together in a blender and blend then pour it in the graham cracker pie crust pan.
2. Pour some water into the Instant Pot and place a steaming rack in it.

3. Put the pan on the rack and seal the lid. Set to cook for 35 minutes at high pressure. Chill in the fridge then serve.

Nutrition Facts per Serving
Calories: 413; Fat: 13.85 g; Carbs: 68.5 g; Protein: 6.1 g; Fiber 4.8

Sweet Cinnamon Apples with Raisins

Prep + cook time: 15 minutes; Serves: 2

Ingredients:
- 2 apples; cored
- ½ tsp. cinnamon
- 3 tbsp. raisins
- ¼ cup of sugar
- ¼ cup red wine

Instructions:
1. Mix all the ingredients in the Instant Pot and seal the lid and the valve.
2. Set to "Manual" to cook for 10 minutes.
3. Press "Cancel" and natural release the pressure for 8 to 10 minutes.
4. Open the pot and serve.

Nutrition Facts per Serving
Calories: 377; Fat: 0g; Carbs: 62g; Protein 3.5g; fiber 11.5g

Sweet and Sour Oreo Cheesecake

Prep + cook time: 30 minutes; serves: 3

Ingredients:
- ¾ cup Oreo cookies
- 3 tbsp. unsalted butter
- 1 ½ pack (8 oz.) cream cheese
- 6 tbsp. sugar
- 1 tsp. vanilla
- 1/3 cup sour cream
- 2 eggs

Instructions:
1. Coat the pan with butter. Heat the oven to 350°F. Crush the Oreo cookies and mix with the melted butter.
2. Press the buttery cookie crumbles in the bottom of the pan and bake for 10 minutes in the oven.
3. Mix the cream cheese until smooth and add the sugar, vanilla, and sour cream.
4. Mix in the eggs, one at a time then pour it on the crust. Cover the pan with a foil.
5. Pour some water into the Instant Pot and add a steaming rack. Place the pan on the rack and seal the lid.
6. Set to "Manual" to cook for 20 minutes at high pressure. Press "Cancel" and natural release the pressure.
7. Remove the cheesecake and lift the sides with a knife but don't remove the cake yet.
8. Cover with a plastic wrap and chill for an hour.

Nutrition Facts per Serving
Calories: 677 g; Fat: 53 g; Carbs: 41.3 g; Protein: 12.1

Creamy Fudge Balls with Nuts

Prep + cook time: 10 minutes; serves: 2

Ingredients:
- 1 (14 oz.) can condensed milk
- 1 (12 oz.) package semi-sweet chocolate chips
- 2 cup of water
- ½ cup walnuts
- ½ cup almonds
- 1 tsp. vanilla

Instructions:
1. Mix the chocolate chips with the milk in a bowl and cover it with a foil.
2. Pour the water into the Instant Pot and place a rack inside it. Put the bowl on the rack and seal the lid. Set to "Manual" to cook for 5 minutes.
3. "Cancel" the pot and quick release the pressure.
4. Mix in the nuts and the vanilla and mold into balls on a wax paper. Cool and enjoy it.

Nutrition Facts per Serving
Calories: 156; Fat: 8g; Carbs: 18g; Protein 3.5g; fiber 0.5g

Sour Vanilla Cheesecake

Prep + cook time: 35 minutes; Serves: 2

Ingredients:

- 1 prepared graham cracker crust in an aluminum pan
- 1 package cream cheese; softened
- 2 tsp. vanilla
- ½ cup sour cream
- 2 eggs
- 2/3 cup sugar
- 2 tbsp. cornstarch

Instructions:

1. Mix all the ingredients together and pour them in the pan.
2. Pour water in the Instant Pot and put a rack in it. Place the pan on the rack and seak the lid to cook for 25 minutes at high pressure.
3. Cool before serving.

Nutrition Facts per Serving

Calories: 523; Fat: 23.78 g; Carbs: 69.89 g; Protein: 7.37 g; fiber 0.9g

Cocoa Vanilla Pot Cake

Prep + cook time: 30 minutes; serves: 2

Ingredients:

- ½ cup butter
- 1 cup of sugar
- 2 eggs
- 1 tsp. vanilla
- 2/3 cup flour
- 1/3 cup cocoa powder
- ½ tsp. baking powder
- ½ tsp. salt

Instructions:

1. Whisk the butter and sugar in a bowl and mix in the eggs one at a time. Add the vanilla and mix some more. In another bowl, mix the flour, cocoa powder, baking powder, and salt together.
2. Mix dry and wet ingredients together and pour into a baking pan that fits the pot.
3. Put a rack into the pot and pour in some water. Place the pan on the rack and seal the lid to cook for 20 minutes.
4. Serve warm.

Nutrition Facts per Serving

Calories: 524; Fat: 26.25 g; Carbs: 70.72 g; Protein: 6.45 g; Fiber 2.7g

Lemon Banana Bread

Prep + cook time: 40 minutes; serves: 4

Ingredients:

- 1/3 cup milk
- 3 tsp. lemon juice
- 1/3 cup butter
- ¾ cup of sugar
- 1 egg
- 2 mashed bananas
- 2 cup flour
- 1 tsp. baking soda
- ½ tsp. baking powder
- A pinch of salt

Instructions:

1. In a bowl, combine the milk and lemon juice. Add the butter, sugar, egg, and mashed bananas and mix.
2. In another bowl, mix the flour, soda, baking powder, and salt.
3. Slowly pour the butter mixture into the flour mixture while stirring.
4. Pour into the pan and cover with a foil tightly.
5. Pour some water in the pot and place a rack into it. Put the pan on the rack and seal the lid. Set to "Manual" to cook for 30 minutes at high pressure.
6. Press "Cancel" and natural release the pressure. Open, let cool and serve.

Nutrition Facts per Serving

Calories: 267 g; Fat: 20.4 g; Carbs: 6.6 g; Protein: 13.7

Fruit Jumble

Prep + cook time: 20 minutes; serves: 2

Ingredients:

- ¼ cup coconut; shredded
- 1 plum; chopped
- 1 pear; chopped
- ½ tsp. cinnamon
- 3 tbsp. coconut oil
- 1 apple; chopped
- 2 tbsp. granular stevia or sugar
- 1 cup of water
- ¼ cup pecans; chopped

Instructions:

1. Mix all the ingredients in a heat-proof bowl except the pecans and the water.
2. Pour the water into the pot and place a rack over it. Put the bowl on the rack and seal the lid.
3. Set to "Manual" to cook for 10 minutes.
4. Press "Cancel" and quick release the pressure.
5. Share into bowls and serve topped with pecans.

Nutrition Facts per Serving

Calories: 150; Fat: 4g; Carbs: 13.5g; Protein 6.5g; fiber 4g

Lemon Tapioca

Prep +cook time: 16 minutes; serves: 2

Ingredients:

- ½ cup tapioca pearls; rinsed and drained
- ½ tsp. sweetener Stevia
- 1 tbsp. lemon zest
- 1 ¼ cup milk
- 1 ½ cup water
- ½ lemon; sliced

Instructions:

1. Pour 1 cup of water into the Instant Pot and put the rack inside the pot.
2. Mix all the ingredients except the lemon slices in a baking dish until the sweetener dissolves and put it on the rack. Seal the lid.
3. Set to "Manual" to cook for 6 minutes at high pressure.
4. Press "Cancel" and quick release the pressure. Pour into pudding cups and serve with lemon slices.

Nutrition Facts per Serving

Calories: 214 g; Fat: 3.2 g; Carbs: 41.8 g; Protein: 5.1g

Creamy Oatmeal with Strawberries

Prep + cook time: 25 minutes; serves: 3

Ingredients:

- 1 tbsp. butter
- 1 cup steel-cut oats
- 3 tablespoons brown sugar
- ¼ cup cream
- 4 cups of water
- ¼ teaspoon salt
- 1 ½ cups fresh and sliced strawberries
- 4 tbsps. chia seeds

Instructions:

1. Press Sauté on the Instant Pot and add the butter to the pot.
2. Mix in the oats and cook continuously for 3 minutes while stirring.
3. Mix in the sugar, cream, water, and salt.
4. Seal the lid and set to cook for 10 minutes at High Pressure.
5. Natural-release the pressure and open the lid. Mix in the strawberries and chia seeds. Serve.

Nutrition Facts per Serving

Calories 246, Fat 10.3g, Carbs 37.4g, Protein 6.3g

Cheesy Mushroom Egg Dish with Chives

Prep + cook time: 15 minutes; serves: 4

Ingredients:

- 2 tbsps. butter
- 5 lightly beaten eggs
- 2 tbsps. Minced chives
- ½ cup coconut milk
- 1 ½ cups sliced mushrooms
- ½ tbsp. cheddar cheese
- 1 chopped bell pepper
- 1 chopped onion

Instructions:

1. Press Sauté on the Instant Pot and add the butter to melt. Beat the eggs in a bowl until it is well combined.

2. Mix the rest of the ingredients with the eggs and pour it into the pot and cook for 2 minutes.

3. Seal the lid and set to cook for 8 minutes more.

4. Quick-release the pressure and open the lid. Serve.

Nutrition Facts per Serving

Calories: 229, Fat: 18.9g, Carbs: 7.8g, Protein: 9.4g

Ginger Cinnamon Squash

Prep + cook time: 28 minutes; serves: 2

Ingredients:

- 1 (1¼ pounds) whole squash
- 2 medium apples, cored and chopped roughly
- ½ tsp. ground cinnamon
- ⅛ tsp. ground ginger
- ⅛ tsp. ground cloves
- ½ cup chicken broth
- 2 tbsps. maple syrup
- 2 tbsps. gelatin
- Pinch of salt

Instructions:

1. Put the squash, apples, cinnamon, ginger, cloves, and broth and mix everything well. Seal the lid and the valve.

2. Set to Manual to cook for 8 minutes.

3. Press the Cancel button and Natural-release the pressure for 8 to 10 minutes.

4. Open the lid and remove the squash. Place it on a chopping board and cut in half lengthwise and remove the seeds.

5. Put the squash, apple mixture, maple syrup, gelatin, and salt in a blender and puree till smooth. Serve warm.

Nutrition Facts per Serving

Calories: 312; Fat: 0.8g; Carbs: 44g; Protein 13.5g; Fiber: 9g

Cheesy Ham and Potatoes Egg Dish

Prep + cook time: 30 minutes; serves: 6

Ingredients:

- 1 cup whole milk
- 10 eggs
- ½ diced onion
- 4 red potatoes
- 1 cup chopped ham
- 1 tsp. salt
- 1 tsp. pepper
- 2 cups shredded cheddar cheese
- 2 cups of water

Instructions:

1. Spray the Instant Pot with cooking spray and choose a glass bowl that will fit into the Instant Pot.

2. Whisk the milk and the eggs in the bowl until it is well combined then add the potatoes, ham, onions, salt, pepper, and cheese. Gradually mixing as added.

3. Cover the bowl with a foil and put a rack into the pot. Pour in 2 cups of water and put the bowl on the rack.

4. Seal the lid and the valve and set it to Manual to cook for 25 minutes.

5. Quick-release the pressure and remove the dish then serve with your desired topping.

Nutrition Facts per Serving

Calories: 205, Fat: 14.3g, Carbs: 5.1g, Protein: 12g

Cheesy Bacon and Zucchini Fritters

Prep + cook time: 15 minutes; serves: 3

Ingredients:

- 1 chopped scallion
- 1 chopped zucchini
- 4 tbsps. shredded cheddar cheese
- 2 cooked bacon slices
- ¼ tsp. lemon-pepper seasoning
- 3 eggs
- ¼ cup almond milk
- Pepper and salt to taste

Instructions:

1. Pour 1 cup of water into the Instant Pot and place a steaming rack in the pot.
2. In a bowl, whisk all the ingredients together until it is well combined.
3. Pour the mixture into silicone molds and put it on the rack. Seal the lid and set to cook for 5 minutes at High Pressure.
4. Quick-release the pressure and open the lid. Serve.

Nutrition Facts per Serving: Calories: 228, Fat: 17.7g, Carbs: 4.5g, Protein: 13.9g

Sweet Quinoa with Blueberries and Apples

Prep + cook time: 11 minutes; serves: 2

Ingredients:

- ¾ cup of water
- ¾ cup white quinoa
- 1 small cinnamon stick
- 1/8 cup raisins
- ½ cup apple juice
- ½ cup apples; grated
- ½ tbsp. honey
- ½ cup plain yogurt
- ⅛ cup pistachios; chopped
- 3 tbsps. blueberries

Instructions:

1. Rinse the quinoa and strain with a mesh strainer.
2. Open the lid and add the water, quinoa, and cinnamon stick in the Instant Pot.
3. Seal the lid and the valve and set to cook at Manual for 1 minute.
4. Press the Cancel button and Natural-release the pressure for 8 to 10 minutes.
5. Open the lid and remove the cinnamon stick then serve the quinoa into a bowl.
6. Mix in the apple, apple juice, raisins, and honey and put it in the refrigerator for at least 1 hour or overnight.
7. Mix in the yogurt and serve topped with pistachio and blueberries. Serve.

Nutrition Facts per Serving
Calories: 418; Fat: 6.5g; Carbs: 44.5g; Protein 14g; Fiber: 7g

Instant Pot Boiled Eggs

Prep + cook time: 6 minutes; serves: 2

Ingredients:

- 1 ½ cups of water
- 6 eggs

Instructions:

1. Pour the water into the pot and put the eggs in a steaming rack and put it over the water.
2. Seal the lid and set to cook at High Pressure for 5 minutes.
3. Natural-release the pressure and remove the eggs to a cold bath. Peel and serve.

Nutrition Facts per Serving
Calories: 470; Fat: 13.22 g; Carbs: 81.95 g; Protein: 13.04 g; Fiber: 10.1 g

Ginger Rice with Potatoes and Sausage

Prep + cook time: 18 minutes; serves: 3

Ingredients:

- 1 ½ tbsps. olive oil
- 1 ½ tbsps. finely chopped green onions
- 1 tbsp. finely chopped green onion; to garnish
- 4 slices ginger
- 2 lean sausages, thinly sliced
- 5 small yellow potatoes, peeled

- 2 cups long-grain rice
- 1/6 tsp. ground black pepper
- ¼ tsp. chicken broth mix
- 3 cups of water
- 1 tsp. salt

Instructions:
1. Press Sauté on the Instant Pot and add the olive oil, onions, and ginger to cook for 2 minutes.

2. Mix in the sausages to cook for 1 to 2 minutes. Mix in the potatoes and cook for 2 minutes then add the rice and stir.
3. Mix in the rest of the ingredients and seal the lid and the valve.
4. Set to "Rice" to cook for 4 minutes.
5. Press the Cancel button and Natural-release the pressure for 8 to 10 minutes. Open and serve.

Nutrition Facts per Serving
Calories: 377; Fat: 12g; Carbs: 55.6g; Protein 13.7g; Fiber: 4g

Spicy Garlic Polenta

Prep + cook time: 15 minutes; serves: 2

Ingredients:
- 1 tsp. minced garlic
- 1 tbsp. olive oil
- 1 bunch green onions
- 2 tbsps. cilantro
- ½ tsp. cumin
- 1 cup broth
- ½ tsp. oregano
- 1 ½ tsps. chili powder
- 1 cup boiling water
- ½ cup cornmeal
- Pinch of cayenne
- ¼ tsp. paprika

Instructions:
1. Press Sauté on the pot and add the oil, garlic, and onions to cook for 2 to 3 minutes.
2. Add the rest of the ingredients and stir to combine then seal the lid and the valve.
3. Set to Manual to cook for 5 minutes until the timer stops.
4. Press the Cancel button and Natural-release the pressure for 8 to 10 minutes. Open and serve.

Nutrition Facts per Serving
Calories: 98; Fat: 1.5g; Carbs: 6g; Protein 4g; Fiber: 3g

Ginger Lentils with Tomatoes

Prep + cook time: 55 minutes; serves: 3

Ingredients:
- 2 tbsps. avocado oil
- 1 tbsp. cumin seeds
- 1 large onion; chopped
- 1 ½ inches ginger; minced
- 6 garlic cloves; minced
- 1 tsp. Garam masala
- 1 tsp. turmeric
- 1 tsp. cayenne
- 1 bay leaf
- ½ tsp. black pepper
- Salt
- 2 tomatoes; chopped
- 3 cups of water
- 1 cup whole and split lentils; soaked for 12 to 14 hours and drained
- 2 tbsps. ghee or butter
- Cilantro leaves

Instructions:
1. Press Sauté on the Instant Pot and add the oil and cumin seeds to cook for 1 minute, mix in the onions to cook for 8 to 10 minutes until it is soft.
2. Mix in the ginger, garlic, spices, and tomatoes to cook for 5 minutes then mix in the lentils and the water.
3. Seal the lid and the valve and set to Beans/Chili to cook for 30 minutes until the timer stops.
4. Press the Cancel button and Natural-release the pressure for 8 to 10 minutes.
5. Serve into containers with ghee and garnished with cilantro.

Nutrition Facts per Serving
Calories 210; Fat: 14g; Carbs: 15g; Protein 6.9g; Fiber: 5.7g

Appendix 1 Measurement Conversion Chart

VOLUME EQUIVALENTS(DRY)

US STANDARD	METRIC (APPROXIMATE)
1/8 teaspoon	0.5 mL
1/4 teaspoon	1 mL
1/2 teaspoon	2 mL
3/4 teaspoon	4 mL
1 teaspoon	5 mL
1 tablespoon	15 mL
1/4 cup	59 mL
1/2 cup	118 mL
3/4 cup	177 mL
1 cup	235 mL
2 cups	475 mL
3 cups	700 mL
4 cups	1 L

VOLUME EQUIVALENTS(LIQUID)

US STANDARD	US STANDARD (OUNCES)	METRIC (APPROXIMATE)
2 tablespoons	1 fl.oz.	30 mL
1/4 cup	2 fl.oz.	60 mL
1/2 cup	4 fl.oz.	120 mL
1 cup	8 fl.oz.	240 mL
1 1/2 cup	12 fl.oz.	355 mL
2 cups or 1 pint	16 fl.oz.	475 mL
4 cups or 1 quart	32 fl.oz.	1 L
1 gallon	128 fl.oz.	4 L

TEMPERATURES EQUIVALENTS

FAHRENHEIT(F)	CELSIUS(C) (APPROXIMATE)
225 °F	107 °C
250 °F	120 °C
275 °F	135 °C
300 °F	150 °C
325 °F	160 °C
350 °F	180 °C
375 °F	190 °C
400 °F	205 °C
425 °F	220 °C
450 °F	235 °C
475 °F	245 °C
500 °F	260 °C

WEIGHT EQUIVALENTS

US STANDARD	METRIC (APPROXIMATE)
1 ounce	28 g
2 ounces	57 g
5 ounces	142 g
10 ounces	284 g
15 ounces	425 g
16 ounces (1 pound)	455 g
1.5 pounds	680 g
2 pounds	907 g

Appendix 2 Instant Pot Cooking Timetable

Dried Beans, Legumes and Lentils

Dried Beans and Legume	Dry (Minutes)	Soaked (Minutes)
Soy beans	25 – 30	20 – 25
Scarlet runner	20 – 25	10 – 15
Pinto beans	25 – 30	20 – 25
Peas	15 – 20	10 – 15
Navy beans	25 – 30	20 – 25
Lima beans	20 – 25	10 – 15
Lentils, split, yellow (moong dal)	15 – 18	N/A
Lentils, split, red	15 – 18	N/A
Lentils, mini, green (brown)	15 – 20	N/A
Lentils, French green	15 – 20	N/A
Kidney white beans	35 – 40	20 – 25
Kidney red beans	25 – 30	20 – 25
Great Northern beans	25 – 30	20 – 25
Pigeon peas	20 – 25	15 – 20
Chickpeas (garbanzo bean chickpeas)	35 – 40	20 – 25
Cannellini beans	35 – 40	20 – 25
Black-eyed peas	20 – 25	10 – 15
Black beans	20 – 25	10 – 15

Fish and Seafood

Fish and Seafood	Fresh (minutes)	Frozen (minutes)
Shrimp or Prawn	1 to 2	2 to 3
Seafood soup or stock	6 to 7	7 to 9
Mussels	2 to 3	4 to 6
Lobster	3 to 4	4 to 6
Fish, whole (snapper, trout, etc.)	5 to 6	7 to 10
Fish steak	3 to 4	4 to 6
Fish fillet,	2 to 3	3 to 4
Crab	3 to 4	5 to 6

Fruits

Fruits	Fresh (in Minutes)	Dried (in Minutes)
Raisins	N/A	4 to 5
Prunes	2 to 3	4 to 5
Pears, whole	3 to 4	4 to 6
Pears, slices or halves	2 to 3	4 to 5
Peaches	2 to 3	4 to 5
Apricots, whole or halves	2 to 3	3 to 4
Apples, whole	3 to 4	4 to 6
Apples, in slices or pieces	2 to 3	3 to 4

Meat

Meat and Cuts	Cooking Time (minutes)	Meat and Cuts	Cooking Time (minutes)
Veal, roast	35 to 45	Duck, with bones, cut up	10 to 12
Veal, chops	5 to 8	Cornish Hen, whole	10 to 15
Turkey, drumsticks (leg)	15 to 20	Chicken, whole	20 to 25
Turkey, breast, whole, with bones	25 to 30	Chicken, legs, drumsticks, or thighs	10 to 15
Turkey, breast, boneless	15 to 20	Chicken, with bones, cut up	10 to 15
Quail, whole	8 to 10	Chicken, breasts	8 to 10
Pork, ribs	20 to 25	Beef, stew	15 to 20
Pork, loin roast	55 to 60	Beef, shanks	25 to 30
Pork, butt roast	45 to 50	Beef, ribs	25 to 30
Pheasant	20 to 25	Beef, steak, pot roast, round, rump, brisket or blade, small chunks, chuck,	25 to 30
Lamb, stew meat	10 to 15		
Lamb, leg	35 to 45	Beef, pot roast, steak, rump, round, chuck, blade or brisket, large	35 to 40
Lamb, cubes,	10 t0 15		
Ham slice	9 to 12	Beef, ox-tail	40 to 50
Ham picnic shoulder	25 to 30	Beef, meatball	10 to 15
Duck, whole	25 to 30	Beef, dressed	20 to 25

Vegetables (fresh/frozen)

Vegetable	Fresh (minutes)	Frozen (minutes)	Vegetable	Fresh (minutes)	Frozen (minutes)
Zucchini, slices or chunks	2 to 3	3 to 4	Mixed vegetables	2 to 3	3 to 4
Yam, whole, small	10 to 12	12 to 14	Leeks	2 to 4	3 to 5
Yam, whole, large	12 to 15	15 to 19	Greens (collards, beet greens, spinach, kale, turnip greens, swiss chard) chopped	3 to 6	4 to 7
Yam, in cubes	7 to 9	9 to 11			
Turnip, chunks	2 to 4	4 to 6	Green beans, whole	2 to 3	3 to 4
Tomatoes, whole	3 to 5	5 to 7	Escarole, chopped	1 to 2	2 to 3
Tomatoes, in quarters	2 to 3	4 to 5	Endive	1 to 2	2 to 3
Sweet potato, whole, small	10 to 12	12 to 14	Eggplant, chunks or slices	2 to 3	3 to 4
Sweet potato, whole, large	12 to 15	15 to 19	Corn, on the cob	3 to 4	4 to 5
Sweet potato, in cubes	7 to 9	9 to 11	Corn, kernels	1 to 2	2 to 3
Sweet pepper, slices or chunks	1 to 3	2 to 4	Collard	4 to 5	5 to 6
Squash, butternut, slices or chunks	8 to 10	10 to 12	Celery, chunks	2 to 3	3 to 4
Squash, acorn, slices or chunks	6 to 7	8 to 9	Cauliflower flowerets	2 to 3	3 to 4
Spinach	1 to 2	3 to 4	Carrots, whole or chunked	2 to 3	3 to 4
Rutabaga, slices	3 to 5	4 to 6	Carrots, sliced or shredded	1 to 2	2 to 3
Rutabaga, chunks	4 to 6	6 to 8	Cabbage, red, purple or green, wedges	3 to 4	4 to 5
Pumpkin, small slices or chunks	4 to 5	6 to 7	Cabbage, red, purple or green, shredded	2 to 3	3 to 4
Pumpkin, large slices or chunks	8 to 10	10 to 14	Brussel sprouts, whole	3 to 4	4 to 5
Potatoes, whole, large	12 to 15	15 to 19	Broccoli, stalks	3 to 4	4 to 5
Potatoes, whole, baby	10 to 12	12 to 14	Broccoli, flowerets	2 to 3	3 to 4
Potatoes, in cubes	7 to 9	9 to 11	Beets, small roots, whole	11 to 13	13 to 15
Peas, in the pod	1 to 2	2 to 3	Beets, large roots, whole	20 to 25	25 to 30
Peas, green	1 to 2	2 to 3	Beans, green/yellow or wax, whole, trim ends and strings	1 to 2	2 to 3
Parsnips, sliced	1 to 2	2 to 3			
Parsnips, chunks	2 to 4	4 to 6	Asparagus, whole or cut	1 to 2	2 to 3
Onions, sliced	2 to 3	3 to 4	Artichoke, whole, trimmed without leaves	9 to 11	11 to 13
Okra	2 to 3	3 to 4	Artichoke, hearts	4 to 5	5 to 6

Rice and Grains

Rice & Grain	Water Quantity (Grain: Water ratios)	Cooking Time (in Minutes)	Rice & Grain	Water Quantity (Grain: Water ratios)	Cooking Time (in Minutes)
Wheat berries	1:3	25 to 30	Oats, steel-cut	1:1	10
Spelt berries	1:3	15 to 20	Oats, quick cooking	1:1	6
Sorghum	1:3	20 to 25	Millet	1:1	10 to 12
Rice, wild	1:3	25 to 30	Kamut, whole	1:3	10 to 12
Rice, white	1:1.5	8	Couscous	1:2	5 to 8
Rice, Jasmine	1:1	4 to 10	Corn, dried, half	1:3	25 to 30
Rice, Brown	1:1.3	22 to 28	Congee, thin	1:6 ~ 1:7	15 to 20
Rice, Basmati	1:1.5	4 to 8	Congee, thick	1:4 ~ 1:5	15 to 20
Quinoa, quick cooking	1:2	8	Barley, pot	1:3 ~ 1:4	25 to 30
Porridge, thin	1:6 ~ 1:7	15 to 20	Barley, pearl	1:4	25 to 30

Appendix 3 Recipe Index

Made in the USA
Columbia, SC
08 April 2022

58682311R00080